The Age of Fire Is Over fills a critical void in our strategic thinking about the future of the world, and the role that energy plays in it. The author lays out a robust framework for navigating the interlinkages across sectors, society, innovation and our relationship with Nature. Vincent Petit has once again pulled together a compelling perspective for each of us to reflect on, learn from, and incorporate into our thinking.

Douglas Arent, Ph.D., MBA
Executive Director, Public Private Partnerships,
National Renewable Energy Laboratory

The Age of Fire Is Over is one of those books which gets you to challenge every assumption that you hold about the way that the energy system works and the best way to accelerate the urgent transformation of the system that we need to see. By challenging those assumptions, *The Age of Fire Is Over* expands the solution space and ultimately inspires a credible, more hopeful future.

Jeremy Oppenheim
Co-founder, SYSTEMIQ

In *The Age of Fire Is Over*, Vincent Petit paints an exhilarating and optimistic picture of what the transition to a low carbon economy might look like. With a firm grasp of the data, this wellresearched book shows that a demand driven transition may happen much faster than most experts predict and that we may avoid the worst scenarios of climate change.

Mike Rosenberg, Ph.D., MBA
Professor of the Practice of Strategic Management,
IESE Business School

THE AGE OF
FIRE IS OVER

A New Approach
to the Energy Transition

THE AGE OF FIRE IS OVER

A New Approach
to the Energy Transition

Vincent Petit

Schneider Electric, Hong Kong

World Scientific

NEW JERSEY · LONDON · SINGAPORE · BEIJING · SHANGHAI · HONG KONG · TAIPEI · CHENNAI · TOKYO

Published by

World Scientific Publishing Europe Ltd.

57 Shelton Street, Covent Garden, London WC2H 9HE

Head office: 5 Toh Tuck Link, Singapore 596224

USA office: 27 Warren Street, Suite 401-402, Hackensack, NJ 07601

Library of Congress Cataloging-in-Publication Data
Names: Petit, Vincent, author.
Title: The age of fire is over : a new approach to the energy transition /
    Vincent Petit, Schneider Electric, Hong Kong.
Description: London ; Singapore ; Hackensack, NJ : World Scientific, [2022] |
    Includes bibliographical references and index.
Identifiers: LCCN 2021014317 | ISBN 9781800610361 (hardcover) |
    ISBN 9781800610378 (ebook for institutions) | ISBN 9781800610385 (ebook for individuals)
Subjects: LCSH: Renewable energy sources. | Energy policy. | Energy industries.
Classification: LCC TJ808 .P485 2022 | DDC 333.79--dc23
LC record available at https://lccn.loc.gov/2021014317

British Library Cataloguing-in-Publication Data
A catalogue record for this book is available from the British Library.

For any available supplementary material, please visit
https://www.worldscientific.com/worldscibooks/10.1142/Q0305#t=suppl

Desk Editors: Anthony Alexander/Michael Beale/Shi Ying Koe

Typeset by Stallion Press
Email: enquiries@stallionpress.com

Foreword

In 2020, the world was hit by a global pandemic of the likes we had not seen for over a century. As COVID-19 spread desolation across continents, the deadly virus shook the balance of our global order across many of its components: political, economical, and societal. Countries reacted differently to the crisis, often in their own way. Some found themselves better prepared than others, with greater capacities to face spikes in hospitalizations. Some also found support in traditional habits and cultural behaviors, which others did not. Despite everyone having to deplore terrible loss counts, each country reacted to the pandemic in its own way, and the crisis exposed each one's strengths and vulnerabilities. Every government also had to strike a careful balance between opening and closing, within the borders and across, in a world poised by global exchanges at all levels. In fact, many businesses, particularly those dependent on global exchanges, travels, or social interactions, simply ceased to operate from one day to the other, leaving many in distress. And many have not reset their operations yet, a year after the initial outbreak. Finally, COVID-19 also hit different categories of populations in different ways, exposing many differences and issues — isolated elderly who could not rely on family support anymore, a young generation called into the line of fire, critical differences between those able to retreat to their countryside estate and those forced into lockdown in small apartments downtown. One year into the pandemic, the world has changed forever, and it will likely take a few more years for everyone to realize the extent of those transformations.

I want to retain one transformation here, however, that of a renewed sense for sustainable development. While, at the beginning of 2020, the term often fell off the headlines, the crisis soon taught all of us its biggest lesson: that the virus had hit us unprepared, despite early warnings for many years. It was thus becoming critical to "build back better", and mitigate for other issues, including, the mother of all, climate change. 2020 was therefore also a marked year when it came to climate change with the first two economies of the world making firm commitments to reach a net-zero economy by around mid-century, joining the European Union and the United Kingdom which had led the way thus far. 2021 will be the year of turning those commitments into concrete plans around the world, to firmly take us on a course toward a net-zero economy by mid-century, which the IPCC considers the only route to maintain a global Earth temperature increase limited to 1.5 degrees in the long-run. In this regard, the COP26, due in November in Glasgow, will be a critical turning point.

And the challenge is daunting: greenhouse gas emissions need to reduce every year till 2050 by a similar level as what the global economic disruption from COVID-19 delivered in 2020. In fact, emissions only fell by a few percent in 2020, an indication of the considerable inertia built in our system. At the heart of the problem lies our energy system, fueled by global and cheap access to fossil fuels for over 2 centuries. Energy transitions have happened in the past, but it typically took 60 to 70 years for a transition to reach maturity, and only in parts of our energy system. What the world is now facing is a transition across all sectors of activity, in a timeframe twice shorter.

The key question is thus how to do it successfully, and in time, without creating a considerable burden for everyone, particularly those who are most exposed and fragile in the face of rapid changes. Debates are therefore raging around the world on the best course of action. *The Age of Fire Is Over* is a new contribution to these debates. What makes it valuable is that it departs from most scenarios developed in recent years. The main argument of the book is that energy transitions have always been driven by transformations of demand patterns, a result of key innovations (or industrial revolutions) that included but were not limited to new energy uses.

What Vincent Petit sets out to do here is to sketch possible demand evolutions that have barely been anticipated in current projections and look at the way the 2050 energy system could look as a result. The first conclusion of this book, likely provocative, is that the future energy system might in fact be very different from what we think.

There is also a second and more important conclusion. As the world races to achieve in 30 years a transition that would otherwise take much longer to materialize, *The Age of Fire Is Over* suggests that the only way to do it in time is to shift focus toward the demand side of the energy system, and accelerate these transformations, which inherently serve the cause of decarbonization, while providing greater abundance for all.

This challenge and the way our generation responds to it will certainly be what future generations will remember of this time, and what will be taught in classes around the world in 50 years and beyond. *The Age of Fire Is Over* will certainly bring a meaningful contribution to the debates at hand.

Jean-Pascal Tricoire
Schneider Electric Chief Executive Officer and Chairman of the Board

About the Author

 **Vincent Petit** is Senior Vice President Global Strategy Prospective and External Affairs at Schneider Electric. With 20 years of experience at Schneider Electric, Vincent has had a diverse career in both operational and corporate roles, from driving contracting activities to offering development positions in global business organizations. In 2011, he moved to Russia where he led contracting operations for the CIS zone. In 2015, he was appointed Senior Vice President of Energy Automation, in charge of global smart grid applications. Since 2017, he has focused his time on reinforcing the global prospective activity of the group and later extended his role to government relations and industrial affairs.

A recognized expert in the field of energy, he is also the author of three previous books.

He holds a Master's degree from French engineering school Supéléc and a Master's in Electrical Engineering from the University of Texas, Austin.

Contents

List of Figures

Part 1
Setting the Debate Right

CHAPTER 1

What Truly Drives Energy Transitions Is Not What We May Think

"All sciences are vain and full of errors that are not born of experience, the mother of all knowledge." (L. da Vinci)

Since the Intergovernmental Panel on Climate Change's foundation in 1988, the topic of climate change has become front and center. As science advanced to better understand its root causes, the topic of a necessary energy transition progressively emerged, as energy was unequivocally identified as the major origin of anthropogenic emissions. Since then, a multitude of scenarios, detailed studies, and forecasts have been drawn up to propose alternative pathways that would help mitigate the rise in the planet's temperature. Energy experts have gathered at conferences, provided the results of their studies, and engaged with government officials to design the proper policies to be put in place to change the harmful course that the world appears to be set on. The consensus is that the world needs to reach a net-zero carbon economy by 2050. More importantly, our current emissions of greenhouse gases need to be halved by 2030. Only a decade to go!

This book is another contribution to these debates. Yet, it departs from previous studies. On the coming pages, we will develop an alternative approach to the current debate, largely revolving around what needs to be done to best transition away from fossil fuels. We will build on evidence from past energy transitions to better grasp the true dynamics at play in every energy transition, from the past and into the future, and assess how these dynamics are most likely to change the energy system. We will realize that considerable changes are at play in our world and its energy system, which are largely overlooked in today's conversations. These changes make current forecasts and scenarios for the most part irrelevant, or at least inaccurate predictions of what will probably happen and what effectively needs to be done to stop climate change. Pressure in the system is mounting, with the world caught between dystopian "realistic" scenarios that all fail to mitigate climate change in time and "forceful" scenarios, which all appear increasingly unrealistic considering the sheer size of the transformation needed in a short time.

Is there an alternative course that could be charted, building on lessons from the past?

As we dive into this complex issue, we first need however to describe the terms of our discussion. What is energy? What is a transition?

I will start with this friend of mine, an American physicist. After a long day of hiking in the Rockies, he takes a breather on the top of the mountain he has just ascended. Exhausted, quieted by the spectacular view, he takes a moment, looks around and contemplates the vast view before his eyes. He is able to distinguish and describe all these tiny energy flows that connect every single activity on Earth, be it the slight wind that agitates the branches of the trees down the slope, the little rocks that are falling from under his feet, the majesty of the rays of sunlight that irradiate the surrounding nature, and the growing plants that turn to it for life. At this moment, he is able to comprehend a superior order of the world. He may regret that he is unable to translate his emotions as beautifully as he would like to. His language is that of arduous mathematical equations, accessible to only a few. He shares his passion every Monday morning with his class, using a blackboard and writing down, enthused, a set of equations that his students can hardly decipher. He sighs, turns back to me, checks the time on his watch and turns around. The sun will set in a couple of hours. Time to head back. It lasted only a second, but I was watching him. I saw the intense emotion, the wonderment. Like a poet, he had a vision, and he is now reflecting on how best to transmit it to others. He knows that it will be difficult — maybe impossible. Yet, he just needs to catch the attention of one student and pass the torch of amazement so that the long chain of knowledge continues. Energy is not about oil, natural gas, coal, or renewables. It is not about deposits, reserves, and complex artificial transformations; it is about much more than that. Energy flows in multiple forms fuel all life on Earth, transmuting from one form into another in a harmonious ballet of complex entanglements.

What Is Energy?

Energy in physics represents a property transferred to an object in the form of work or heat. This is a very wide concept that takes on many different forms. Energy can be stored in fuel or materials; we talk about chemical energy. Wood or fossil fuels (which are nothing less than old biomass) store vast amounts of energy that can be released when burned. Plants also store energy; a form of energy that is vital to human and animal life. Less obvious is that energy is also determined by the position of a specific object in a force field. Take the famous apple of Isaac Newton. The apple falls from the tree because of the attraction from the gravitational field of Earth. Yet, an apple hanging from the same tree is equally pulled, but retained by the branch that holds it. We talk about potential energy. The same applies to water held in some form. Ice sheets on top of a mountain prevent water from flowing down to the valley. They also store loads of potential energy. The same is true for water dams. They retain water at a certain altitude, storing potential energy. Considerable amounts and forms of energy are thus stored in different systems.

The law of the conservation of energy, one of the primary principles of physics, states that the total energy of an isolated system can be neither created nor destroyed. It remains constant over time. When the apple falls of the tree branch, its potential energy (or stored energy) is converted into another form of energy: the speed at which it falls to the ground, kinetic energy. The same applies to a car in motion. The gasoline (a powerful form of energy storage) is burned and converted into heat. This heat pressurizes gas, which is then used to move a piston and eventually rotate the crankshaft. Through the power-train, this motional force is transferred to the wheels, which put the car in motion. The chemical energy has been converted into kinetic energy. Part of it has been wasted, in the form of unusable heat, released through the exhaust pipe or through the heat radiation of various mechanical parts of the engine. Another example is human life itself. Food is a form of chemical energy. It is this energy that enables proper body functioning, the essential fuel of our organs and brains. Chemical energy is converted again and everything humans do — be it thinking, working, or traveling — proceeds from this daily energy intake.

Nothing is lost: energy is simply converted from its original form into other forms of suitable energy (Energy Information Administration, 2020).

Earth is not an isolated system. Yet, it acts almost as if it is. The sun provides huge energy volumes, around 430 Exajoules (EJ) per hour. This figure may not mean anything, but let's compare it to the final energy demand of the world today. The two figures are around the same, except that the world's final energy demand is — per year. Hence, the sun strikes Earth with enough energy in one hour to fulfill all human needs in one year. Things are not that simple, however. A large portion of the sun's energy (around two-thirds) is actually reflected back directly by the atmosphere and the clouds. Only one-third of it is "absorbed" by the atmosphere, in the form of heat and radiation. Eventually, Earth radiates that heat back at night, when the planet cools down, and diffuses it back to space. The balance is nearly zero. No energy is created or destroyed.

There are many forms of energy conversions. Sun irradiation (the main source of energy on Earth) is converted into chemical energy through photosynthesis, heat through absorption, and even electricity through the use of photovoltaic cells. Chemical energy can be processed into heat through combustion (such as through gasoline in cars) or used to store electricity (such as in batteries). Thermal energy can be used to produce electricity (when rotating a turbine into a magnetic field) or converted into kinetic energy through thermal expansion (of gas). Electrical energy itself can be turned into a magnetic force through radiation, or converted into chemical energy through electrolysis, as well as heat through the Joule effect. We owe the magnificence of our modern civilization to the ability of humankind to learn how to harness energy and master its conversions to its own benefit.

I will stop here and not go into details further. Yet, you have understood. Energy is everywhere. It is the bloodline of everything that happens and of life itself, and, like the poet, the physicist deciphers these underlying flows of life that connect anything to everything, in a permanent conversion and transmission process.

What, then, are energy transitions?

A Brief History of Energy Transitions

The origins

We humans are part of these energy flows and depend on them. Like all other animals, we have been living on it. On the savannahs millions of years ago, where our distant ancestors first stood on their hind legs, humans foraged for food: plants, berries, beans. All these proceeded from and depended on photosynthesis. Later, humans began to hunt other animals, which depended on the same energy flows. Smil (2017) has brilliantly explained the energy equation that our ancestors faced. How much energy is needed to hunt and forage for food, versus the corresponding energy intake? Humans mastered fire about 450,000 years ago. This enabled a massive increase of energy intake through the cooking of food, particularly meat, and was the mother of all energy transitions. Then, 10,000 years ago (at the beginning of the Holocene), agriculture emerged in at least seven locations on three continents at approximately the same time (Smil, 2017). Humans began to settle down.

The roots of this revolution are lost to history. Yet, a combination of factors, stemming from environmental change (global warming) and social evolution (increased population) likely led to diminishing returns on food gathering and hunting in these locations, prepping the transition to a new form of living based on sedentarism and agriculture. Though some believe this transition has been essentially detrimental to humanity, it did transform it more fundamentally than any other, partly removing humankind from the cycles of nature and fueling a population explosion and the fundamental transformation and sophistication of societies (Hariri, 2014). However, at the dawn of the agricultural revolution, humankind continued to rely on fire, traditional energy sources from plants and crops, and essentially human effort.

Later, people learned to domesticate animals and use them as an alternative energy resource. The work carried out by animals (cows, horses, donkeys, and mules) could top three to seven times that of a human adult. This was the second energy transition. Harnessing the power of domestic animals helped improve agricultural yields, but did much more than that. Improved agricultural yields helped reduce the burden of growing crops, releasing parts of the population from it, which could then turn to other forms of work, such as artisanal manufacturing. It also enabled humans to realize works such as the construction of large cities and monuments. They would have been unable to engage in this without the support of these domestic animals.

Waterwheels or windmills progressively emerged as new forms of energy harvesting. Waterwheels were first reported in the first century BCE, but emerged at a larger scale during the Middle Ages. So did windmills. Despite their number and the progress they entailed, triggering modern industry for some, these ingenuous solutions never represented more than 1 percent of the total primary energy consumed by humanity, according to an estimate by Smil (2017).

The reality is indeed that the combination of energy fire from wood and animal power has remained the dominant principle of the energy system for humanity until only very recently, and one could argue that it is still the dominant system for millions around the world. At the beginning of the nineteenth century, wood still represented 90 percent of primary energy demand in France, and it remained the largest source of energy in the United States until the late 1880s. There were still millions of mules in the South of the United States in the 1950s, and the administration actually stopped counting them only in the 1960s.

The first industrial revolution

It is precisely around the early to mid-nineteenth century that a new energy transition occurred. The Chinese Han started using coal for iron smelting 2,000 years ago. However, it took centuries for coal to emerge as a dominant source of energy. The United Kingdom began to shift from wood to coal in the seventeenth and eighteenth centuries (with traces of early transitions as far back as the fourteenth century). The reason for this transition was the increased depletion of forests, which forced the United Kingdom to import vast quantities of wood from the Nordics, threatening their energy independence, security, and very development (Rhodes, 2018; Smil, 2017). They turned to coal, an energy source with an energy density higher than wood that the nation could source locally, preserving its independence. However, coal did much more than that.

In the eighteenth century, the first prototypes of steam machines emerged. Rhodes (2018) has explained that steam was initially used to remove water from coal mines, but that soon the systems were perfected, and it was not long before lighter and portable steam engines were designed. This was the real trigger point. Until then, the transition had been limited. The United Kingdom needed coal as an alternative to depleted wood. Steam was used to pump water out of mines, enabling miners to dig deeper into the ground for the precious fossil resource. At first, wood was used to generate the steam, then coal replaced it. And finally, as these pumps were perfected, steam engines emerged. The quality of the technology continued to improve, and the size of the engines decreased. Coal also needed to be transported. Someone had the idea to use these portable steam engines to pull wagons on rails, as an alternative to road or river carriages. The railroad system of the United Kingdom was born. And it changed everything. Within a few decades, distance was erased. Land planning took on a completely different dimension. While millions of villagers had been living in relative isolation from one another in the kingdom, barely traveling beyond the borders of their county, a world of opportunities emerged — and the economy was set on fire. The rest of Europe followed.

This "industrial revolution," although it was largely incremental and progressive (contrary to what is often stated), changed the world forever. While people in the early 1800s were living not so differently from those of the early 1700s, the young man of the early 1900s had a completely different life. He most certainly had left the village of his ancestors, and the farm on which his parents and grandparents had been living their entire lives. He had settled in a new neighborhood of the capital city of his county (Birmingham, Manchester, maybe London). The building blocks were new but poor. He had a room, a small coal-fired stove, and a bed. He would be working 60 hours a week in a factory, for a small salary (Economic History Association, 2020). On Sundays, after mass, he could travel to the city and visit it, amazed at its beauties, before returning to his neighborhood and getting a drink at the local pub.

This great transition is also the story of all our ancestors. The grandfather of my father was the first person to leave his small village of "La Chapelle d'Aurec" (try finding it on the map!) in Auvergne, France, for the city nearby, and four generations later, I am writing this book from Hong Kong. It was the 1890s. France was a good half-century behind the United Kingdom. I visited this small village, lost in the forests of Auvergne, bewildered and touched by the memory of such ancient times, which are not so far away in time after all.

Coal and steam dominated the 1800s. Railways erased distances and propelled the Industrial Revolution. This is also what durably transformed the United States and led to the spectacular "conquest of the West," turning the nation into one of the dominant world economies. With this revolution, the need for steel rapidly increased, and this period became the age of steel, celebrated by the erection of the Eiffel Tower in Paris for the "Exposition Universelle" of 1889.

The second industrial revolution

Yet, new energy transitions were to happen. Since ancient times, nighttime was mysterious; a time of evil spells, susceptible to all sorts of imaginary thoughts, legends, and fears. There was light of course, but it was expensive and in scarce supply. People used plants, or wax from bees, and built candles. They would burn for some time and fight the surrounding darkness before inevitably fading away. Life at night was impossible. People thus developed other ways of procuring light. One of the most famous techniques was to use oil from whales. Herman Melville's famous novel illustrated the race to hunt whales in the Northern Atlantic in the 1800s in order to obtain sperm whale oil, a superior fuel for lamps. Other techniques involved the use of town gas, particularly in Europe and large urban centers. However, these techniques were eventually surpassed by a new emerging technology: electricity. Electricity had been known for millennia already: 600 years BCE, Thales wrote down his observations on static electricity. However, electricity became a serious object of research only from the seventeenth century onward. William Gilbert published a study on electricity and magnetism. This was followed by numerous research experiments throughout the seventeenth, eighteenth, and nineteenth centuries. In the mid-1700s, Benjamin Franklin was the first to correlate lightning with electric power. In 1800, Alessandro Volta designed the first electric storage system, the voltaic pile. From then on, everything accelerated. Hans Christian Oersted and Andre-Marie Ampere discovered electromagnetism in 1820; a year later, in 1821, Michel Faraday developed the first electric motor. In the early 1860s, James Clerk Maxwell linked electricity and magnetism once and for all. This discovery — the famous Maxwell's equations — would lead to the design of the first transistor in 1947, which led to the emergence of electronics and the modern IT industry.

Throughout the late nineteenth century, electrical engineering accelerated, leading to major new applications designed by people such as Alexander Graham Bell, Lord Kelvin, Werner von Siemens, and, maybe more importantly, Thomas Edison, George Westinghouse, and Nikola Tesla. Thomas Edison built the first industrialized light bulbs and developed the first electric substation in Pearl Street, New York, in 1882. He was quickly followed and eventually surpassed by George Westinghouse and Nikola Tesla, who developed large-scale power generation (hydroelectric dams) and contemporary electric networks. The first main application of these developments was to bring light to houses in cities and eventually throughout the country. Life at night became possible, leading to a score of possibilities and new developments that took civilization a step closer to where it is today. From its onset, the development of electricity became unstoppable. It did not stop with lighting. Electric welding enabled humans to build robust and larger infrastructure: steel-made ships, bridges, etc. Electric motors brought considerable motion power alongside automated work. Electricity was instrumental to the development of modern communications, enabling greater precision and uniformity. The world entered the electric age.

At the same time, oil emerged as a new energy resource as well. Oil was already familiar to Mesopotamians — who used it as asphalt for their buildings — and to the Chinese, who used it to evaporate brine and produce salt. Yet, its formidable development started in North America. In 1850, Abraham Gesner created kerosene from oil refining. The fuel burned more cleanly than competing products and was less expensive. And so the modern development of oil extraction and refining began. Yet, it is only when the first combustion engines were developed that the demand for oil truly exploded. Various developments in combustion engines since the late 1700s had occurred. It was however only in the late 1870s that German engineers (Nicolaus Otto, Gottlieb Daimler, Wilhelm Maybach, and later Karl Benz and Rudolf Diesel) developed the first series of commercial gasoline engines. Smil (2017) notably recalls the ideas of Diesel, who sought to deploy his engines in small workshops. He thought that by doing so, he would ease the burden of many factory workers. Yet, his invention led to something completely different, which took a few decades to develop. At first, automobiles were expensive and would often run out of fuel. Yet, the concurrent development of electricity made it possible to build more infrastructure, and thousands-kilometers-long pipelines could now be installed, connecting extraction sites to refining stations and end-user demand, flooding the world with oil. Oil became even cheaper, and then the Ford T by Henry Ford entered the stage. Introduced in 1908, its cost per horsepower was already ten times lower than that of a normal carriage. And this was just the beginning. A decade later, costs had dropped fourfold (Arbib and Seba, 2020).

The outcome was clear. Within a decade (1910–20), most horses serving as means to transport people within New York were replaced by cars. The world had entered the oil age. Individual transportation emerged as a new paradigm, and, once again, distances shrank, leading to a whole new relationship with mobility and the development of large suburban areas. Civilization advanced at rocket speed. Over the next decades, ship construction also improved, and by the mid-1900s, the first commercial flights became available. In 2018, there were more than 4.3 billion air passenger trips every year (International Civil Aviation Organization, 2019).

A historic moment of innovation

Within a century, humanity had developed all the technologies that it founded its rapid progress on, with three consecutive transitions occurring in parallel: that of coal and steam, that of electricity, and that of oil. These transitions first revolutionized transport and erased distances. Doing so, they also largely erased cultural differences. These discoveries moreover pushed economic productivity to levels that would have been hard to imagine a century before. Agriculture, industrial manufacturing, and infrastructure construction changed forever. Everything became possible. And with this, development advanced, improving living standards and changing conditions for the better. There is no better summary of this progress than the one that Vaclav Smil gave in his momentous work on the history of energy (2017). I summarize it in the following graph, which provides the power output of dominant technologies at different periods in history, to which I have added the evolution of the world's population (Our World in Data, 2020) (Figure 1). Careful though: this is a logarithmic scale! What it shows is the unprecedented development of technology of the last two centuries, and how it contributed to an also unprecedented explosion of the world's population.

And indeed, the period of the late 1800s is probably one of the most innovative eras of all times. All the building blocks were here — they had been researched since the 1700s — but they all combined during this period to accelerate the development of civilization and create and fuel new uses, transforming lives for the better but also for the worse. The twentieth century lived up to it. These technologies then continued to expand and improve. The first nuclear reactors were designed in the mid-1900s to produce gigawatt volumes of electric power. The Maxwell equations led to the creation, in 1947, of the first transistor, the core building block of modern electronics. This progressively led to the build-up of the IT industry and our modern information systems and the Internet. However, the twentieth century was also the century of two world wars fought between industrial powers. The atrocious level of casualties (an estimated 70 million in

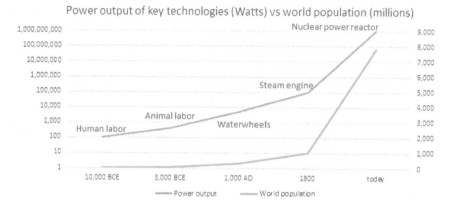

Figure 1   Power output of key technologies

World War II) was to a large extent the result of industrial grade killing capabilities. It was also during the twentieth century that pollution levels from burning fossil fuels increased to alarming levels. In the early 1980s, a significant thinning of the ozone layer (a key constituent of Earth's atmosphere) was discovered over Antarctica. It soon became clear that this was the result of the mass diffusion of aerosols by the modern economy at that time, and it took a global ban on these dangerous substances to prevent the worst from happening. Nowadays, scientists from the Intergovernmental Panel on Climate Change (IPCC) have accelerated research on climate change and established with near certainty that massive greenhouse gas emissions (75 percent of it being carbon dioxide — CO_2 — from the combustion of fossil fuels) and their build-up within the atmosphere are having an impact on the climate on the surface of the planet.

What does this very brief review of the history of energy transition tell us about the upcoming one?

Long, Complex and Entangled, Demand-Driven Transitions

Energy transitions overlap

Time to make sense of it all. First, we can observe that energy transitions actually overlap. New forms of energy do not necessarily substitute previous energy forms, at least not immediately. They emerge and then complement other historical uses of energy. Never in history has one source of energy quickly substituted another in all its final uses. When the first gasoline engines emerged and led to the development of cars, they did not substitute animal use everywhere. It took four more decades to fully mechanize agriculture. Even during

World War II, the use of horses remained largely prevalent, at least in the German army. The example of New York's substitution of horses by cars within a decade is often quoted as an example of disruptive innovation, and to a large extent it is. But horses remained domesticated animals that were used in many areas of the economy long after the revolution happened there.

Another way to look at this fact is to contemplate the primary energy mix of the world today, more than a century after these transitions took place. Bioenergy (essentially made from traditional biomass, or wood) still represented 10 percent of total primary energy demand in 2018, coal 27 percent, and oil 31 percent. Primary energy demand stands for raw resources. Some of them are converted (into electricity, gasoline, etc.) to fuel final demand needs. In terms of final energy demand: in 2018, oil represented 41 percent of final demand, electricity 19 percent, bioenergy 11 percent, and coal 10 percent (International Energy Agency, 2019). Traditional energy sources like wood continue to be used as the primary resource in many new economies, despite the tremendous developments witnessed for over a century. Oil, thanks to its high energy density and high transportability, has won the battle in the transport sector. Coal remains largely used in heavy industries such as steel mills or cement plants and sometimes for household heating in certain economies, including modern ones! Electricity and gas pretty much share the rest of uses. Electricity is more versatile and fuels all appliances and some electric motors and heating systems, but not in a dominant way. Gas is primarily used as a heat source in mature economies' households and as a substitute to coal in a number of heavy industries. Lags in development across the world and specific local decisions on fuels of choice are the true reasons for this complex energy mix. Transitions are thus always imperfect substitutions and are more complex than one would initially imagine.

Energy transitions take time and build on the old system

There may be another reason for this complex energy landscape: transitions take time. Smil (2017) argues that it typically takes 50 to 60 years for a new source of energy to peak in terms of use (if it peaks at all). Some of the Shell experts tend to confirm this trend. They argue that it takes 20 to 40 years for a technology to reach maturity and 1 percent of world energy demand, then another 30 years to move from 1 percent to 10 percent or more (Shell, 2014).

The other critical paradigm is that these new technologies actually build on the previous system before they replace it. An example would be the initial stationary steam machines that used to pump water out of coal mines. Initially powered by wood, they were eventually powered by coal. The same could be said of modern renewable power. The manufacturing of solar photovoltaic panels or wind turbines consumes significant amounts of energy, which is delivered by the system in place — coal-fired power plants for the most part. Indeed, an argument often raised against these modern technologies is that they create a lot of pollution in their manufacture, but that argument does not hold a second when we look at the experience of history. It could not be otherwise, and it does not preclude the long-term sustainability of these technologies. I will come back to this.

Another interesting argument from Smil is that innovation follows critical dynamics: what he calls 50-year innovation "pulsations" (Smil, 2017, p. 411). He argues that these "pulsations" are often triggered by economic depressions. He notes that most of these "innovation clusters" fall "almost perfectly into the midpoints of Schumpeterian downswings": the diffusion of mobile steam engines between 1843 and 1869, the arrival of commercial electricity between 1898 and 1924, and the modern developments of commercial transport and modern electronics post–World War II. The question that we could ask ourselves though is this: can these cycles now be accelerated, as the world has clearly entered a new era where access to information and trade is truly globalized? I will come back to this question further below as I progress through the argument.

Energy transitions are a byproduct of demand innovations

Yet, there may be an even more striking conclusion, and I again quote Smil (2017, p. 426):

> As far as fuels are concerned, history would have taken a different course if coal had been used merely as a substitute for wood in open fireplaces, or if crude oil had remained limited to kerosene for lighting. In most cases it has not been the access to abundant energy resources or to particular prime movers that made the long-term difference. Decisive factors were rather the quest for innovation and the commitment to deploying and perfecting new resources and techniques and finding new uses.

Indeed, what truly drives energy transitions is not so much the emergence of new energy supply technologies but more so what people do with these. Of course, these technologies play a decisive role. Would they not exist, there would be no innovation. Yet, what history teaches us is that the "pulsations" of innovation are driven by "new uses," or, in other words, social progress. And social progress manifests itself with greater abundance: in the form of access to services at a fraction of past costs or access to new services that did not exist before, and ultimately in the ability to achieve more and dedicate more time to new activities as traditional ones become simpler and cheaper to execute. Energy transitions are part of this much broader context, which I could refer to as "industrial revolutions" (even though the term is likely limiting). They are driven by innovations in usage. And these innovations in usage are made possible by new technological developments. Energy technologies are part of it, but one part only.

Let me illustrate this. The first industrial revolution would not have happened without coal. Yet, it is not coal that defined the first industrial revolution, but rather the invention of the steam engine and the great idea to put it on rails to transport goods and later people. It is when the demand for these new innovations emerged that the energy system began to transform at a rapid pace, pulled by demand. Another example would be lighting. Lighting existed before electricity. But electricity delivered it at a fraction of its previous cost and with a great deal of convenience previously unmatched. This changed everything, because enjoying light at night became ubiquitous, effortless, and convenient, transforming people's habits and modes of life. This time it was not about a "new use" but rather about an existing service that could suddenly become widely accessible and hence be generalized. And with lighting came the demand for electricity. The same could be said about the transition to oil for transport. When cheap oil was combined with standardized and light combustion engines, transport by car became possible. All of a sudden, there was no longer the need to remove manure from the streets of New York, or to take care of the animals that people depended on so much. Automotive transport skyrocketed. It was more convenient, more accessible, and cheaper. In this case, an existing service (transport) was substituted by a better one as well. And the continuous perfection of the engineering generalized car adoption as years passed, while new opportunities (or new services) emerged, such as commercial flights. And with private transport came the demand for more oil.

This specific pattern of energy transitions is probably also one of the causes of the earlier conclusions I drew. Since not all demand shifts at the same time, energy systems tend to overlap in a complex energy mix and take more time to complete. In summary, demand drives the supply of energy, which decides the pace and extent of energy transitions. This is the analysis of demand pattern evolutions that can help predict upcoming transitions.

The Upcoming Energy Transition Will Not Be as Experts Currently Frame It

This conclusion, as obvious as it may seem in light of the above, might be received as a revolutionary statement by the small circle of energy experts.

I devote a large part of my professional and personal time to reviewing energy and climate transition scenarios. Guess what? None of them actually go into demand-side evolutions in depth. In general terms, most of these scenarios take demand as a bulk inelastic exogenous factor that the supply system must adapt to by maximizing its potential and minimizing constraints to it. Yet, as we have just seen, demand is not exogeneous to the energy supply system. The central point of the energy system is demand. To be provocative, I would argue that the energy system is merely a byproduct of a score of innovations that actually have little to do with energy. This is probably why all these scenarios are challengeable from the start. This is probably also why in the past, they often failed to identify the true disruptions that were emerging, and why in the future, they will continue to do so unless they truly pivot to analyzing possible demand evolutions in depth. It is moreover the potential reason that they are failing to identify reasonable pathways to decarbonization, the big "theme" of the current energy transition conversation that is promoting unreliable or extremely expensive options. This while maybe another course could be charted: one that is faster and cheaper and that advances civilization. In other words, most of these scenarios look at replacing like-for-like one energy source by another, without any change in the economic structure, while history has shown that both advance together.

I acknowledge the severity of my argument regarding existing scenarios and forecasts. Yet, when one forecasts as far in time as 2050 or 2070, it is nonsense to not integrate such evidence. And when it comes to the countless discussions around climate change, it is time to understand that the objective is not to replicate the "old system" like-for-like with a new portfolio of decarbonized energies, but rather to change the system itself. This is, by the way, an inevitable reality. Whether policies are efficient or not, our environment will transform, as humanity seeks greater abundance and innovates accordingly. Policies are useful in helping to make those transformations proceed as quickly and smoothly as possible. The energy transition is then a natural consequence.

This new approach to the upcoming energy transition is what I set out to explore. In the following chapters, I will try to outline some of the possible developments in demand and how they could ultimately transform the energy supply system.

Let me finish this chapter with a reflection on where our energy system stands today and on the reason why we are currently having heated debates on the decarbonization of the economy. Back in the early 1900s, global final energy demand was around 8,000 TWh. It was roughly twice that of the early 1800s. By the end of the twentieth century, global demand rose to around 80,000 TWh, or nearly tenfold (based on Ritchie and Roser, 2015 and Tverberg, 2012). This is due to a combination of factors. First, the population expanded, from around 1.6 billion to 6 billion people by the early 2000s. Second, energy demand per capita exploded, driven by all the developments I described above. It stood at around 5,000 kWh annually in 1900 (a global average; industrial economies likely saw energy demand per capita that was two to three times higher, and the rest of the world two to three times lower). By 2000, this figure was 12,000 kWh per year, or 2.5 times larger. The combination of both explains the rise in energy demand. Now, let's take us a century forward. Demographic projections tell us that the population will keep increasing until it hits the 11–12 billion mark. There are obviously great uncertainties to such forecasts, but demographers have traditionally been proven to issue reliable projections (Camdessus, 2017). Global energy demand per capita in mature economies is today much higher than in new economies. It stands at around 20,000 kWh per year in Europe, and twice as much in the United States (though the country has seen a progressive drop over the last decades) (International Energy Agency, 2019). Let's estimate for the sake of the exercise that the world demand for energy will stabilize at around 30,000 kWh per year per capita (lower than current US levels) and that, by the end of the century, all nations of the world will have reached comparable economic development levels. This would lead to around 330,000 TWh of energy demand, or four times the 2000 levels and 40 times the 1900 levels.

With an energy system similar to the one in 2000 (with 25 $GtCO_2$ yearly emissions), that would translate into over 100 $GtCO_2$ per year, or an accumulation of carbon dioxide in the atmosphere that would probably top everything the planet has known for millions of years. It has already exceeded average levels of the last 800,000 years. At this level, would deniers of climate change still hold on to the inanity of human-driven climate transformations?

There are around 200 years of fossil fuel reserves, if we include retrievable reserves (i.e., those that have not yet been proven to be economically viable; Petit, 2017). With an energy demand four times the level of 2000, these reserves would be nearly exhausted by 2100, forcing the transition — an unprecedented event in history.

The bottom line of this argument is this: Humanity has grown large and wealthy, and it will continue to do so in the coming decades, as billions of people reach middle-class levels and standards of living that approach those of modern economies. The current of history is unstoppable. The impact on the energy system will be momentous, with global energy demand expected to reach — if no change — levels where it will face "systemic" and truly "global" issues, be it in terms of the planet or of the energy reserves available, in stark contrast with past energy transitions. And some of these growing issues might well become reasons for change, hence reasons for innovation. In the end, we can safely posit that it is more than ever critical to offer a fresh perspective on the subject, one that will focus on demand evolutions.

References

Arbib, J. and Seba, T. (2020). *Rethinking Humanity: Five Foundational Sector Disruptions, the Lifecycle of Civilizations, and the Coming Age of Freedom*. RethinkX, June. https://www.rethinkx.com/humanity.

Camdessus, M. (2017). *Vers le Monde de 2050*. Paris: Fayard.

Economic History Association. (2020). "Hours of Work in US History." EH.net Encyclopedia. https://eh.net/encyclopedia/hours-of-work-in-u-s-history/.

Energy Information Administration. (2020). "What is Energy?" Last updated June 18, 2020. https://www.eia.gov/energyexplained/what-is-energy/.

Hariri, Y. N. (2014). *Sapiens: A Brief History of Humankind*. London: Harvill Secker.

International Civil Aviation Organization. (2019). "The World of Air Transport in 2018." In *Annual Report of the Council*. https://www.icao.int/annual-report-2018/Pages/the-world-of-air-transport-in-2018.aspx.

International Energy Agency ©. (2019). *World Energy Outlook*. November 2019. Paris: IEA. https://www.iea.org/reports/world-energy-outlook-2019.

Our World in Data. (2020). "World Population since 10,000 BCE." https://ourworldin-data.org/grapher/world-population-since-10000-bce-ourworldindata-series.

Petit, V. (2017). *The Energy Transition: An Overview of the True Challenge of the 21st Century*. Cham, Switzerland: Springer.

Rhodes, R. (2018). *Energy. A Human History*. New York: Simon & Shuster.

Ritchie, H. and Roser, M. (2015). "Energy." Our World in Data. https://ourworld indata.org/energy.

Shell. (2014). *The Colours of Energy. Essays on the Future of Energy in Society*, edited by G. J. Kramer and B. Vermeer. Amsterdam: Shell. https://www.shell.com/energy-and-innovation/the-energy-future/colours.html.

Smil, V. (2017). *Energy and Civilization. A History*. Cambridge, MA: MIT Press.

Tverberg, G. (2012). "World Energy Consumption since 1820 in Charts." The Oil Drum, Institute for the Study of Energy and Our Future, March 16, 2012. http://theoildrum.com/node/9023.

CHAPTER 2

The Current So-Called Energy Transition Has Not Yet Started

"If you have always done it that way, it is probably wrong." (Charles Kettering)

The Initial Kick

Energy transitions are demand-driven. The history of the successive transitions that have occurred in the last centuries has shown a repeating pattern. In the beginning, there is always the search for greater abundance in everything we do and consume. Ultimately, humanity innovates to improve its condition and create social progress. Innovations are developed by visionary scientists and engineers who build on the latest technological advancements, including energy technologies, but are not limited to them. Energy technologies are obviously a powerful enabler, but technological improvements in other resources may also prove vital in reframing value chains: what materials are being used and how they are produced and then used in the manufacturing of all the essential goods we consume. Beyond resources, another key area of technological enhancements has to do with how the system is designed; in other words, how global trade is organized. This spans across both physical flows (transport of people and goods) and nonphysical ones (namely information). Ultimately, these technologies can drive innovations, and innovations will frame new services or deliver better existing services, be it with more convenience or at a fraction of their past cost (or both!). It may take decades to get there. Yet, when these innovations finally emerge and "make sense," they get adopted. And it is only when this happens that the energy mix begins to evolve. Over a few decades, these perfected existing uses or new uses penetrate the economy at an increasing pace, change behavioral patterns, and ultimately transform the system in which we operate. Very often, they also influence adjacent sectors of the economy and transform them as well. In doing so, they dictate the energy mix evolution, which grows in line with these new needs.

The example of the oil revolution described above is emblematic of this process. The world did not actually undergo an "oil revolution" per se; instead, it underwent an "individual transportation revolution," of which oil was one of the core building blocks. Cheap refined oil emerged in the last part of the nineteenth century, as we have seen, but it was only when oil was combined with combustion engines and — more importantly — when it was made easily accessible (through electrically welded pipelines) that all constituents of the disruption were finally assembled. From then on, it took only a few entrepreneurs to build the model, and within a decade, all horses from New York City were replaced by cars. The "individual transportation revolution" was on a revolutionary course. Motorized transport did not apply to cars only. It also transformed naval transportation and enabled commercial air transportation. When this occurred, the globalization of trade became inevitable. And it did not stop here either. Petrochemical factories were also built, which used oil products as well to deliver new materials. The plastics revolution, which transformed packaging and redefined supply chains, but also led to plastic becoming a core material component in pretty much everything, emerged from it. After a century of continuous improvements in the model, oil now represents around 40 percent of final energy demand. The energy transition to oil has reached maturity, and the world is now addicted to it.

What about a new energy transition then?

This theme has been front-page news in the last years, notably with the rise of renewable power. The rationale is this: findings from the Intergovernmental Panel on Climate Change (IPCC) over the last decades have raised government officials' and, more importantly, broader society's awareness of the impact that fossil-fuel-based human activities have had on the climate. The quality of the IPCC's content has been criticized in the last decades, although the IPCC has always made it clear that climate change was a new field of science, with scores of questions to be investigated. Growing access to mass computing has made it possible to make rapid progress in climate modeling and further refine the original conclusions. The IPCC is truly a unique multilateral science effort aimed at pulling all climate scientists' work into a single narrative to properly inform governments around the world of a truly global phenomenon at hand. What did they find out? In short, they have clearly established that recently observed climate change — while potentially influenced by several astronomic factors and albedo (the reflection of ice sheets and land and absorption by vegetation and oceans) — was mainly the product of anthropogenic emissions; in other words, human activities. Our fossil-fuel-based civilization has been accumulating massive quantities of greenhouse gases in the atmosphere since the inception of the industrial revolutions. Total concentration in the atmosphere has now reached 3,000 GtCO$_2$, around 30 percent more than in 1750, or an additional 1,000 GtCO$_2$. This is less than what was ejected in total: land and oceans today absorb around half of total emissions. This level of absorption was probably higher at the beginning of the Industrial Revolution, when volumes of emissions were lower (Intergovernmental Panel on Climate Change, 2007, 2014). The theme of this book is not to review climate change in itself. Let's just say that the global acknowledgment of the negative effects of human activities has triggered the current debate on a necessary energy transition, away from fossil fuels.

We have seen before that reducing carbon emissions will be one driver among many others, and that failing to apprehend the others (without discarding this one!) would lead to wrong scenarios and pathways. Yet, one question could be posed. Could it be that the next energy transition will be forced on us, notably by massive policy changes?

I will come back to this question at the end of this chapter. First, however, it is important to acknowledge that — as a result of this growing threat — innovation has been spurred in every lab around the world, trying to solve the energy dilemma. And for over a decade, a score of new ideas and projects has emerged. The whole purpose of this research is to find ways to harness energies that are alternatives to fossil fuels and come up with a solution that could be efficient and cheap enough to trigger a switch. This is a fascinating time for scientists around the world, if one can say that there has ever been a time that was not fascinating for those who spend their entire lives trying to push the boundaries of knowledge. I remember the excitement surrounding some of these early works 20 years ago when I was a graduate student at the University of Texas, Austin. Labs were always busy on weekends, as students from the Electrical and Computer Engineering department would get together to go on with their experiments, with a handful of passionate professors to mentor them. Since then, the level of excitement has only grown. In 2019, I visited the National Renewable Energy Laboratory in Denver, Colorado, and spent a day hanging out with their specialists and meeting a cohort of students working in jeans and sneakers on very advanced new projects. I could not help but think: who knows? We might well pull this thing off in the end! And I wished I had been 20 years younger…

Not-So-New Energy Sources

My takeaway from visits like the one I just mentioned is that there are essentially four energy flows that scientists intend to harness: solar irradiation, other renewable sources (geothermal, winds, ocean tides), heat, and nuclear energy.

Most of this research looks at converting these energy flows into electricity, the most pervasive and ubiquitous energy vehicle of our modern civilization. Yet, there are also projects that look at adjacent solutions, such as converting one of these primary energy sources into heat or chemical energy (fuels), but they are not mainstream. I will come back to the inherent benefits of electricity in a later chapter.

"This giant [free] nuclear reactor in the sky" (E. Musk)

Solar irradiation is probably the most promising source of primary energy. As I explained in the first chapter, the sheer amount of energy that the sun transfers to Earth is beyond imagination and could — if properly harnessed — largely exceed everything humanity may need to survive and thrive, now and forever. The dominant form of solar power conversion is photovoltaics, building on the photoelectric effect, where absorbed light causes the excitation of electrons. This creates voltage and current that can then flow through a semiconductor. Other forms of conversion include the direct conversion of solar irradiation into heat for locally distributed purposes in households or replicating the photosynthesis effect. Yet, these development areas are not mainstream compared to photovoltaics, so I will not look into them in further detail. However, as this book is largely focused on innovation, it is important to mention them. Who knows?

The photoelectric effect was discovered in 1839 by a French scientist: Edmond Becquerel; another centuries-old discovery from the greatest period of innovation in history. Photovoltaic panels were initially used in space, when the first satellites were launched. It was indeed easier to generate power directly from the sun's energy (and store its excess in batteries) than to load up on fuel for 20 years of operation, a nonstarter. Today's dominant types of photovoltaic panels are crystalline silicon modules. Their efficiency averages around 15 percent (they capture 15 percent of solar irradiation) and they are around 200 micrometers thick. They are the first generation of solar photovoltaic panels. Deployed globally, they represent around 90 percent of existing installations. Their production is relatively complex, as near pure silicon must first be produced before it is cut into wafers.

Yet, the repetitive aspect of solar cells (the more you produce, the more electric power you build) has enabled mass economies of scale as production ramped up. This is what explains the dramatic cost reduction (over 80 percent) in the last decade. In addition, this solid-state technology, with no moving parts, has proved to be extremely robust, ensuring decades-long lifetimes with minimum maintenance. This is also why we can talk about an infinitely scalable technology, with costs expected to collapse way below those of other traditional technologies.

But solar photovoltaic technology has not yet reached maturity. Research is at its climax, and many new discoveries and solutions are on their way. Second-generation solar technologies are based on thin-film technologies, where a thin layer of photovoltaic material is deposited on a substrate such as glass or plastic. These layers are typically around 1 micrometer thick, or less. For a long time, their deployment has been limited by poor efficiency. Yet, significant progress has been made in recent years, and their cost is lower than that of conventional silicon panels because of a much simpler production process. They however barely reach 10 percent of worldwide production today, and their share has actually declined in recent years with the mass flow of first-generation silicon panels onto the market. This could however evolve going forward. At first sight, these technologies offer a broad range of new applications. Because of their gauge, they can be integrated almost everywhere — notably on flexible surfaces — and even laminated in windows.

Third-generation solar photovoltaics might offer the opportunity for this breakthrough. They follow the same principle as second-generation solar cells. They are very thin and could even be used in special kinds of paint, offering a broad range of very low-cost new applications (Power Technology, 2014). This kind of technology breakthrough would bring a whole new level of decentralization to energy supply. Perovskite-based solar cells are the most promising option, and they have received tremendous attention over the last years. Their efficiency has made remarkable headway, but research still needs to focus on lifetime expectancy, as these materials tend to degrade quickly. Atomic-scale research (bio- and nanotechnologies, see below) will play a critical role in enabling the further development of materials with increased photovoltaic capabilities (Hockfield, 2019).

To date, third-generation photovoltaics have mainly been used as a complement to traditional silicon solar cells, namely to enhance performance. The deployment of such technologies has in effect been limited by the lack of an adequate business model. Traditional applications such as large arrays of solar panels continue to dominate. This is why historical technologies have kept increasing in share. But, and I will come back to that, nothing is defined forever, especially when innovation kicks in.

Finally, some research is focused on infrareds. Traditional photovoltaics capture only the visible part of the light spectrum. Several scientists around the world are now investigating the potential of infrared light, which could boost efficiencies way over 50 percent. In addition, Earth refracts the infrared spectrum of light back at night. Hence, in theory, such panels could produce electricity at night. We are still at an early stage of development though.

To wrap up, solar technologies are among the most promising energy sources. Traditional photovoltaics are infinitely scalable and highly decentralized.

What is even more promising is that, because of these patterns, these technologies tend to show increasing rates of return over time. Let's take the example of a solar panel deployed on a rooftop. That panel provides energy for 20 years. Then, it is replaced by a new panel, which — thanks to technological enhancements — provides better energy yields. In other words, more solar energy can be extracted from the same surface over time. This starkly contrasts with traditional extractive activities, such as oil and gas extraction or coal mining, where energy resources are depleted over time. In this case, resources increase over time.

Other well-known renewable energies

There are other renewable energy flows that scientists consider harnessing, beyond solar power. The first that may come to mind is wind flows. Wind turbines have been around for ages. Windmills in the Middle Ages were the first kind of such applications. Modern wind turbines follow essentially the same principle, except that they convert wind energy into electricity, rather than directly into mechanical power. Modern wind farms have reached cost levels that are extremely competitive with conventional power plants and have therefore received a lot of attention. They have been deployed in all mature economies at a rapid pace. Yet, today, they still represent a minor share of the power mix. One of the main drawbacks of wind power has been the rather large social opposition to their deployment because of land-use planning issues. Wind farms tend to take up tremendous space, often near coastal areas, and in some areas, they have been reported to endanger biodiversity. Offshore wind farms could thus be more promising. In addition to solving some of the critical issues of traditional wind farms, they also have the advantage that they can reach much higher efficiency levels, because ocean winds are usually steadier than those onshore. They are obviously more expensive to deploy, however, although their costs have significantly decreased in the last decades.

Beyond wind, there are other energy flows that scientists look at. One of them is geothermal energy. Harnessing the heat from Earth's crust has been around for decades in regions blessed with high volumes of low-depth heat. The very first project that I worked on when I started my engineering career was that of a new geothermal plant in Guadeloupe, 15 kilometers away from the Soufriere volcano. This project harnessed high-temperature heat (250°C) at a relatively low depth of 300 meters; hence the profitability of the project. Geothermal expansion has proven to be difficult, however, as its success mainly depends on regional characteristics. Unless large volumes of heat are accessible at low depths, the corresponding electricity produced may never prove competitive. Geothermal energy has nevertheless been in use in a number of smaller-scale applications around the world to provide low-density heat in households. There, the principle is simpler: there is no production of electricity. Heat is pumped out of the ground to a household. The gradient in temperature is often enough to significantly reduce the need for electric or gas-based heating. The beauty of such installations is that the same flows help provide cooling in summer.

Other scientists have been working on tidal energy. Harnessing ocean current flows to run turbines and produce electricity is a fascinating idea. The regularity of these flows also promises to produce constant quantities of energy. The largest tidal power station provides 254 MW of electricity. It is based out of South Korea. Yet, tidal power has never really found its market, and its development today remains mostly at the pilot stage. For reasons similar to those of geothermal energy development, tidal power progress has been limited by geography, preventing tidal energy from being adopted at a mass scale and hence reducing costs.

Another energy flow that scientists consider is that of heat itself and its conversion into electricity. Heat is everywhere. It is, first, a byproduct of solar irradiation, but it turns out to also be the largest part of energy wasted in human-driven processes. The operation of an engine, the transport of natural gas through a pipeline, and the smelting of iron all produce vast quantities of heat that are lost to the atmosphere. Consequently, a number of researchers have looked at harnessing this wasted energy and converting it into usable electricity. This is what is often referred to as thermoelectric generation. Again, the thermoelectric effect was discovered at the dawn of the nineteenth century by the Baltic German physicist Seebek. The main issue with thermoelectric generation, however, has been its very low efficiency: below 10 percent. Nevertheless, scientists are now exploring new solutions that increase its yield to much higher efficiency levels (Becker, 2016). To date, most applications considered relate to very small-scale and distributed applications, with low power requirements. For example, thermoelectric generation devices are used for large oil or gas pipelines' monitoring, removing the need to bring power to some of the remote places this infrastructure crosses.

The most recent energy source, the atom — but not mature yet

It is striking to see that most of these developments have actually built on scientific discoveries made in the nineteenth century. Some of them have made great strides since the beginning of the twentieth century, such as electricity or electromagnetism, while others have been lagging to date and are still being studied in university labs around the world by enthusiastic cohorts of researchers. I will finish this quick overview of new energy technologies with one scientific discovery made in the twentieth century: nuclear power. The Manhattan Project, which took place during World War II, led to the creation of the first nuclear weapons. It was directed by Robert Oppenheimer and built on experiments in the 1930s by Lord Rutherford and Enrico Fermi and the eventual 1938 discovery of nuclear fission by two German scientists: Otto Hahn and Fritz Strassmann.

It is after the war that research on peaceful applications of nuclear power really started. The scientific community was very excited at first. Nobel Prize laureate Glenn Seaborg dreamed up the perspective of an entirely nuclear-powered world; a world where there would be "nuclear powered earth-to-moon shuttles, nuclear powered artificial hearts, plutonium heated swimming pools for scuba divers, and much more" (Geddes, 1945). This excitement turned into massive investments in the development of a civil nuclear industry. First-generation reactors were built in the 1950s and 1960s, but nuclear power truly reached its fame in the 1970s, when the two oil crises led to a rush toward diversifying away from fossil fuels and reducing dependencies on the Middle East. At its peak, there were nearly 200 new reactors under construction in the world. At this point in time, enthused scientists projected that civil nuclear power would reach 5,000 GW by 2000 (or the equivalent of installed worldwide power capacity). This prospect was proven wrong, as nuclear power reached 350 GW by that date (International Energy Agency, 2019). Here is why. First-generation technologies (Light Water Reactors — LWR, which then evolved into Pressurized Water Reactors — PWR) directly built on military research. The sensitivity of this industry, its limited capability (as it was tied to military research), and the overall scarcity of the competency pool that resulted from it implied a "lock-in" on this type of technology (McGlynn, 2019).

Military-derived technical solutions presented three main flaws that the industry never recovered from. Safety was the first of these. Other designs would have been safer to operate but were discarded early in the process, mainly for financial reasons. Later, safety systems would grow in complexity following some of the incidents that occurred in nuclear power plants, lifting costs dramatically to constitute up to 25 percent of total capital costs of modern nuclear power plants.

Next, efficiency. With the advent of nuclear power, concerns over the scarcity of uranium resources arose. Though this never materialized, designs evolved over time (notably in the latest generation) to reduce dependency on uranium. Expensive designs thus made it possible to reduce the need for what turned out to be a rather broadly available material that represents only a fraction of total costs of nuclear power plants.

The last of the critical flaws that hampered the development of nuclear power was competency. Scarce and limited, the competency pool decreased even further when enthusiasm for nuclear power vanished in the 1980s and the

1990s. This made a reboot of nuclear power plant construction extremely complex and expensive and led to an economic catastrophe for most new attempts in Europe and the United States in the 2000s and 2010s.

The history of nuclear power is that of an industrial disaster. Today, around 40 reactors are estimated to be under construction, mostly in China and India, and only one new project was started in 2019 (Schneider and Froggatt, 2019). The cost of new nuclear power plants has increased over the years. From a low US$1,000/kW in the 1970s, they would today cost around US$2,000/kW (in China's most favorable conditions) and US$10,000/kW (in the United States and Europe), very far above the costs of alternative renewable technologies. Nuclear power also has the dubious honor of being the only industry that has experienced negative learning rates over its history, i.e., an increase in manufacturing costs over time.

Does this mean that this industry is dead? Let me be rather straight in my answer here: yes, it is, under current conditions. Nuclear power today is not competitive and consequently, the outlook for its further expansion is very bleak. Of course, most of this cost burden has come from excessive regulations and a dramatic loss of competency, and a serious set of measures could partially help the sector recover. Yet, one could argue that this would be an expensive revival, coming at a time when the pressing need to move away from fossil resources is greater than ever, while alternative options have already proven to be better. A difficult undertaking for any government.

Does this mean that nuclear technology is dead?

The answer is, of course not. Nuclear power delivers momentous volumes of energy with very high density, several orders of magnitude above what humankind has used in its history. It is thus possible that nuclear power eventually finds its place in the energy mix, provided it can come up with a way to truly develop at scale. For that, the fear of nuclear proliferation and the stranglehold of authorities would have to be solved in one form or another. Many innovations have begun to emerge in an attempt to save this industry from disappearance if not irrelevance. One of the directions of work has been to develop new reactor types, leveraging fast neutrons or alternative designs such as molten-salt reactors. Yet, the most promising perspective seems to focus on miniaturizing and modularizing these reactors in order to dramatically cut costs. Small Modular Reactors (up to 300 MW — or one-third of traditional plants) and Micro Modular Reactors (1–10 MW) could be much easier to deploy and build at a much lower price, if they prove to be safe. This approach is not far off from the original dream of Glenn Seaborg. Fusion reactors, which could typically offer unlimited amounts of energy, are also under research, with many nuclear scientists and a handful of celebrities-backed startups working on it.

The bottom line is that nuclear power finds itself in the midst of an existential crisis after decades of poor strategic choices. In my view, this means that it will play only a very limited role in the short term and will likely not play a large part in the current debates on the energy transition. However, the scientific potential of this spectacular form of energy remains. I will leave you here with this thought: it took electricity around 100 years from initial research works to reach an industrial scale. It also took electromagnetism nearly 100 years from its initial discovery to create the first transistors. It might thus take another few decades for nuclear power to truly finds its way. Energy transitions come in waves. It might just not be the time for the nuclear wave yet.

Now that I have completed this brief overview of new energy technologies, how should we compare them one with an another? We can use three key factors to contemplate the benefits and limitations of each technology: density, energy return on investment, and reliability.

Energy density: Is it really a problem?

First, density. Density can be measured in both energy terms and power terms. Energy density represents the amount of energy "stored" in a given volume or mass. It is typically measured in Joules per unit of volume or mass (liter or kilogram). Power density refers to the "rate at which energies are produced (…) per unit of area" and is typically expressed in watts per square meter (Smil, 2017, p. 10). Energy density is a key factor explaining the giant step forward of the nineteenth century. A simple figure helps explain it. Wood energy density averages below 20 MJ/kg. Oil energy density averages above 40 MJ/kg. Coal is in between, around 30 MJ/kg. Hence, civilization kept moving from low energy-density solutions toward higher density alternatives.

Power density comparisons are even more striking. Here, I will refer to Vaclav Smil's extremely detailed review of power densities (2015). According to his analysis, wood's power density averages well below 1 W/m², while that of coal and oil (at least in their beginnings, when the easiest resources were extracted) numbered above 10,000 W/m². Conventional thermal electricity generation has a similar number. The nineteenth-century energy transitions have hence also been massive steps toward accessing new ultra-dense energy contents.

Now, where do these new energy technologies stand?

Here is the problem: they all average well below current coal and oil densities. In fact, they are "low power density" technologies by design. Smil has put these into perspective wonderfully: wind barely numbers around 1 W/m², photovoltaic solar around 10 W/m², and geothermal energy around 50 W/m².

Hence, their power densities are up to four orders of magnitude below those of oil, coal, and traditional thermal electricity. Nuclear power falls into that last category, essentially because nuclear power plants are thermal power generation systems that use the heat content of nuclear fission to propel a turbine, very much like a coal-fired or gas burner would do. From an energy density standpoint, the analysis does not make much sense. Solar irradiation, wind power, or even geothermal heat indeed have no real energy densities, since no "mass" is associated with them. Measuring the energy produced by a kilogram of solar panel does not really mean anything. We therefore essentially rely on power densities. Nuclear is a bit different, since we can associate an energy density with uranium fission that is about one million times that of oil.

Smil's study has basically served as a basis to counter proponents of renewable energies, even though it was probably not the intent. Yet, many large energy organizations have used these arguments to make the case that renewable energy forms, because of their low power densities, will eventually never amount to anything more than a complementary solution to our fossil-fuel-based modern civilization, and that alternative research should focus on higher density options. This argument was also used by Bill Gates to criticize the "buzz" surrounding wind and solar energy. In an interesting interview in 2019, he mentioned that a city like Tokyo would never be able to be fully supplied by such energy sources (Global Warming Policy Forum, 2019). More recently, environmentalists such as Michael Moore and Michael Shellenberg have also in part referred to this argument to criticize wind and solar energy, stating that these energy options, despite being "clean," are actually a threat to biodiversity because of the vast land they use (Gibbs, 2020), and that we need an energy transition that will "save the climate without destroying the environment" (Shellenberg, 2019).

These arguments are undebatable. They are science-based. However, I would point out that, again, demand needs have been overlooked, and that this is a fundamental issue. Energy demand is not homogenous. It is not a factor that is exogenous to the energy transition; it is right at the core of every energy transition. It is a given that wind farms and geothermal power plants are by design utility-scale technologies. They are to compete against conventional and nuclear power plants, and density is a key limiting factor, particularly for onshore wind. When it comes to large centralized utility-scale solutions, demand can almost be considered as exogenous. Supply systems adapt to an aggregated demand that they blindly supply.

Yet, photovoltaic solar and distributed geothermal heat are of a different nature. These technologies are made to be distributed. It is their distributed nature that explains the massive drop in costs of solar photovoltaics. Solar panels are produced by the square meter. Hence, the more the industry produces, the greater scale effect it obtains, and the lower the prices. More importantly, these one-meter large and wide panels can pretty much be dispatched anywhere, generally closer to the source of demand. In such a different paradigm, the nature of demand becomes a critical factor. And it turns out that a significant share of demand can actually be served by low power-density resources, as they are in effect low power-density loads.

Let's take an example and look at the energy mix of a typical home in the United States. Here, 45 percent of the demand comes from space heating and cooling, while nearly 20 percent comes from water heating. The rest, nearly 35 percent of total demand, is devoted to cooking, lighting, and other appliances (International Energy Agency, 2013). These ratios significantly evolve across regions and building types. In Europe, for instance, two-thirds of energy needs correspond to space heating, while the share devoted to cooking, lighting, and other appliances is below 20 percent. In commercial buildings, this share is closer to 50 percent across most geographies. Most of these needs are actually low-density needs. Modern lighting bulbs typically measure below 40 W, and LEDs less than 10 W. The aggregated power demand for lighting within a household therefore barely exceeds 1 kW. Every other appliance (washing machines, dryers, electric oven, and potentially heat pumps or air-conditioners) does not exceed a few kilowatts either. Taken together, the power demand of a typical residential home rarely exceeds 7–10 kW, and average demand (over the course of a day) falls in the range of 2 to 4 kW. We have seen above that the power density of a solar panel is around 10 W/m^2 (lower bound estimate). In fact, this is an average, which considers the capacity factor (utilization rate) of the solar panel across a year. Indeed, a solar panel does not produce electricity at night and produces less when the weather is not optimal. The actual maximum power output of a solar panel at a given instant is around 150–200 W/m^2, which means that a 20 m^2 surface of panels (on a roof) could fulfill most power needs of the house. Considering the lack of lighting and the ability of the solar panel to operate only a fraction of the day (say on average four hours per day at maximum capacity, a conservative estimate), it would take 120 m^2 and a storage system to fully supply the power demand at any time of the day. A nice two-story, 250 m^2 family house typically offers a roof surface of about that size. Of course, many of us actually live in apartments. There, the roof surface is unlikely to be sufficient. Picture a five-story apartment building, with ten apartments in it. The average power demand ranges from around 20 to 40 kW and would therefore require a 1,200 m^2 solar panel surface. However, the roof is not expected to exceed 200–300 m^2. Only 25 percent of the power demand could be met by solar panels on average, although there could be times with near autonomy of the building.

It is this type of analysis that has triggered claims that solar photovoltaics would not be able to constitute much more than a minor, complementary share of the future energy mix, but this misses the point. A study by Taminiau and Byrne (2018) has for instance demonstrated that New York City could be home to around 10 GW of rooftop solar photovoltaics, which could in turn supply 25 percent of electricity demand (and over 50 percent of daytime needs). The main finding here is that distributed solar energy has the potential to significantly contribute to typically low power-density demand needs. The debate is not about solar photovoltaics replacing conventional power plants with much higher energy densities, but rather about such distributed installations' ability to partly offset low power-density demand.

The next order of business is obviously the cost of such installations. As I explained in the first chapter, such a transition only comes if it provides increased benefits, in this case in terms of costs. The cost of conventional electricity generation represents 50 percent of the total cost of electricity (without tax). A huge share of the cost is actually its distribution, and it is largely incompressible. On the other hand, solar panel costs have plummeted and are expected to continue to do so, while storage technologies appear to follow a similar pattern. When is the tipping point? According to many external agencies, particularly BloombergNEF (2019), many countries have already reached parity, and more are to follow. On top of that, costs continue to drop, and second- and third-generation solar technologies could increase the spread in costs even further, while improving the usable surface of photovoltaics through a concept called building-integrated photovoltaics, where thin-film technologies could play a major role. While power density is a critical element to consider when weighing different technologies, and since recent history has shown a transition from low density to higher density energy fuels, I argue here that it will not actually matter this time because of the naturally distributed nature of the upcoming transition. And, as we have seen above, an energy transition is not only about replacing an existing system like-for-like. The centralized system will continue to coexist with new distributed approaches, which will progressively offset a sizable share of aggregated demand.

Energy return on investment

A second critical factor often brought up by renewable-energy detractors is that of the EROI, or the energy return on investment. Once again, this is a very interesting metric, which assesses the volume of energy delivered over the lifetime of a given energy solution to that required to produce it. A society relying on an energy system with an EROI below one would collapse, since more energy would be required to produce the needed energy to run its economic activity. The higher the EROI, the better.

Traditionally, an EROI above 10 is considered as necessary to maintain sustainable and vibrant economic activity (Hall *et al.*, 2009). Once more, figures vary widely across different sources. This is because assumptions differ greatly from one study to another. The general consensus is however that current solar technologies (first generation) require around 500 kWh of energy to be manufactured and have energy paybacks of around two years, or an EROI of 10 (if we assume 25 years' lifetime). Yet, figures range between 3 and 40. In the upper bound, technologies such as Cadmium Telluride appear to offer the greatest potential. Wind power would average around 20 (Bhandari *et al.*, 2015; Celik *et al.*, 2017; Conca, 2015; Fraunhofer Institute for Solar Energy Systems, 2019; Understand Solar, 2016). Celik *et al.* (2017) also expect that upcoming breakthroughs such as Perovskite could lead to an EROI of nearly 100 in the coming years.

How does this compare to traditional energy sources?

Conventional power technologies have an EROI of around 30 and nuclear power of around 70. Oil is said to have ranged around 100 initially and would now be down to 20 or less, because most of the easily accessible resources have already been extracted. Again, this metric has been widely used to criticize emerging technologies as being essentially nonprofitable. The EROI would be too low to ensure a sustainable economy in the long run.

Recent criticism has however emerged on the way fossil fuels' EROI is actually computed. They would be artificially inflated, making a much stronger case for emerging renewable technologies (Griffith, 2020). Whatever the exact EROI of fossil fuels, this argument fails anyhow to take into account that many of these new emerging technologies are still in development. The paper by Celik *et al.* (2017) is a good reflection of the actual potential of technology development in the coming decades and its impact on EROI. Silicon-based solar photovoltaics indeed require large quantities of energy to purify the silicon. The manufacturing process of thin-film solutions is much simpler and far less energy-intensive. These new energy technologies offer considerable potential for technology improvement and hence an increase in EROI, while traditional technologies relying on fossil resources buried in the ground have been on the decline since their inception.

A more subtle argument behind the criticism on new energy technologies' sustainable development is that of the strain on metals they represent. A complete transition to these new technologies would lead to a significant rise in demand for the metals necessary to manufacture these new solutions that are able to harvest and store renewable energy (Deloitte, 2020). And with increasing extraction, rising costs (and energy demand) will come that will decrease the EROI, exactly as in the case of oil mentioned above. Again, this argument, as relevant as it is, fails to include potential technological evolutions. Recent developments in energy batteries for instance indicate that not only is the dependency on metals decreasing, but also new technologies are emerging that could completely change the perspective on needed resources. I do not intend here to discard current concerns about metal dependencies and their potential negative effect going forward; on the contrary (for more, see Petit, 2021). However, conversations on the EROI should take stock of the critical difference between these new energy technologies and the traditional ones. On the one hand, fossil fuels are extracted from the ground, and hence follow a declining EROI course. On the other hand, these new technologies harvest renewable energies. Their EROI is defined by the actual energy (and resources) required to manufacture the infrastructure. It is critical to understand this difference, because in the latter case, technology improvements kick in and help further reduce these dependencies. This is not to say that a solid understanding of energy and resource dependencies should not be developed, but the future is not a prisoner of the past.

Finally, a broader factor is the actual cost of a given source of energy, which is typically measured as a Levelized Cost of Energy (LCOE). The LCOE tells a broader story because it also includes the manufacturing cost dynamics. Scale effects (which are huge for solar photovoltaics, as we have seen) are hence accounted for, alongside the actual costs of energy required to manufacture the new solution. And LCOEs also tell a very different tale in terms of the competitiveness of these emerging technologies. BloombergNEF (2019) has conducted a detailed quantitative analysis and provided some forecasts. Over the coming decades or so, LCOEs of solar photovoltaic solutions will drop to around US$20/MWh, far below conventional system levels, which range between US$50/MWh in the best cases (coal-fired power without negative externalities included) and US$100–125/MWh. In many countries, the tipping point has already been passed.

We can challenge forecasts at will. For sure, these figures stand for utility-scale solar, not the solar panels deployed on rooftops; they do not account for additional storage solutions; they compare conventional systems with suboptimal capacity factors; and they assume favorable costs of capital. Yet, the conclusion from the study holds strong: emerging technologies are on a collision course with conventional ones. They will eventually be cheaper, and there is evidence for it. The conclusion is that — despite a possibly lower EROI (discounting further improvements) — it would still be cheaper to operate a system based entirely on such technologies.

Energy is good as long as it is there

A final critical factor is reliability. The intermittency of new renewable technologies such as wind or solar power has often been criticized because it makes them less reliable. Proponents of the "status quo" typically argue that demand is inelastic, and that supply should thus be designed to be flexible, or "dispatchable." They also argue that the integration of such energies into a centralized network could have dramatic impacts on overall stability.

Yet, recent studies tend to prove the opposite (Brown *et al.*, 2018; Sek *et al.*, 2018). Brown *et al.* (2018), for instance, assume a 100 percent renewable system, and they actually conclude that not only can the system be operated safely, but it can also be done at an economically viable cost. The bottom line is that a lot can be done to ensure a stable operation of the system.

One of the things to do is to rely more and more on electronics. Indeed, if solar panels or wind farms can produce electricity only when the sun is high or the wind is blowing, they can also be controlled to be dispatchable thanks to electronic systems. These technologies are indeed not directly "synchronized" with the grid, and they typically go through a series of electronic converters, where controls can help respond to overall frequency changes or load demand accordingly. Electronics play a critical role in the development of these new technologies, and with the growing reliability of such systems, they are bound to eventually displace traditional electromechanical approaches.

Going further, one of the main ways to tackle intermittency is electricity storage. Electricity storage has been around for decades, with electrochemical batteries. Yet, it has proven to be relatively expensive and inefficient. More recently, the development of portable electronic devices (such as our modern smartphones) has led to a surge in demand for small batteries, which are based on lithium-ion technologies. The same technology also served as the foundational technology for the first electric vehicles, except that batteries were much larger in size. This development led to a sharp drop of lithium-ion battery costs, mainly driven by China's industrial development (as said, an infinitely scalable technology). This new development has translated beyond portable devices and electric cars into stationary storage, and some have started to argue that photovoltaic solar combined with storage would create a dispatchable energy resource and that it would eventually be competitive with other options. It would be — according to enthusiasts — the holy grail of the energy transition. In my example above, with the right volume of solar photovoltaic panels combined with storage, off-grid operation could theoretically become possible. Everyone would then switch to solar and storage, and away from oil, coal, and gas. I will come back to this.

Let's just say at this point that electricity storage has been undergoing its own revolution. From an industry at a standstill, which barely interested anyone 20 years ago, battery design has become front and center as one of the core pillars of modern research. Indeed, a lot can be done, and one can hope that this renewed interest and massive investment will eventually lead to technology breakthroughs. As a matter of fact, such discoveries may be closer than we think. The Rocky Mountain Institute has published a comprehensive report on this in 2019 (Mandel and Stone, 2019). The institute is located in a net-zero energy building in Boulder, Colorado, its staff not very far from its colleagues in the National Renewable Energy Laboratory that I mention above. It is always a very fulfilling experience to spend time in Colorado, which — beyond the magnificent scenery of the Rockies — has become a hotbed of energy innovation. Bloch *et al.* (2019) notably explain that, while traditional lithium-ion technologies are expected to continue to make progress (with a doubling of battery energy in the coming decade), new chemistries such as zinc air, lithium sulfur, or lithium air, just to mention a few, could increase energy by up to five times its current levels, with costs possibly dividing by two to three, depending on the technology. More recently, Bill Gates announced that one of the startups its Breakthrough Energy fund backed (Form Energy) has been able to pull off a low-cost, long-duration 1 MW/150 MWh storage system, or 150 hours of storage available (an order of magnitude beyond what current lithium-ion technologies have been able to realize), using an aqueous air battery.

In conclusion, storage innovation is booming, with new technologies at cost-defying levels emerging everywhere. And this is changing the entire equation regarding renewable energies' intermittency. There remains however a critical issue with batteries, and this is their material intensity. A detailed investigation by Benjamin Pitron (2018) has clearly established the worrisome consumption of raw materials (whose extraction is polluting) that constitute modern battery designs. But yet again, technology advances. The recent advent of the "million mile" battery from Tesla is one such milestone toward developing more resource-efficient batteries (Delbert, 2020).

A final thought on this issue. All of the above assumes demand to be inelastic, with the supply system having to adapt to its variations. This is often referred to as a "load following" system. This paradigm of traditional energy systems is likely to get increasingly challenged. Dorr and Seba (2020) notably get around the issue of intermittency by exploring a significantly oversized renewable system, where the truly inelastic demand would be met by the fraction of firm power available from intermittent sources at any time, and the remaining energy demand adopting a "supply following" model, adapting in real-time to the intermittent supply. They find this new paradigm to provide massive productivity to the whole economy, while putting to rest concerns on reliability of supply. I will come back to this.

What should we take away from this brief review?

The purpose of this book is not to go into too many details on technology comparisons. Yet, you will have understood that innovation in the energy domain is moving at warp speed. Already, several building blocks of an upcoming transition have emerged: more efficient and ubiquitous solar photovoltaic panels and cheaper and high-performance electricity storage systems are two critical advances that — if not perfect yet — now shape a possible, reliable, and affordable distributed power solution, at odds with the current centralized energy approach. And while conventional energy systems tend to see their cost grow over time because of their reliance on resources that are increasingly hard to extract, these alternative options see their cost plummet with scale and perfected technologies. What will ultimately make these technologies prevail is the fact that they are infinitely scalable, are highly decentralized, and bring increasing rates of return over time. There is not much traditional technologies can do against such an overhaul. And no matter what limits people may put on such technological developments in their long-term projections, these are likely to be beaten sooner rather than later. The ingredients for a disruption are here.

Digital Everywhere — Even Where We Do Not Expect It

Computing supremacy

Yet, not much would probably be possible without another major adjacent innovation, that of digital technologies. Interestingly enough, digital and electricity innovations actually share common roots. Maxwell's equations date back to the early 1860s and enabled science to combine electricity and magnetism for the first time. Less than a century after, in 1947, the first transistor was created, which heralded a new era of electronic development and eventually led to the emergence of the IT industry. Less than a decade later, IBM released the first calculator based entirely on transistors. The decade that followed saw the invention of both semiconductor-based transistors (solar photovoltaic panels are interestingly also based on semiconducting materials) and the first microprocessor. Later, in the 1970s, the first personal computers hit the market: the IT revolution was making great strides and changed everything.

Cofounder of Intel Gordon Moore predicted in 1965 that the number of transistors in an integrated circuit would double every two years on average.

His prediction proved true for the next five decades and became what is often referred to as the Moore's law. And with this daunting increase in computing capacity, costs went down. The first Apple computer used a 5,000-transistor processor. The current iPad Pro (2018) is running on a processor of 10 billion transistors, is much smaller and considerably less expensive. Current smartphones have about 100,000 times the processing power of the guiding system that helped the Apollo 11 mission land on the moon in 1969. In other words, one smartphone could guide 100,000 Apollo 11 missions today.

And this is not the end! Quantum computing is the new frontier of IT development. Quantum computing basically uses quantum-mechanics properties to perform more computation at a faster pace. Google published an article in Nature in 2019 that essentially revealed that their new 54-qubit processor had been able to perform an operation in 200 seconds that would have taken the best supercomputer available 10,000 years to complete. They claimed having reached "quantum supremacy" (Arute *et al.*, 2019). Commercial developments are not there yet, but this illustrates the tremendous progress made in computing capacities. Every decade or so, new applications emerge, some of whom were considered impossible tasks before.

Always on

This is not all though. All this data has also to be shared and exchanged. Arpanet, the ancestor of the Internet, was developed in the 1970s to connect computing facilities across academic and military sites throughout the United States. Commercial networks and enterprises were connected in the early 1990s, propelling the exponential growth of the Internet, which has been one of the defining advancements of our modern societies. All this data connects through networks. And again, tremendous progress has been made over the years. Today's fiber optic cables connecting all large regions of the world can typically offer speeds north of 100 gigabytes per second (Gbps) through multichannels. However, the traditional performance of residential or commercial connections falls in the range of 1–2 Gbps at best.

Wireless networks represent only 10–15 percent of total data exchanges today but are expected to grow in importance as most digital services become portable and distributed. The emerging 5G technology is expected to yield a connection performance of around 10 Gbps (or ten times what we currently enjoy in our fixed connections at home!). This would be around 10–20 times faster than the previous 4G generation, which was itself 250 times faster than the older 3G generation. Within roughly a decade, our wireless network capacity has increased over 2,500 times. Right now, 5G even competes with distributed optical fiber connections because of its speed advantage (which was not the case for 4G), opening up a new realm of nonintrusive distributed applications that are yet to be invented. A couple of years ago, I met with a senior executive from a large and renowned telecommunications company at a forum. He explained the rationale for getting rid of optical fiber networks in cities in order to promote 5G networks instead. They would save a lot on the civil engineering required to pull cables within large trenches in the middle of the street, he said. But yet again, his worry was that this would also disrupt the traditional business model of these companies, which are essentially based on civil engineering works in constrained environments. And this is again just the beginning. What should we expect in the coming decades with further enhancements, and the advent of 6G, 7G, and more?

Digital everywhere, for better or for worse

With more computing power and more broadband capacity to distribute and share data, digital technologies are becoming entirely ubiquitous and pervade every aspect of our lives. The International Data Corporation (2019) expects the number of connected devices to reach 40 billion by 2025, generating nearly 80 zettabytes of data. This is to be compared to the current "data universe" of around 40 zettabytes in 2020 (an estimate of the full amount of data available that was generated since the inception of computers). Of that data, 90 percent would moreover have been created in the last couple of years, as the growth in data generation happens to be exponential (Petrov, 2020). After the Internet of people, here comes the Internet of Things, or IoT.

Think of it a minute and remember the old "Matrix" movie. Within five years, it is expected that connected objects could generate twice as much data as what the "Internet of people" has created over the last 40 years or so. And with this massive "universe" of data come new ways of handling it, such as artificial intelligence (AI). But AI is not new. It was founded as an official academic scientific field in the 1950s and went through a series of enthusiastic and disappointing periods in the last six decades. More recently, improvements in computing and data-harnessing capabilities have brought this field of computer science back to the forefront.

Yet, AI is difficult to describe. It is usually defined as the study of intelligent agents, or devices capable of perceiving their environment and acting on it independently, but the definition is so vague that some argue AI is pretty much everything that has not been invented yet. Typically, AI systems include reasoning, representing knowledge, processing language, and the automated ability to move objects in an evolving environment, among other things.

Many applications are emerging in healthcare (telemedicine), transport (autonomous vehicles), government (security, administration), finance, the military, and even homes. Yes, in a nutshell: pretty much everywhere.

And let's not underestimate it: AI will be a game changer. In large supercomputing facilities, AI will be used to push the boundaries of knowledge. But it will also be distributed across all appliances we humans interact with, and this will change our relationship with our environment, for better or for worse. Some would say we will lose touch with reality. They argue, and those are reasonable concerns, that information asymmetry and fake news may significantly hamper the proper functioning of democracies while reinforcing inequalities. In a 2018 survey, the Reuters Institute for the Study of Journalism (2018) notably revealed that up to 50 percent of the population of some countries was exposed to fake news. They also argued that digital addiction is growing, and that its devastating effects on human capabilities are yet to be seen. After all, the average time people spend on smartphones per day has increased 50 percent in the last five years. People in Brazil for instance spend nearly five hours a day on their phone, and nearly 20 percent of the world population checks their smartphone when waking up at night (Armstrong, 2017; World Economic Forum, 2016). China comes second, with nearly three hours per day, and I can testify to it since I live in Hong Kong and take the subway every morning to get to work. It is hard to make your way through crowds of people going in all directions without looking! Yet, there is another possible outcome. Connected speakerphones with embedded AI for language processing, such as Amazon's Alexa, were first released in 2014. Today, they take the form of a speakerphone installed right in the middle of the living room. Tomorrow, all connected appliances could be interconnected via this central interaction system, and — as Eric Schmidt and Jared Cohen from Google put it — the home will become an "electronic orchestra" at the service of its dwellers (Schmidt and Cohen, 2013). This inspiring description of the future of our homes is in no way a degradation of humankind, but rather an advancement of civilization. In other words, progress. And it could well be that these kinds of developments would put an end to our current addiction to small phone screens. Who knows?

Science fiction, for real

Digital technologies are here to stay, and they will significantly change lives and our relationship with services and products in the coming decades. But let's take a step back and reflect on the key elements that truly bring disruption in usage, beyond the obvious.

First, these technologies are highly decentralized. With them pervading every object we interact with, daily use will possibly be increasingly reliant on the Internet and data. The example of the home "electronic orchestra" is an inspiring vision of such a development. Yet, the same could apply to industries, with much greater customization, real-time production, and efficiency in manufacturing processes. I will come back to this in greater detail in later chapters, yet you will have grasped it: immense decentralized computing capabilities will change every single thing that humans do for the better, whether in terms of living, entertainment, or work. Efficiency, real-time response, granularity of controls, and customization will improve every single process that we run, every single offer or product that we manufacture and use. As a matter of fact, we have seen only the beginning. Ubiquitous virtual interaction will be the norm and sooner than we think.

The second element is the platforming of value chains and the scalability effects (or network effects) it drives. Platforms enable us to connect various actors of an ecosystem to each other and essentially streamline supply chains and remove friction. There are many examples of what platforms help realize. I could start with the previous example of the home "electronic orchestra." In essence, all home-related activities — from entertainment to information, online shopping, managing everyone's agenda, schooling support, cleaning, and paying bills — could be centralized in one platform. Every external actor of the ecosystem could eventually place offers and interact almost instantaneously with its consumers (or the house's residents) through the platform. The final user (or resident in this case) would essentially connect to one system and access everything they need to pretty much run their life. Yet, platforms largely go beyond the living space. The disaggregation of supply chains is the next major outcome of digital platforms. Two obvious examples are Amazon and Google. Amazon is in the process of entirely reshaping goods' deliveries. On the one hand, online shopping has become completely genuine and intuitive. There is no more need to go to a shop and look for a product, or to have that same shop order what you are actually looking for. Everything is instantaneously available, as producers and consumers are virtually connected through the Amazon platform, everywhere in the world. The cascade of intermediaries is disrupted by this incredible horizontalization of supply chains. The beauty of such a platform is that it truly advances commerce beyond boundaries in a way that has not been known in history. And the larger the platform becomes — or, in other words the greater the adoption — the larger the positive effects on opportunities and costs. This is another example of an infinitely scalable technology providing increasing rates of return.

Take a step back for a second and imagine what it was like to procure spices in the Middle Ages, when merchants had to travel for years along the Silk Road. Even in the late twentieth century, it took weeks for goods to travel from one region to another, and most advanced goods available in one country were often inaccessible to people in other areas. The Internet and Amazon have transformed this for the better. A good manufactured in Malaysia or Brazil can now be sold over the Internet and distributed to someone in Europe or the United States, and this can be achieved through a few clicks on one's desktop or smartphone.

Google is another striking example of such horizontalization. The entire world's available knowledge and information is now distributed to everyone in an efficient manner. Google makes sense of these zettabytes of data that I mentioned earlier and organizes them so that everyone can find their way through them and access the relevant information they seek, instantaneously. To a large extent, this book would not have been possible without the tremendous access to information that Google has provided me with. Yet, there are also drawbacks. People are concerned that Google, through its perfected algorithms, may actually influence the "search" process in a way that optimizes its commercial objectives, and some people argue that the platform has actually turned into a public good and should no longer be considered a commercial enterprise, notably given its monopolistic situation.

Platforms offer immense benefits in that they facilitate trade at a level unknown in history, while removing all tedious friction of the past world. This however comes at the expense of traditional value chains, which are completely broken up.

Digital technologies hence provide a totally new paradigm of near real-time, highly personalized, ultra-efficient, optimized, and frictionless interactions with both the physical environment and other human beings. In short, they are infinitely scalable and highly decentralized technologies. And as in the example of solar technologies, their rate of return tends to increase over time with further technological enhancement and adoption. The stunning pace of technological development also invites a reflection on what formidable new developments lie ahead of us. For the most part, these advancements will be beneficial to humanity. Obviously though, with them come a number of questions that will have to be addressed.

Working at an Atomic Scale

There is a last area of technological innovation that should also be considered: what I refer to as atomic-scale technologies, which include both biotechnologies and nanotechnologies.

The term biotechnology was first coined by Karl Ereky in 1919, while using living organisms to produce raw materials. Yet, biotechnology has always been around. Using natural fertilizers or selected crops to optimize agricultural yields is a form of biotechnology. The development of computing capabilities has however fueled the accelerated development of biotechnology applications as well as a renewed interest in them, particularly in terms of working at the genome level. DNA sequencing cost US$100 million in 2000, and still US$10 million in 2008. Today, it costs around US$1,000, a much sharper drop than that of the traditional Moore's law that applies to electronics (National Human Genome Research Institute, 2020).

On the flip side, ideas on nanotechnologies were discussed by Richard Feyman in the late 1960s, but it is not until the 1980s that this new field of technology truly developed. First, there was the invention of scanning tunneling, which made it possible to improve visualization at the atomic level, followed by the discovery of fullerenes: very specific carbon structures that gave way to research on graphene materials and carbon nanotubes.

These new fields of research are now able (and this is recent) to competitively break boundaries of traditional industrial applications. They provide the opportunity to design new materials with new properties. It is very possible that in the coming decades, new materials will emerge that will replace the traditional building blocks we have been using all along, with dramatically improved properties. As Chad Mirkin (director of the Northwestern University's Institute for Nanotechnology) puts it: "Instead of taking what nature gives you, we can control every property of the new material we make." This new ability is expected to disrupt a variety of fields of research over time: think of solar irradiation capture, energy storage technologies, or the entire field of electronics and communications, just as examples of some of the technologies we have discussed above (National Nanotechnology Initiative, 2020). In other words, they are infinitely scalable technologies with likely enhancements that will dwarf current incremental improvements in traditional technologies and uses.

In addition, nanotechnologies enable the manufacturing of devices at the nanometer level (while biotechnologies work at the genome level). The smallest nanoelectronics device is now 3 nm long. This is opening entirely new areas of innovation, such as in medicine. Why not develop specific microchips that would be so small they can be installed directly in our body to monitor our health? Yuval Noah Hariri has wonderfully described this scenario in his *Sapiens: A Brief History of Mankind*, alongside the concerns that it raised in terms of ethics and inequalities in the face of death (Hariri, 2014). In the context of the energy transition, nanotechnologies are already at the heart of ongoing research on third-generation solar photovoltaic materials, and they have played a growing role in research on new types of electricity storage batteries. The same could be said about biotechnologies when looking at the development of new medicine and new agricultural crops, but could also soon apply to other fields, such as energy, as discussed by Susan Hockfield, President Emerita at the Massachusetts Institute of Technology, in her latest book (2019).

The bottom line of all this is that the current ability to work at an atomic scale is redefining the boundaries of what is and is not possible. In short, the fundamental building blocks we have been using for centuries may now be revisited. This has been facilitated by the gigantic leap forward in terms of computing capacity, and is expected to diffuse across all sectors of activity, in particular offering new capabilities in energy technologies. As for energy and digital technologies, atomic-scale technologies show similar patterns: they are also infinitely scalable and enable high decentralization. With significant achievements in technology, they bring increasing rates of return.

Nothing Has Happened Yet

Time now to wrap up this brief overview of major emerging technologies. As we have seen in the first chapter, energy transitions are driven by demand evolutions. Yet, since at least two decades, climate change has become a growing area of concern, which has spurred international cooperation and innovation, and we have just had a glimpse of this. Back to the question I posed earlier on then. Could it be that the next energy transition will be forced on us?

In the seventeenth and eighteenth centuries, the United Kingdom did switch from wood to coal because of its depleted stock from centuries of deforestation. This was the origin of the first industrial revolution, one that built on new technologies such as coal and steam and eventually a revolution in transport with the emergence of railway networks. Yet, if the origin of the energy transition was the heavy constraint that applied to the United Kingdom's economy, it did not trigger the transition toward a completely different energy system. It was innovations, and their combination, that changed the energy paradigm for good. Today's climate change forces a new kind of threat on us, global in nature. Governments around the world have already taken significant measures to tackle it. As of today, around 49 percent of global GDP is covered by carbon neutrality commitments, with the European Union leading the way (ECIU, 2020). Over half of the 169 signatories to the Paris Agreement have also submitted specific pledges, notably referring to the use of carbon pricing, an attempt to integrate climate externalities into the economy to better facilitate the transition toward solutions not based on fossil fuels (World Bank Group, 2018). Massive subsidies have been granted to promote a quicker adoption of new technologies such as wind or solar power. In the European Union, this represented over €100 billion in subsidies for renewable energies in 2016, a figure that should be compared however to the remaining €60 billion in subsidies to fossil fuels

(Trinomics, 2018). A forced transition away from fossil fuels thus seems on the way. However, decades after the first alarming messages from the IPCC, half the world's economy has still not made any commitments to reaching carbon neutrality, and an even lower share has actually kicked off the transition. As a matter of fact, and despite all the buzz surrounding renewable energies, new technologies such as wind and solar still represent less than 10 percent of electricity demand today (BloombergNEF, 2019). In total energy terms (electricity represents around 20 percent of final energy demand), that is a couple of percentage points of the entire energy system, a rather poor result after decades of investment. The conclusion should jump out at us. The energy transition has in fact not started.

So, 30 years after the first commitments related to climate change, renewable energies still represent only a fraction of total energy supply. Some could argue that I am overly pessimistic and that renewable energies are very much reaching the beginning of the famous "S" curve of accelerated growth, now that they are becoming competitive with other technologies. Possibly. Yet, many experts around the world have raised concerns about the "true" costs of these intermittent and low-density energies, not to say their material intensity, arguing that such a transition will come at a cost for society. Among other projections, the International Energy Agency has for instance estimated that the cost of curbing carbon dioxide emissions by moving away from fossil fuels would require an extra 20 percent of energy capacity investments (International Energy Agency, 2019). More subsidies would thus be required, and some companies would make a fortune.

Yet, the argument fails to recognize the true pattern of energy transitions. In fact, solar and wind are new energy technologies, which government subsidies support in order to accelerate their deployment. But these will not trigger the energy transition by themselves. For them to develop at scale, innovations building on these technologies and others will need to kick in to provide increased benefits. When this happens, then adoption will accelerate and the transformation of the energy mix, the energy transition, will truly begin.

Does this remind you of the transition that took place in the United Kingdom in the seventeenth and more importantly the eighteenth and nineteenth centuries?

The nation was forced to move away from wood and adopt coal for some of its usages, in order to maintain its security and build the British fleet, which would soon dominate the oceans and world trade. Government-driven incentives propelled this transformation. Some entrepreneurs made a fortune. To a certain extent, coal was imposed as a replacement for wood in some usages. Yet, it is when portable steam engines using coal emerged that railway transportation and the first industrial revolution truly transformed the energy mix.

Let me give a modern example. The largest solar farm in the world has a power capacity of 1,000 MW. The Kurnool Ultra Mega Solar Park, based in India, is spread over 20 square kilometers and reported to be able to supply around 300,000 homes (Summers, 2019). Should we feel impressed with this performance, when a similarly sized nuclear power plant, operating 24 hours a day, requires only 3.5 square kilometers of land on average? The reality of such developments is that they aim at replicating the old model with new technologies. We have switched from one big nuclear power plant to an even bigger solar farm. The world needs to move away from fossil energies, so fossil energies are replaced with renewable energies, without a change in the way the energy system is run. And this exemplifies that the energy transition has not truly started yet. Solar panels are not designed to be assembled in large power farms that mimic other technologies based on fossil fuels. They are designed to be decentralized and deployed everywhere. This however will depend on new applications to emerge, which will build on solar technology's properties as well as other, adjacent technologies (same as coal — and steam engines). Until this combination happens, solar panels' development will essentially rely on government policies, but will not be pulled by market forces. Hence, they will go only as far as governments want them to, and not always with positive effects. Let's just remember that the "Energiewende" in Germany (the energy transition, in German) has yielded an increase in electricity tariffs of nearly 50 percent for households in a little over a decade.

What is true for power generation also applies to a score of other examples. What to say about recent excitement regarding fast-charging infrastructure for electric vehicles (a copy of gas stations, while electricity is by nature ubiquitous and distributed) or hydrogen (a copy of natural gas, distributed through decades-old expensive infrastructure, while many alternatives exist for heating that are simpler and often more competitive) as two emblematic examples of self-proclaimed innovations? These "innovations" are first and foremost experiments in embracing new technologies by mimicking the existing system. They will possibly be short-lived.

The true energy transition will thus begin when — as I discussed in the first chapter — a combination of innovative technologies is finally able to either create a new demand pattern or provide the ability to better supply a given service, and notably at a fraction of its previous cost. The companies who first come up with such a combination and make adoption frictionless will truly trigger the transition, while traditional actors relying on subsidies will be washed away. This is as inevitable as the fact that the sun rises and sets every day; a simple lesson of the history of energy transitions. When it happens, these new demand patterns will skyrocket and in turn impact the upstream energy-supply-chain. The two questions we can then ask are: when will it happen? And what will it be like? I argue in this book that this transition will accelerate in the coming decade because of the potential of existing technologies, which are on the verge of bringing true benefits to the market if they have not done so already. New renewable (notably solar) technologies, digital technologies, and atomic-scale technologies have already made significant strides in the last decade, and they are now reaching tipping points that make their adoption inevitable, be it because of their cost or the ubiquity with which they can now be deployed. These technologies actually share common patterns. They are infinitely scalable and highly decentralized, and by their nature bring increasing rates of return over time as their capabilities improve. These characteristics make their further development largely inevitable, and we have not yet seen the extent of their potential unfolding. Only time will tell, but one can already realize that the world they will shape will probably differ considerably from the current one.

A last reflection before I close this chapter. I spend a considerable time in external meetings and forums gathering energy experts from various companies such as mine. I have diligently been attending all of those for the last few years. And I am extremely thankful for these opportunities, because they gave me the idea for this book. In none of these meetings have I ever seen someone stand up and reflect on what past energy transitions are telling us about the upcoming one and how we got it all wrong. Here and there I have been able to promote this alternative vision, but despite past transitions' successes, these were seldom picked up as further subjects of research. I can see two reasons for this. First, there is some level of endogamic design in energy transition scenarios. When you put energy experts in a room, they tend to talk about their common subject of passion, which is energy. Despite very high-level conversations, they naturally set boundaries around their area of expertise. In doing so, they always overlook adjacent innovations outside of their field of expertise. It turns out that, as a result, the conversation always fails to fully embrace the broader context of changes at play, hence leading to wrong outcomes.

I would refer to the second reason as reverse anachronism. If anachronism is the traditional mistake of judging the past with the eyes and beliefs of the present, reverse anachronism is all about anticipating the future with these same eyes, disregarding the efforts of future generations to build on new advancements to make their life better. By doing so, experts tend to project the future as a linear trend, and obviously fail to fully anticipate the nonlinear advancements of civilization. Back to my example of current smartphones, which have 100,000 times the processing power of the Apollo 11 guiding system. What should this tell us about what to expect for 2050 or 2070?

This has unfortunate consequences, since energy companies are those advising governments on energy policies. Let's just be clear then: an energy transition will kick off in the coming decade, and we are only at the beginning of it. This transition has not been properly anticipated and has not been accurately forecasted by the energy world, while it could in fact be the missing clue to reach the stringent targets of mitigating climate change that are upon us. In the end, this ecosystem could likely undergo the transition rather than lead it. Others might well drive it for them.

References

Armstrong, M. (2017). "Smartphone Addiction Tightens Its Global Grip." *Statista*, May 24. https://www.statista.com/chart/9539/smartphone-addiction-tightens-its-global-grip/.

Arute, F., Arya, K., Babbush, R., Bacon, D., Bardin, J., Barends, R., Biswas, R., *et al.* (2019). "Quantum Supremacy Using a Programmable Superconducting Processor." *Nature*, 574: 505–10. https://doi.org/10.1038/s41586-019-1666-5.

Becker, T. (2016). "12 Emerging Technologies That May Help Power the Future." *Georgia Tech Research Horizons* 1. https://rh.gatech.edu/features/12-emerging-technologies-may-help-power-future.

Bhandari, K., Collier, J., Ellingson, R., and Apul, D. (2015). "Energy Payback Time (EPBT) and Energy Return on Energy Invested (EROI) of Solar Photovoltaic Systems: A Systematic Review and Meta-Analysis." *Renewable and Sustainable Energy Reviews* 47: 133–41. http://dx.doi.org/10.1016/j.rser.2015.02.057.

Bloch, C., Newcomb, J., Shiledar, S., and Tyson M. (2019). *Breakthrough Batteries: Powering the Era of Clean Electrification*. Report, Rocky Mountain Institute. https://rmi.org/insight/breakthrough-batteries/.

BloombergNEF. (2019). *New Energy Outlook*. Report, Bloomberg New Energy Finance. https://about.bnef.com/new-energy-outlook/.

Brown, T., Bischof-Niemz, T., Blok, K., Breyer, C., Lund, H., and Mathiesen, B.V. (2018). "Response to 'Burden of Proof: A Comprehensive Review of the Feasibility of 100 Percent Renewable-Electricity Systems.'" *Renewable and Sustainable Energy Reviews*, 92: 834–47. https://doi.org/10.1016/j.rser.2018.04.113.

Celik, I., Philips, A., Song, Z., Yan, Y., Ellingson, R., Heben, M., and Apul, D. (2017). Energy Payback Time (EPBT) and Energy Return on Energy Invested (EROI) of Perovskite Tandem Photovoltaic Solar Cells. *IEEE Journal of Photovoltaics* 8, no. 1 (January): 305–9. https://doi.org/10.1109/JPHOTOV.2017.2768961.

Conca, J. (2015). "EROI — A Tool to Predict the Best Energy Mix." *Forbes*, February 11. https://www.forbes.com/sites/jamesconca/2015/02/11/eroi-a-tool-to-predict-the-best-energy-mix/#5ea22d55a027.

Delbert, C. (2020). "Elon Musk Reveals Plans for His Million-Mile Battery." *Popular Mechanics*, May 18. https://www.popularmechanics.com/cars/hybrid-electric/a32576671/elon-musk-tesla-million-mile-battery/.

Deloitte. (2020). "Les batteries pour la mobilité." Report, June. https://www2.deloitte.com/fr/fr/pages/sustainability-services/articles/batteries-pour-mobilite.html.

Dorr A., Seba T. (2020). *Rethinking Energy 2020–2030*, RethinkX. https://www.rethinkx.com/energy.

Fraunhofer Institute for Solar Energy Systems. (2019). *Photovoltaics Report.* September 16. Freiburg. https://www.ise.fraunhofer.de/content/dam/ise/de/documents/publications/studies/Photovoltaics-Report.pdf.

Geddes Donald. (1945). *The Atomic Age Opens.* Pocket 340. First edition. https://www.amazon.com/Atomic-Opens-Donald-Porter-Geddes/dp/B000OMEZZA.

Gibbs, J., dir. (2020). *Planet of the Humans.* Documentary film, produced by M. Moore. https://planetofthehumans.com.

Global Warming Policy Forum. (2019). "Bill Gates Slams Unreliable Wind and Solar Energy." YouTube video, February 18. https://www.youtube.com/watch?v=9xe3BWPsBTU.

Griffith, S. (2020). *Rewiring America.* Rewiring America, November. https://www.rewiringamerica.org/handbook.

Hall, C., Balogh, S., and Murphy, D. (2009). "What Is the Minimum EROI That a Sustainable Society Must Have?" *Energies* 2, no. 1: 25–47. https://doi.org/10.3390/en20100025.

Hariri, Y. N. (2014). *Sapiens: A Brief History of Humankind.* London: Harvill Secker.

Hockfield, S. (2019). *The Age of Living Machines: How Biology Will Build the Next Technology Revolution.* New York: W. W. Norton & Company.

Intergovernmental Panel on Climate Change. (2007). *Climate Change 2007: Synthesis Report. Contribution of Working Groups I, II and III to the Fourth Assessment Report of the Intergovernmental Panel on Climate Change.* Edited by the core writing team, R. K. Pachauri, and A. Reisinger. Geneva, Switzerland: IPCC. https://www.ipcc.ch/site/assets/uploads/2018/02/ar4_syr_full_report.pdf.

Intergovernmental Panel on Climate Change. (2014). *Climate Change 2014: Synthesis Report. Contribution of Working Groups I, II and III to the Fifth Assessment Report of the Intergovernmental Panel on Climate Change.* Edited by the core writing team, R. K. Pachauri, and A. Reisinger. Geneva, Switzerland: IPCC. https://www.ipcc.ch/site/assets/uploads/2018/02/SYR_AR5_FINAL_full.pdf.

International Data Corporation. (2019). "The Growth in Connected IoT Devices Is Expected to Generate 79.4ZB of Data in 2025, according to a New IDC Forecast." Press Release, June. https://www.idc.com/getdoc.jsp?containerId=prUS45213219.

International Energy Agency ©. (2013). *Technology Roadmap. Energy Efficient Building Envelopes.* December. Paris: IEA Publishing. https://www.iea.org/reports/technology-roadmap-energy-efficient-building-envelopes.

International Energy Agency ©. (2019). *World Energy Outlook*. November. Paris: IEA. https://www.iea.org/reports/world-energy-outlook-2019.

Mandel, J., and Stone, L. (2019). "Making Our Existing Buildings Zero Carbon: A Three-Pronged Approach." Rocky Mountain Institute, December 4. https://rmi. org/making-our-existing-buildings-zero-carbon-a-three-pronged-approach/.

Mcglynn, D. (2019). "The Future of Nuclear Energy." *Phys.org*, November 28. https:// phys.org/news/2016-11-future-nuclear-energy.html.

National Human Genome Research Institute. (2020). "The Cost of Sequencing a Human Genome." NHGRI Fact Sheet. https://www.genome.gov/about-genomics/ fact-sheets/Sequencing-Human-Genome-cost.

National Nanotechnology Initiative. (2020). "Benefits and Applications." https://www. nano.gov/you/nanotechnology-benefits.

Petrov, C. (2020). "25+ Impressive Big Data Statistics for 2020." *Tech Jury*, last updated September 10. https://techjury.net/stats-about/big-data-statistics/#gref.

Pitron, B. (2018). *La guerre des metaux rares. La face cachée de la transition énergétique et numérique*. Paris: Editions Les Liens qui Libèrent.

Power Technology. (2014). "Six of the Most Promising New Green Power Technologies." March 19, last updated July 30. https://www.power-technology.com/features/ featuresix-of-the-most-promising-new-green-power-technologies-4199646/.

Reuters Institute for the Study of Journalism. (2018). *Digital News Report 2018*. http:// www.digitalnewsreport.org/survey/2018/overview-key-findings-2018/.

Schmidt E., and Cohen J. (2013). *The New Digital Age: Reshaping the Future of People, Nations and Business*. London: John Murray.

Schneider, M., and Froggatt, A., eds. (2019). *World Nuclear Industry Status Report 2019*. https://www.worldnuclearreport.org/IMG/pdf/wnisr2019-v2-hr.pdf.

Shellenberg, M. (2019). "Why Renewables Cannot Save the Planet." *TEDxDanubia*, YouTube video, January 4. https://www.youtube.com/watch?v=N-yALPEpV4w.

Smil, V. (2015). *Power Density: A Key to Understanding Energy Sources and Uses*. Cambridge, MA: MIT Press.

Smil, V. (2017). *Energy and Civilization. A History*. Cambridge, MA: MIT Press.

Summers, J. (2019). "5 Largest Solar Farms in the World." *Origin*, March 5. https:// d1ilckqk9cr8k7.cloudfront.net/blog/5-largest-solar-farms-in-the-world/.

Taminiau, J., and Byrne, J. (2018). "City-Scale Urban Sustainability: Spatiotemporal Mapping of Distributed Solar Power for New York City." *WIREs Energy and Environment*, 9: e374. https://doi.org/10.1002/wene.374.

Trinomics. (2018). *Study on Energy Prices, Costs and Subsidies and their Impact on Industry and Households*. Study for European Commission, September. https:// ec.europa.eu/energy/sites/ener/files/documents/energy_prices_and_costs_-final_ report-v12.3.pdf.

Understand Solar. (2016). "Solar Uses More Energy to Manufacture Than It Produces?" February 8. https://understandsolar.com/solar-uses-more-energy-to-manufacture-than-it-produces/.

World Bank Group. (2018). *State and Trends of Carbon Pricing 2018*. Report, May. Washington DC: World Bank. https://openknowledge.worldbank.org/bitstream/handle/10986/29687/9781464812927.pdf.

World Economic Forum. (2016). *Digital Transformation of Industries: Societal Implications*. White Paper in collaboration with Accenture, January. http://reports.weforum.org/digital-transformation/wp-content/blogs.dir/94/mp/files/pages/files/dti-societal-implications-white-paper.pdf.

CHAPTER 3

The Upcoming Energy Transition Will Be a Byproduct of Greater Changes at Stake

"It's better to walk alone than with a crowd going in the wrong direction." (Gandhi)

We have already reached two important conclusions. These conclusions, as obvious as they may appear in line of the above demonstration, could already seem quite provocative in some circles, considering that they are never discussed. Both of them are indeed somewhat disruptive and bring many consequences with them, which I will review in later chapters.

First, energy transitions are driven by innovations in demand. New energy sources may appear, but the real shift occurs when new demand emerges or when an existing service can suddenly be supplied in a better way, and notably at a fraction of the previous cost or effort, in a quest toward greater abundance for humanity. This shift happens based on a combination of technological advancements, including in energy. Hence, energy transitions are merely a byproduct of broader transformations. This pattern has repeated itself over and over again in the last centuries. These transformations were called industrial revolutions, and they implied energy transitions. This is also the reason why over time, the energy mix has turned into a complex mix of different energy sources serving different purposes. The current energy system is an almost perfect representation of various stages of technological progress in how to use energy. Layers of such progress overlap and, like a paleontologist studying stratified layers of fossils in bare rock while looking for an answer to evolution theory, the energy expert can retrieve various innovation "pulsations" in the energy system's modern diagram. Transport has essentially shifted to fossil fuels, notably oil and its derivatives. Electricity has pervaded many uses, from lighting to motion, but is still produced largely from coal. Heating and cooking still rely heavily on traditional wood or coal, even though in mature economies they have shifted mostly to natural gas and electricity. Steelmaking still largely relies on coal and has made little progress in the last hundred years. Aluminum production however mainly relies on electricity, and has to a large extent depended on the invention of electricity. And the list goes on.

The second important conclusion is that the current energy transition, which has been discussed for the last decade or so, has not started yet. Considerable progress has been made on new energy sources, particularly renewable technologies. Research on alternative energy sources has boomed in the last decades, given the growing concern on the impact of fossil fuels on climate change. Solar photovoltaics and wind turbines have constituted the lion's share of such early developments, largely supported by government subsidies. Costs have gone down, to a point of near parity with historical technologies, fueling a narrative that the great transition away from fossil energy is in sight. Yet, these new energy sources basically represent only a few percent of today's energy demand, and they essentially have come as a substitute to traditional energies, with no change in demand. The massive subsidies devoted to them have helped bring the costs down and create a space for these technologies, but they have not triggered a large-scale transformation yet. Renewable farms are deployed worldwide, and they replace conventional power plants. They enable electricity production without carbon emissions (if we do not account for the embodied emissions of manufacturing solar panels or wind turbines), but they also come at the possible expense of reliability (renewable energies are intermittent) and, according to some, biodiversity (with large wild areas being transformed into renewable farms, disrupting local ecosystems). They end up producing electricity, which fuels the daily needs of people with little change to their habits and little positive impact on the cost of the services they get from electricity, if any. And this is likely the reason why the changes have been slow thus far. As the world engages on a race to decarbonize the economy by 2050 to mitigate climate change, this conclusion stands out as a major lesson from history. The only way to meet the deadline will be to focus on the inner drivers of energy transitions, i.e., demand innovations that provide greater abundance.

Yet, research keeps advancing, and we have seen that solar photovoltaic technologies and electricity storage technologies offer tremendous perspectives in the years to come. In parallel to energy research, digital technologies are also pervading every aspect of our daily lives, and the potential of transformation is spectacular, even beyond what the Internet revolution has already changed in our way of living, entertaining, interacting, and working. Finally, atomic-scale technologies hold the massive potential to redefine the building blocks that humanity has been using for millennia to build progress.

Will a combination of these technologies therefore eventually trigger some demand transformations and eventually start the energy transition for good?

Together, these technologies share patterns that make their further deployment largely inevitable: they are infinitely scalable and highly decentralized, and they provide increasing rates of return over time. The question is thus not if, but rather when new combinations of these technologies will enable innovations to emerge that will transform existing services for the better, while possibly yielding new services that have not been invented yet.

How then to identify these innovations? My view is that they will necessarily build on current issues or opportunities that manifest themselves in the current course of the world, be they related to the economic, social, or broader environmental landscape. This will include climate change for sure, but by no means will it be limited to it. I would argue that today's economy is largely inefficient, that our society has grown extremely fragile, and ultimately that we are reaching a worrying turning point in our civilization's ability to sustainably maintain its position and continue to thrive on the planet. It is by looking at these three themes that we can best identify potential upcoming innovations.

An Inefficient Economy

Massive waste

I will make a first argument here that our current economy as it stands is extremely inefficient. We could start with our energy system.

I recall the first time I discussed how inefficient our energy system was. I was sitting on a panel when I made that comment, and I remember being asked a barrage of questions as a result. The surprise, not to say shock, that it created in the audience was because of the lack of common understanding and proper communication on how energy systems are being designed and used.

What do I mean by inefficient? The International Energy Agency (2019) is the global reference when it comes to computing energy data. It tells us that in 2018, the world consumed around 170,000 TWh of primary energy (or 14,000 megatons of oil equivalent of energy). Fossil fuels (oil, coal, natural gas) accounted for around 80 percent of this; traditional biomass (wood, plants, etc.) for around 10 percent, and the remaining 10 percent was provided by nuclear energy and various renewable energies, including hydroelectric power. New renewable energies came in at a little over 2 percent. Within fossil fuels, oil accounted for 31 percent, natural gas 23 percent, and coal for a stunning 27 percent. Our modern energy system hence keeps relying for 10 percent on wood and other biomass and for 27 percent on coal (the energy of the first industrial revolution).

These stunning figures should already surprise the uninformed reader and suggest — as it did to me — that something is not quite right. These raw resources are then converted into modern energy sources that can be consumed by all the machines and equipment that we use in our daily lives. Around 40 percent of it is actually used to produce electricity. Coal, gas, nuclear energy and renewable energies come in there. Coal is "burned" to produce vast amounts of heat, which is then used as a way to create steam (yes, steam, like in the 1800s!) to rotate a turbine that in turn activates an alternator, which converts that mechanical power into electricity through the electromagnetic effect. The yield of such installations is 30–40 percent on average, with the best operating plants ranging slightly above 50 percent (Petit, 2018). Natural gas is also burned and used in turbines. Combined cycle gas turbines use steam in addition, with slightly better yields. Overall, this means that between half and two-thirds of the primary energy is actually wasted and released in the atmosphere as unusable heat. Out of around 70,000 TWh of primary energy per year, that represents around 40,000 TWh of waste, to produce around 27,000 TWh of electricity. Electricity is then distributed through large networks. Typical dissipation within long-distance cables is around 10 percent globally, with some regions experiencing even higher levels of losses and a handful of regions lower levels. The actual electricity consumed is thus closer to 23,000 TWh per year. The rest of primary energy is either directly used or converted into usable fuels. When it is converted into fuels, the level of losses (outside of the energy required to process it) is extremely low. It is notably low for oil refining. With regard to coal conversion, it can be much higher. We assume approximately 5–10 percent of losses in these conversion processes. These conversions apply to the total remaining primary energy (not devoted to electricity production), or around 100,000 TWh. 5–10 percent of losses mean that around 5–10,000 TWh are wasted in the process, a fraction of electricity production losses. Losses in the distribution of these fuels are negligible. For gas distribution, losses typically measure below 5 percent. We can assume that there is around 1,000 TWh in methane leaks worldwide, a conservative estimate.

Overall, these various conversion and distribution processes lead final energy demand to average around 120,000 TWh, with around 50,000 TWh of losses, mostly coming from the production of electricity. Usually, most energy reports stop with this analysis. The final energy demand is essentially the oil that fills the tank of a car, or the natural gas that reaches the furnace of a household. Yet, there is a third step to look into: the conversion into useful energy. The useful energy is what actually matters. It is the energy effectively used to heat (a household or an industrial process), to activate motion (a car, an electric motor, etc.), or to run an appliance (a laptop, lighting, etc.). And the analysis of the conversion process from final energy to useful energy reveals a number of issues. Liquid refined fuels are typically used in modern combustion engines. Their yield is around

20 percent, which means that around 80 percent of the energy (in the tank) is actually wasted in the combustion process. Gas or coal heaters are typically 80 percent efficient, with wide disparities between gas and coal and the technology's maturity levels. Finally, electricity is by far the most efficient energy at end-use, with nearly 100 percent efficiency for heating and 90 percent for electric motors. We take a 90 percent proxy in our calculation. The rough exercise we have done above yields a total useful energy of around 70,000 TWh, with further losses of around 50,000 TWh, for the most part in traditional combustion engines and to a lesser extent in fossil-based heating systems.

The bottom line of this exercise is that, for the world to spend 70,000 TWh of useful energy per year, 170,000 TWh of primary energy resources are needed, or a waste of nearly 60 percent, as various forms of unusable heat! The vast majority of these losses comes from electricity production and liquid fuel combustion in traditional engines, while the conversion of crude primary resources and conventional heating take the rest. Another takeaway from this is that there are equal volumes of losses in primary conversion to final energy demand as there are in the actual use of energy — which is reported nowhere! Saul Griffith (2020) finds similar numbers in his recent handbook Rewiring America, as he runs a very detailed analysis of the energy system of the United States. A final lesson, and maybe the more important one, has to do with how we waste those precious primary energy resources, and it all boils down to one key realization: we burn things. Despite all the modern developments of the last couple of centuries, we continue to burn primary resources to create energy. We burn coal or gas in power plants to produce electricity; we burn refined oil in combustion engines to run our cars, ships, planes, cranes, etc. And every time we burn fuels, we create immense wasted heat that ends up in the atmosphere, unusable. Ten thousand years ago, our ancestors were burning wood and crop residues to light, cook, and heat. Our energy system has not changed a bit, despite all discoveries made in the bright nineteenth century. At the heart of our energy system still lies the old habit of igniting finite raw materials to make a living. The "Age of Fire" is not over.

Energy is thus a very good example of what I mean by an inefficient economy. What is true for energy is however also true for other resources that we consume. Since the 1970, we have nearly doubled our material consumption (per capita), with very limited productivity in material use (UN Environment Programme, 2019). Not only have we not made significant productivity gains in material use during half a century, but we continue to waste considerable amounts of material in producing and manufacturing goods. Let's just take one example: 15 percent of materials are wasted in the construction industry, while buildings are overspecified, requiring 20–30 percent more material use than effectively needed (Material Economics, 2018). Do the math! While the construction industry probably stands out as a very inefficient one because of its fragmented nature and the harsh conditions of its development, the same also applies to all our existing industrial processes, even if at different levels.

Beyond the way we manufacture goods, our economy is also inefficient because of what we do with these products or assets we manufacture. A couple of statistics should help illuminate the case here: the world produces around two billion tons of waste each year, as 99 percent of the products and goods consumed are trashed within six months (Petit, 2021). In other words, we keep manufacturing goods (for which we extract resources in mines) that we end up trashing and wasting in landfills.

Significant assets underutilization

But there is more than waste. Another critical inefficiency lies in how the assets we build are utilized. Do we really optimize what we build? The answer comes as a shock. Cars are used less than 5 percent of the time. Commercial buildings (particularly offices) are generally unoccupied for up to 30–40 percent (JLL, 2020). Factories, even in the most optimized sectors, typically run below 60–70 percent of utilization (Roland Berger, 2016). What to say about the common goods we use in our own dwellings? And what is true for machines, buildings, factories, also applies to our large energy infrastructure. Since energy demand is largely inelastic, supply needs to be available at any time. What this translates into is oversized assets to cope with peak demands. Large storage facilities mitigate this to a certain extent, notably for oil, which can be stored at both supply and demand levels (the oil tank). For natural gas, it is already more complicated. For electricity, large storage capabilities are not yet available. As a consequence, these energy infrastructures must cope with peak demand while operating at much lower levels most of the time. Hence, they are underutilized. To take a couple of examples, we could consider gas infrastructure, which provides heating in buildings and homes. This only operates in winter (six months a year) and during parts of the day. Its utilization rate is therefore considerably low. The same could be said of electrical grids, which typically have to cope with "valley to peak" ratios of demand of 1 to 2, and rates of utilization that are often below 70 percent (a raw approximation due to the lack of public studies on the topic, see Petit, 2018).

Everything we do and build is therefore traditionally wasted or underutilized. Our entire economy is built on the principle of "consumerism," or the insatiable appetite for new things to buy and old things to dispose of, whether we use them or not. And as I stated, this fact of life is generally overlooked.

Economists typically estimate that the two main drivers of economic growth are labor workforce evolution and industrial productivity. The more labor, the greater the economic output. The more industrial productivity, the lower the capital needed to manufacture a new good, hence the greater the demand for and adoption of this good, and the greater the reallocation of capital to new goods or services. Yet, as valid as these two drivers are, they overlook sustainability of demand. They take for granted that demand for goods and services grows over time, together with economic wealth, in an insatiable and wasteful race for more goods. What if this was not the case? What if a different economic approach could look at reducing the need for goods and products while providing a similar experience? The consequences of such a structural change would be considerable. What if over time the world needed fewer products or goods? This would constitute a true paradigm shift from the last centuries and the way industrial revolutions initially developed.

A Fragile Society

Energy and resources

A second critical consideration is the inherent fragility of our societies. Let's start once more with energy to illustrate this.

Our energy system is largely dependent on fossil fuels. The spectacular rise in demand for fossil fuels over the last century has triggered a race to access resources where they were abundant and cheap, in a globally integrated market. Alas, these resources are not universally distributed, with the potential exception of coal. These are carbon residues (from crops and plants) that have developed over millennia in specific geological formations. You do not find them everywhere! The underlying architecture of the planet beneath us enables their formation — or not. The greatest reserves of oil can be found in North America, in the deserts of the Middle East, and in the vast plains of Eurasia. Natural gas is slightly better distributed, with the largest share of resources in Eurasia and the Middle East, but also with important reserves in both North and South America, as well as Asia and Africa. The largest coal reserves are in North America, Eurasia, and, to a lesser extent, Europe and China (Petit, 2017).

The historic development of these resources has a lot to do with their region of origin, and the political power and will in place at the time of their discovery. Looking back in time, coal mining was developed because of depleted forests in the United Kingdom of the seventeenth and eighteenth centuries. This fueled an industrial revolution that began in Europe and led the continent to dominate world exchanges for two centuries. While most European countries have acknowledged that they will move away from coal, these vast resources are a powerful incitation to continue to burn coal. It is cheap and it is locally available, hence ensuring energy security. This is a particularly interesting test for Germany, which holds massive reserves in its ground. Today, modern China literally runs on it, with over 50 percent of its primary demand based on coal, consuming 50 percent of the world's coal production in the process. Yet, China's resources are getting depleted, and the country has only a few decades of reserves left at the current pace of production (Petit, 2017), a situation quite similar to that of the United Kingdom centuries ago with wood. The same goes for oil. North America developed refined oil products in the nineteenth century that led to a new industrial revolution a few decades later. This development started with locally abundant energy sources. This tells another interesting tale on how innovation is always primarily driven by local observations and discoveries. This assertion might no longer hold in today's interconnected world, but one must acknowledge that energy security — or the ability to locally source the energy resources required to operate the economy — has always been among the main topics on the agenda of nations. I would also argue that the system has now become so big that its foundations are back in question.

Indeed, the significant increase in our energy needs has dramatically changed the equation. For most countries around the world, it has become impossible to rely entirely on local energy resources. Whoever holds the key of the door to these massive reserves has considerable geopolitical leverage. The "Great Game" in the nineteenth and early twentieth centuries that the British, Russians, and French played in the Middle East was largely driven by a quest to access oil reserves (Frankopan, 2016; Yergin, 2009). The Americans took over during World War II, when Roosevelt signed a historical agreement with the new Saudi regime from Ibn Saud on the US warship Quincy. They have not left since, despite the development of giant reservoirs of nonconventional oils in the US in the early 2000s that have progressively made their presence less imperative. Today, energy exchange represents the vast majority of trade (in dollar terms) across regions.

Notably, oil would represent almost half of this trade by itself (Furfari, 2007). The oil market is global, with nearly 60 percent of oil that is traded. The coal market is slightly more regional, with 30 percent of the coal consumed traded across regions, in two almost independent markets (the Atlantic and Pacific markets). The natural gas market is much more regional, with less than 20 percent of natural gas traded across regions and critical dependencies between Russia and Europe, and the Middle East and Asia (Petit, 2017). The bottom line of this is that energy is now a global commodity that depends largely on multilateral agreements and their enforcement.

Alas, no such thing exists, and geopolitics remains a cruel and grueling power game. There have thus been significant incidents in the trade of energy over the last decades, and these have mostly fueled wars, conflicts, and chaos of various kinds. It is striking to contemplate the evolution of energy prices over the last decades. Until the 1970s, oil prices remained below US$20/barrel (in today's dollar terms). The two oil crises of the 1970s were started by Middle East countries, which formed the OPEC (Organization of Petroleum Exporting Countries) and organized supply-and-demand balance in order to increase prices and generate a higher rent for themselves. These oil crises were a shock to importing nations (at the time mainly the United States and Europe). They gave new breath to oil exploration (Europeans for instance developed their resources in the Nordics and the North Sea) and led to significant investments in decreasing the West's reliance on oil (the civil nuclear programs of the 1970s were pretty much a direct consequence of these emergencies). Since these crises, prices have continued to fluctuate: up to US$122/barrel at the end of the 1970s to US$30/barrel in the middle of the 1980s and US$18/barrel in 1998, then up again to US$164/barrel in 2008 prior to the global financial crisis, down to US$36/barrel in 2015, slightly up again and then down to a low US$18/barrel during the height of the Covid-19 2020 crisis, and back up since (Macrotrends, 2020).

Ritchie and Roser (2020) have mapped the price index of all fossil fuel resources (oil, but also natural gas and coal) from the 1980s to 2015. The volatility of these fuel prices is patent and a clear representation of the geopolitical issues associated with producing and distributing energy across regions. Oil is often cited as an example of a volatile energy resource, but it is striking to see that coal has been even more volatile over the last few decades, with a price that nearly quadrupled during the first decade of the twenty-first century — before it was divided by nearly three in the second — while oil only tripled and natural gas doubled. These price swings result from geopolitical or economic crises, but more importantly, they lead to huge economic shocks in both importing and exporting countries. During the 2015 oil crisis, which was triggered by rising production from OPEC in a context of already increasing production from US shale oil, nearly US$1,000 billion in wealth shifted from importing regions to exporting ones. In other words, exporting countries such as the Middle East or Russia lost around US$1,000 billion in revenues, while importing countries made huge savings on their energy bills and trade deficits. While this kind of shock might have benefited economic growth in China or Europe in the short run, it can also have the opposite effect and significantly hamper economic cycles. At the same time, volatility is never good for business, and such dependencies and uncertainties tend to slow down investment cycles and overall consumer trust and appetite to spend. Let's not forget this: energy is a means to an end, nothing more. What matters is what countries, businesses, and people do with it. How they use cheap and reliable access to it to develop new ways to do the same things in a better way, or to simply do new things that we did not know we would need or did not dare dream about!

The bottom line is that the current energy system has turned out to be a drag on economic development. It has grown so big and so interconnected that the slightest hiccup in global trade or relations turns into massive price swings, and risks (or fears — which matter almost as much) of disruptions. In short, a fragile construct.

And what is true for energy also applies to most (if not all) resources that the modern world depends on. Take the case of China. One of the many reasons of its current rise in international affairs today, and that of its military, partly has to do with its huge imports of resources of all kinds from Southeast Asia, Russia, Africa, and Latin America, which often represent more than half of global commodity trade (Petit, 2021). The increase of interdependencies in a globally interconnected economy is unfortunately often synonymous with increasing political and possibly military confrontations. This has large implications for sustainable economic development as well. Uncertainty, threats, and foreign postures have a large impact on the peaceful development of economic ties, relations, and wealth.

And the situation is not close to improving, as resources get harder and harder to procure. Following the Ricardo theory (Suman, 2020), the price of a resource equals the marginal cost of the last unit to procure to meet demand. Since all the cheapest resources go first, and have to a large extent been utilized, it becomes increasingly expensive over time to procure these resources, as the marginal cost of the last unit keeps increasing. Our resource-based economy has largely relied on cheap resources, which over time become more difficult to access, hence more expensive. This is what Arbib and Seba (2020) have named the "Age of Extraction." We also talk of decreasing rates of return, which are a foundation of the modern economy and a powerful fuel for innovation. There are no dramatic short-term issues when it comes to access to resources (Petit, 2017, 2018, 2021), but the world is on a clear path toward more expensive resources as time goes, with decreasing returns that slow down economic development.

Our economy is therefore fragile because of its dependency on (we could say addiction to) resources. Unevenly distributed resources create interdependencies and trade disputes across nations. These disputes expand way beyond trade to all foreign policy matters, including the military, which in turn creates uncertainties and threats. Beyond this, our resource-based economy follows the rule of decreasing rates of return, which over time lead to a heavier burden on economic development, and thus wealth creation.

Trade

But fragility is not only about resources. A second aspect of it, which is possibly counterintuitive, would be global commerce. Trade has been around for millennia and is one of the foundations of our history. Frankopan (2016) has wonderfully described the trade between Western and Eastern civilizations along the Silk Road that took place for over two thousand years. He tells a tale of mutual enrichment strewn with wars and conflict among powers for the control over these routes. In fact, trade is not fragile per se, but dependencies exacerbate conflicts, and an imbalance in trade tends to undermine cooperation. Two examples come to mind when contemplating recent history.

The first one is the major trade dispute that emerged between the United States and China at the end of the 2010s. The global trade imbalance between the two giant powerhouses has grown significantly. The United States has reached a US$400 billion per year trade deficit with China, the largest in history (Petit, 2021). Negotiations went back and forth, following many episodes, and they have not been concluded at the time of writing. While these exchanges were beneficial to all in their early days, they became an issue as the imbalance increased and dependencies tightened. What was initially a good trade deal became a dispute that turned into a geopolitical conflict. Time will tell how it is resolved.

The second example is that of the Covid-19 crisis, which brought the world economy to its knees in 2020 due to a combined supply and demand shock. The story is fairly simple to understand. Countries touched by the virus almost unequivocally decided to shut down their economies for weeks in an attempt to control its spread and mitigate its impact. As countries shut down, their production capacities were virtually zeroed. Therefore, all importing countries were facing a supply shock, which gravely undermined their own ability to run the economy. As countries shut down, their demand for goods was also crushed, with significant impacts on the exporting economies that depended on those markets. China was first to close down in the early months of 2020, leading to a demand-and-supply shock in other economies. When the virus traveled to Europe, the demand-and-supply shock from the region rippled around all world economies. And despite China coming back online, the reduced demand from one of the first economies of the world had major impacts. The United States came third, and the situation there has also significantly hindered the ability of the world's economy to swiftly get back on track. Moreover, the virus has traveled through all other new economies, annihilating a decade of economic development and social progress. Trade is not fragile, but the interconnectedness of the economy has never been as apparent as in the first half of 2020, triggering declarations from all governments, investors, and company executives around the world on the need to build more resiliency into the economic system, in order to enable the economy to better resist such unexpected shocks.

Social contract

A last issue relates to the social contract. The anthropologist Robin Dunbar is famous for having estimated that a normal person cannot maintain relationships with more than 150 people at the same time. Yet, our social organizations have grown much larger than that. There have been quite a number of studies on the Neolithic transition, which saw the emergence of farming as the new principle of social organization (Arbib and Seba, 2020; Hariri, 2014). There seems to be wide agreement that while sedentary farming brought sustained food intake, enabling the population to expand, it also forced a new social structure on humans that was different from past foraging societies, more hierarchical and centralized. The nations, our modern social construct, are byproducts of this transition to sedentary farming, which saw the emergence of large concentrated and hierarchical powers. And these powers inevitably had to confront one another over time to obtain more land and control over resources.

For these powers to expand, capital needed to be consolidated so that it could be distributed toward high-value political objectives, at scale and in the most optimized and efficient way possible. The other consequence of the verticalization of societies has thus been rising inequalities among people: between those who owned and handled capital, and those who did not. Arbib and Seba (2020) explain that the revolution of the distributed press in the fifteenth century enabled the diffusion of ideas and beliefs across different layers of the population for the first time. This would fuel the religious confrontations in Europe a century later, and then the democratic revolutions. One could have assumed that these democratic revolutions of the seventeenth (United Kingdom) and eighteenth (France, the United States, etc.) centuries, fueled by widely available information, would have put a halt to these rising inequalities. Well, it did not do so at all! Instead, the poor stayed poor, and the wealthy got wealthier. Piketty (2014) has masterfully demonstrated this. Through a thorough analysis of capital allocation over the last two centuries, based on collected archival documents and extrapolations, Piketty was able to demonstrate that in our societies, capital tends to naturally concentrate in the hands of a few. The two World Wars of the twentieth century are likely the true root cause of the decrease in inequalities in recent times. Yet, as Piketty demonstrated, these inequalities have been on the rise again as we moved further away from these terrible times. His demonstration also tends to confirm that the myth of social elevation, which has been the bedrock of modern democracies, is far from a given. This is maybe because the distribution of wealth and power obeys rules that are different from those we find in the legislative code.

What is true for inequalities within a society also holds across nations. The last 20 years have actually witnessed a rise in wealth that was faster in mature economies than in new economies (Petit, 2021). When I make this statement, it always comes as a surprise, because people are so used to hearing that capitalism-based economic development is a success story. But although the long period of peace we have known has enabled a significant increase in wealth, which to a certain extent has benefited all, the distribution of that wealth has largely been unequal. Mature economies, and within them small wealthy groups at the top of the pyramid, have captured the essence of global wealth growth. The rest has shared the crumbs. Let's remember that, in 2020, 30 percent of the world population still lacks access to a convenient form of energy! With information now traveling at light speed across social groups and continents, one can wonder whether this unequal construct will stand the test of time any longer. I argue that it will not. In that sense, it is fragile.

A fragile society

In their latest report, titled *Rethinking Humanity*, James Arbib and Tony Seba (2020) describe single points of failure that served as root causes of civilizational collapses. They notably mention the grain delivery system in the Mediterranean Sea during the Roman Empire, and Rome's extreme dependency on Egyptian fields, which constituted a recurring choke point over the centuries.

Jared Diamond (2011) says the same in his remarkable history of civilization collapses, when he finds five contributing factors: climate change and environment, hostile neighbors and collapse of essential trading partners, and society's response. In other words: resources, trade, and the social contract. One can thus predict that many of the upcoming innovations in the next few decades will certainly aim at mitigating these issues and their effects.

Sinking the Spaceship

Pollution

Oliver Twist, the young hero of Charles Dickens's 1838 novel, was an orphan sold into apprenticeship who made his way to London and gang leader Fagin.

He grew up in dark city streets obscured with smog. The cloudy, dusty, filthy smog that appeared at night in the streets of London is an integral part of most major English novels of the nineteenth and early twentieth century. It was engrained forever in the minds of the time, an essential element of their lives, although it was uncomfortable. They called it "pea-soupers," the smog being "as thick as pea soup." It killed many, even though it took time for people to realize that pollution was the root cause of the deaths. The person reading these novels from Europe today may experience the thrilling sensation of visiting a distant planet and diving into a period of mystery and danger susceptible to drama.

Yet, the smog is no ancient history. The Great Smog of 1952 in London killed 4,000 and led to the Clean Air Act of 1956, which banned soft coal use in certain areas in an attempt to reduce the smog. There is still some of it today, notably from the pollution induced by exhaust pipes, but not to the extent that it used to be. In effect, the smog is a rather old memory in modern London today.

Yet, if old records start in the London area, smog today is an international plague. Most large metropolitan areas are affected by it. These areas are overcrowded, with major transportation congestion and industrial pollution alongside the occasional further contribution from surrounding areas (be it industrial pollution or deforestation, as in the case of most Southeast Asian cities). Smog has become an international reality. This reminds me of when I visited New Delhi some years back. After long hours in an airplane, even longer hours to exit customs and finally reach the hotel in the middle of the night, and an obviously agitated and short sleep, I felt like I needed to freshen up before getting to work. Hence, I decided to go for a quick run in the early and still deserted hours of the morning. I did not pay much attention to the weather, nor did I pay attention to much of anything, and went on with my run in the surroundings. The sun was just rising on the horizon and I was thrilled by the view of the sun shining through the atmosphere and illuminating the last particles of humidity on the leaves of the trees outside. What I had however not fully captured was that this poetic light in the early morning was actually due to pollution. Walking back to the beautiful, air-conditioned room of the palace where I was staying, I grabbed a bottle of water and looked outside. This is where I could contemplate, from high above, the cloud of dust that surrounded the premises, the "pea soup" I had been running in. And I felt its effects the entire day, with a small irritation in my throat that kept me uncomfortable until nightfall. I did not repeat the experience the next day, as you can imagine. A similar thing has happened to me in Beijing, and I have to say that even in modern Paris or London, when I go out for a jog in the morning, I do not feel fully refreshed when I come back.

Why is it then that we have to force ourselves to live in such filthy environments, with our bodies weakened and infected by various particles that penetrate deep into our lungs and eventually cause cancer and other cardiovascular issues? I am sure that, like me, you have always had a particular feeling when reaching the countryside. You may have put that impression down to the fact of finally being on holidays, far away from daily work issues and concerns, being able to relax, etc. But there may be something else too: the ability to finally be able to breathe deeply and fill your lungs with fresh and rejuvenating air. My house is in Brittany, France, and sits on the upper hills near the small city of Tregastel, a few hundred meters away from the sea. You permanently breathe the spray of the sea, charged with iodine, and it feels as if your lungs are opened wide, finally, and this from morning to evening. Over time, you begin to forget the smell, and it is not as obvious every time you go out. However, in the first days, it is reinvigorating, and I have never found anyone who thought otherwise! It is just our human condition that drives these feelings, deep inside the body and cells that form us. Whatever it is, I think I made the case. Why would we still want to live in polluted places when we finally recognize that we are augmented as human beings when we do not? Well, in short, because we have no choice. Business is within the cities. And because cities concentrate many of us, they also concentrate all the pollution we generate.

It is now possible to monitor worldwide air pollution levels in real time. The World Air Quality Index project is a nonprofit started in 2007 (World Air Quality, 2020), which turned into a worldwide real-time air pollution monitoring system. It is a Sunday morning in May as I am writing these lines, and I have checked the website. The overall air quality index in Hong Kong where I live is at 40, which is considered good. This is expected, as it has rained all night, chasing the dust away. The website records all data points since 2014, and it is possible to compare one year to another. This year has been the best one since the creation of the website. One should note that this is also the first year that it has rained so much, and this has been the case for over two weeks at the time of writing these lines, almost day and night. Browsing through the virtual map of the website, it is possible to access similar data from any city in the world. What immediately comes as a shock is the very high level of pollution in the cities of China, India, and several countries in new economies in Southeast Asia, the Middle East, Africa, and South America. This is in stark contrast with Western Europe and North America, which now all enjoy appropriate levels of pollution. The World Health Organization (2016) has notably shown that if fewer than 20–40 percent of cities in Western mature economies exceed standard air quality guidelines, for cities in all other countries this is generally well above 90 percent. Many of the inhabitants of these cities now have to suffer from and battle against the filthy effects of pollution smog. In Beijing today, the smog is reminiscent of some of the darkest times of Oliver Twist's London, over a century ago.

The website of the World Air Quality Index project also holds incredible treasures, such as real-time monitoring of an array of indicators like PM2.5, PM10, ozone, nitrogen dioxide, sulfur dioxide, and carbon monoxide concentration levels. PM2.5 and PM10 refer to matter particles that are below 2.5 micrometers or 10 micrometers respectively. These particles — particularly PM2.5 — can penetrate deeply into the lungs and blood and create health issues, such as strokes, heart disease, lung cancer, and chronic respiratory diseases, especially asthma for children. Between 25 and 40 percent of these diseases can actually be attributed to pollution (WHO, 2016). According to the World Health Organization (2016) and Ritchie and Roser (2019), over six million deaths annually can directly be associated with pollution. More than half of these are related to outdoor air pollution, which essentially comes from energy emissions such as transportation, nearby electricity production (if from fossil fuels such as coal), or direct fossil fuel burning. Another 25 percent comes from household air pollution, essentially from cooking methods that still rely on open fires or simple stoves fueled by kerosene or coal. Around three billion people still cook using such antiquated systems; nearly 40 percent of the world's population!

But pollution is not only about air. Water could become an even bigger issue in the decades to come. Of freshwater use today, 70 percent goes to agriculture, while energy, industrial applications, and domestic use share the rest equally. There is obviously no water treatment for agricultural water use or energy use, and very limited treatment for industrial and domestic water uses. Around 80 percent of domestic water returns to the water system untreated and pollutes freshwater resources. Water used in agriculture is mixed with pesticides and chemical fertilizers; water used in energy, industrial, or domestic uses is similarly polluted with chemical products that further dissolve in rivers and aquifers. The outcomes are horrifying. Today, around 25–30 percent of the global population regularly drinks contaminated water, with obvious major impacts on long-term health (Denchak, 2018; Globe Water, 2020).

Finally, soil pollution is also set to play a major role going forward. To pick just a few numbers: the world loses around 10 million hectares to erosion every year, while 20 million more are abandoned because of soil that is too much degraded (Everything connects, 2013). To put this figure into perspective, there are currently 1.6 billion hectares in use for agriculture (FAO, 2011). In other words, every year, the world loses almost 2 percent of its arable land area, a considerable number! In some geographies, it may already have taken a dramatic toll. In today's China, 40 percent of arable land is said to now be polluted (Marshall, 2011), potentially yielding food-supply security issues. It is therefore no surprise that one of the five pillars of Xi Jinping's long-term policy is that of a "beautiful" China, a healthy environment with low pollution (Bosu, 2018; Kuhn, 2013).

Today, these pollution issues are mainly concentrated in new economies. Overall, over 90 percent of pollution deaths would occur in these countries, which have no alternatives to these extremely polluting supply chains. The cost for the economy is around US$3,000 billion per year, but the Organisation for Economic Co-operation and Development (2016) estimates that it could go up to US$25,000 billion per year by 2060, a major strain on new economies' GDP, with all the unpredictable consequences that we can imagine.

Climate change

And this is not all! All these issues of air, water, and soil pollution and their devastating effects are aggravated by another issue: climate change. I began to discuss this in the introduction of the second chapter. Climate change is part of nature's history and is a relatively new field of science. Remarkable progress in computing power has made it possible to model the climate with greater precision. Yet, the lack of observed data makes it difficult to finetune the models. There is no doubt however that climate science will continue to make dramatic improvements in the coming decades.

However, some conclusions already stand out. While climate change can be induced by a multitude of factors, from astronomical evolutions to atmospheric constitution changes, reinforced or tamed by albedo evolutions (ice cores, biosphere, etc.) over millennia, it has become apparent that the recent changes to the climate (with a nearly 1-degree increase in temperature compared to preindustrial levels) can only be explained — because of the pace at which it materializes — by atmospheric constitution changes. When digging into such changes, the only explanation that seems to prevail today is the extra emissions of greenhouse gases in the atmosphere by human industrial activities of the last couple of centuries (Intergovernmental Panel on Climate Change, 2007, 2014), with carbon dioxide representing the highest share of these.

Some of the gases we emit are actually said to have a cooling effect, notably aerosols (which tend to form clouds that reduce sun irradiation). Yet, aerosols are considered an even bigger source of pollution for people (particles of matter in the air), and many countries around the world have embraced radical reduction programs, which could accelerate further global warming as a result; a "Faustian bargain."

Overall, and as I indicated earlier, the concentration of carbon dioxide in the atmosphere has increased 50 percent in two centuries, reaching around

3,000 $GtCO_2$, caused by the progressive accumulation of anthropogenic emissions that were only in part absorbed by the biosphere and the oceans. With this increase comes greater radiative forcing and hence increased temperatures. The question is what the increase will be, but more importantly, at which pace it will occur. As stated, the planet has seen changes in climate in the past. The question of the pace of change is however dramatic, because time provides the ability to species and the biosphere to adapt or not to the change. A brutal increase of 2 degrees or more during this century could have dramatic consequences for the biosphere. Some of the IPCC reports mention possible losses of 20–30 percent of Earth's species in a scenario above 2 degrees, with ripple effects on entire biospheres and ecosystems, including humans!

Beyond this, these changes would of course strain some world regions with more frequent climate events such as droughts, flash floods, fires, etc. Some regions around the Tropic of Cancer would be particularly impacted (Petit, 2021), but with 40 percent of the world population living near coastal areas, many countries would have to review landscape planning (Sedac, 2020). Some regions are already experiencing transformations of this kind. One of my colleagues told me the story of some of his friends in Florida who purchased a house without checking insurance requirements. Insurance turned out to be around US$50,000 per year, because of the likelihood of weather events that could hit the specific spot they occupied. This is already a reality in the United States and is likely to take precedence in other regions of the world. Responses will of course differ, but adaptation to climate change might become a new norm, and it will impact many regions and lead to changes in habits. It is better not to have invested in those that will eventually be abandoned or largely depreciated.

In 1966, Kenneth Boulding (1966) introduced the concept of Earth as a spaceship. In other words, our species has grown so large that it is impossible to any longer consider the planet as an infinite land of opportunity, as used to be the case in past millennia. Earth is now a finite plot of land that can barely sustain our survival. Boulding's theory was that we were about to engage in a radically new paradigm of making the planet we live on thrive so that we can continue to survive in the big void of the universe. Without falling into counterproductive dystopian scenarios, the perspective I briefly laid out above (and which I will go more into the details of in a later chapter) raises the question: are we sinking the spaceship? And what happens if we fail to stop this?

How to Take It Forward?

Our current energy system is the complex product of a series of industrial revolutions that have emerged over time when a set of new technological advancements (including but not limited to energy) led to innovations that, as they expanded, reshaped demand patterns by either providing new services or simply enabling current services to be provided in a better way, and often at a fraction of their past cost. Energy transitions are not driven by energy; they are a component of greater transformations taking place in our economy, our societies, and our civilizations, which race toward greater abundance.

In the previous chapter, I identified three foundational technological advancements that — as they are today — already offer considerable potential for transformations and improvements. Decentralized renewable energy sources that, if intermittent, also offer access to reliable sources of energy. In most countries of the world, they are already cheaper than conventional sources. Their costs have collapsed thanks to the very nature of these technologies. Dependent on mass small-scale production of small units, their accelerated adoption has brought costs down significantly, following 20 percent learning rates. Rooftop solar technologies in particular offer the largest prospect since they can easily be deployed everywhere people live and work; pretty much everywhere next to where we consume energy. And with this, the significant costs of transporting and distributing that energy (over 50 percent of total costs) become irrelevant, alongside (part of) the considerable infrastructure that has been developed over the past decades. These technologies are only at the beginning of their development, and more is to come. Third-generation solar panels already promise further integration potential and lower costs, possibly near-free energy over time. These technologies are complemented by the fantastic potential of energy storage. For decades, this industry did not experience any major breakthrough. The situation is now reversed, and energy storage has become one of the primary focus points of many energy scientists around the world. Every month, new breakthroughs or advancements are made public, and one can expect mass and cheap energy storage to be within reach. As mentioned, what makes these technologies so promising is also the way they are manufactured. Mass production enables significant learning rates and sharp cost reduction. Small is beautiful!

Then come digital technologies. The Internet has changed lives for the better, connecting billions of people to information, knowledge, and opportunities. And the digital transformation of our lives is only at its beginning, with significant enhancements to come, whether these will be of computing power, communication performance, or miniaturization and pervasive connectivity. This is a world where virtual and physical realities begin to blur, offering significant potential for doing the same things in a better way or doing new things that we have only begun to imagine.

Last, atomic-scale technologies such as nanotechnologies or biotechnologies also hold the promise of tectonic transformations in the way we understand how our current systems operate and the inherent limitations of our models. What if we could produce and manufacture new and better resources that would replace the ones our planet has made available to us? What if we could reach nanometer-level applications that would enable us to solve some of our greatest challenges?

These technologies are also entangled in a positive and reinforcing loop of technological progress. Atomic-scale technological development is highly dependent on the advancement of digital technologies. Significant improvements in computing power of the last decades have enabled the development of affordable atomic-scale research, fueling innovations in this field. Atomic-scale technologies also hold the potential to redefine how we can further harness and store the massive amounts of renewable energy that our planet is endowed with.

Finally, these technologies have key common characteristics. First, they are infinitely scalable. Unlike twentieth-century technologies, they can be directly deployed in the fragmented consumer ecosystem on a very large scale in small components, accelerating adoption and cutting costs at a rapid pace. In this way, they become highly decentralized to a point where they potentially redefine common and engrained boundaries of what we consider feasible: distributed energy provisions in appliances, native connectivity in virtually every device or tool we may tomorrow interact with, and nanometer-scale intelligent devices that could ultimately even be placed in our own bodies. Finally, these technologies provide increasing rates of return. Unlike the current set of technologies, which heavily build on finite resources that need to be procured from depleting deposits (thus yielding decreasing rates of return), these technologies have the potential to remove this dependency, at least in part. And the more the technology progresses, the more benefits and hence returns it offers. A good example of this is the ability to harvest renewable energies with increased yields over time, a major game changer compared to traditional energy extraction activities.

These technologies, when combined, will generate significant innovation in the coming decades, which will in turn transform demand and services. Yet, these innovations, as I explained, will ramp up only if they are first capable of providing existing services in ways that are better than present systems have been able to do, and notably at a fraction of their current cost, thus enabling mass adoption; or of providing new services we have not yet thought of.

To understand where these disruptions will emerge, we must therefore look at the current issues and opportunities our world is facing, because these are what the innovations will primarily target. This is what I reviewed in this chapter, proposing three arguments to explore further.

First, I argue here that there is considerable potential for running our economies in a much more efficient way than we have traditionally done. This argument revolves around two fundamental points: first, we significantly underutilize the assets and products we build and use — be it buildings, factories, the goods we use, our mobility systems (particularly private transportation), and our infrastructure. Second, our economies generate significant amounts of waste, during both the manufacturing process and the final use of the products we consume, as well as in the way we use energy. Can the technologies I described above kickstart innovations toward further efficiency?

Second, I also argue that our societies have grown fragile because of the combined effects of increasing resource and trade dependencies and social inequality. Jared Diamond's history of civilizational collapses is a stark reminder of what has made past societies fail, and it has always revolved around these issues. Will innovation help mitigate those issues going forward, or are we doomed to witness the systemic transformation of our societies, maybe ultimately for the better, but also for the worse in the short run?

Finally, I argue that our civilization is reaching a dramatic turning point because of the burden it puts on the sustainable renewal of the vital resources we need. Pollution and climate change, two entangled issues, already lead to a dramatic depletion of arable land and water resources, without which nothing we base our hopes on can truly thrive. The issue is so bad in some places that it could overthrow current social systems, resetting all of our expectations. Will we continue to deplete the planet until a point of no return, or will we be spurred into innovation and trigger massive and positive transformations toward a more sustainable use of our resources?

In the coming decades, innovation will most certainly revolve around these three arguments, and this is where to look if we want to understand how demand patterns will evolve. And as demand changes, so will the energy system, which is a byproduct of these transformations. This approach contrasts significantly with current approaches to the energy transition, but I argue that this approach allows us to truly capture what the next three decades will look like and to properly predict the shape of the future energy system. Since energy transitions are primarily driven by demand evolutions, and more importantly as these define the pace of change, this exploration will also bring new insights on how best decarbonize our energy system in time. To do that however, we need to break with the paradigm of looking at our current energy system from the standpoint of its greenhouse gas emissions alone, and further embrace all the services it is in fact meant to serve.

The second part of this book will now focus on exploring these issues and opportunities and on understanding what a first set of innovations could look like, including the impact they will ultimately have on demand patterns. Moreover, we will need to understand the true driver of adoption for each of these innovations and the inherent challenges to their deployment. This will give us a perspective on the likelihood of their unfolding. I will therefore fill out the following table as I go through each part separately (Figure 1).

Figure 1   Demand-driven innovations

A word to conclude. Earlier, I already made the point on the excitement that prevails in all conferences gathering energy experts today. When we get together to exchange our views on potential scenarios for a new energy system, we all feel compelled to better comprehend the changes at stake and find solutions to the massive problem that the current energy system poses in terms of climate change. In a way, we feel that we truly contribute to building a better future. Yet, all these discussions, as commendable as they may be, may ultimately be completely forgotten over time. Indeed, what future generations will probably remember from this time and what children will learn about this period in history classes a century from now will rather revolve around the key issues I mentioned above and around how our current generation was able to face them. Instead of discussing an energy transition, they will review the industrial revolutions (or whatever we call these transformations by then) that took place and look at how these helped make the world a better place: a place of greater abundance for all. And that will include climate change, though it will not be limited to it. A century ago, we may well have had similar conferences of energy experts discussing the potentialities of new energy sources such as coal, oil, or electricity, but what we truly remember now is what these changed in the world we live in. We should thus remain humble in how we approach this next part of the book and remember that history is made through a complex entanglement of different factors and hazards, and no one really holds the truth. The best we can do is to contribute to seeing through all this a bit more clearly.

References

Arbib, J., and Seba, T. (2020). *Rethinking Humanity: Five Foundational Sector Disruptions, the Lifecycle of Civilizations, and the Coming Age of Freedom.* RethinkX, June. https://www.rethinkx.com/humanity.

Boulding, K. (1966). "The Economics of the Coming Spaceship Earth." In *Environmental Quality in a Growing Economy*, edited by H. Jarrett, 3–14. Baltimore, MD: Resources for the Future/Johns Hopkins University Press. http://www.ub.edu/prometheus21/articulos/obsprometheus/BOULDING.pdf.

Denchak, M. (2018). "Water Pollution: Everything You Need to Know." *NRDC*, May 14. https://www.nrdc.org/stories/water-pollution-everything-you-need-know.

Diamond, J. (2011). *Collapse: How Societies Choose to Fail or Succeed.* New York: Penguin Books.

Everything Connects. (2013). "Soil Pollution." Last updated: November 20. https://www.everythingconnects.org/soil-pollution.html.

Food and Agriculture Organization. (2011). *The State of the World's Land and Water Resources for Food and Agriculture*. Abingdon, England: FAO United Nations and Earthscan. http://www.fao.org/3/a-i1688e.pdf.

Frankopan, P. (2016). *The Silk Roads: A New History of the World*. London: Bloomsbury Publishing.

Furfari, S. (2007). *Le Monde et l'Energie, Enjeux geopolitiques*. Paris: Editions Technip.

Globe Water. (2020). "Water Pollution Statistics 2018–2019." https://www.globewater. org/facts/water-pollution-statistics/.

Griffith, S. (2020). *Rewiring America*. Rewiring America, November. https://www. rewiringamerica.org/handbook.

Intergovernmental Panel on Climate Change. (2007). *Climate Change 2007: Synthesis Report. Contribution of Working Groups I, II and III to the Fourth Assessment Report of the Intergovernmental Panel on Climate Change*. Edited by the core writing team, R. K. Pachauri, and A. Reisinger. Geneva, Switzerland: IPCC. https://www.ipcc. ch/site/assets/uploads/2018/02/ar4_syr_full_report.pdf.

Intergovernmental Panel on Climate Change. (2014). *Climate Change 2014: Synthesis Report. Contribution of Working Groups I, II and III to the Fifth Assessment Report of the Intergovernmental Panel on Climate Change*. Edited by the core writing team, R. K. Pachauri, and A. Reisinger. Geneva, Switzerland: IPCC. https://www.ipcc. ch/site/assets/uploads/2018/02/SYR_AR5_FINAL_full.pdf.

International Energy Agency ©. (2013). *Technology Roadmap. Energy Efficient Building Envelopes*. December. Paris: IEA Publishing. https://www.iea.org/reports/technology-roadmap-energy-efficient-building-envelopes.

International Energy Agency ©. (2019). *World Energy Outlook*. November. Paris: IEA. https://www.iea.org/reports/world-energy-outlook-2019.

JLL. (2020). "Benchmark Your Way to a Smarter Workplace." https://www.us.jll.com/ en/space-utilization.

Macrotrends. (2020). "Crude Oil Prices — 70 Year Historical Chart." https://www. macrotrends.net/1369/crude-oil-price-history-chart.

Marshall, T. (2001). *Prisoners of Geography: Ten Maps That Tell You Everything You Need to Know about Global Politics*. London: Elliott & Thompson.

Material Economics. (2019). *Industrial Transformation 2050 — Pathways to Net-Zero Emissions from EU Heavy Industry*. Cambridge: CISL. https://materialeconomics. com/latest-updates/industrial-transformation-2050.

Organisation for Economic Co-operation and Development. (2016). *The Economic Consequences of Outdoor Air Pollution*. June 9. Paris: OECD Publishing. https:// doi.org/10.1787/9789264257474-en.

Petit, V. (2017). *The Energy Transition: An Overview of the True Challenge of the 21st Century*. Cham, Switzerland: Springer.

Petit, V. (2018). *The New World of Utilities: A Historical Transition toward a New Energy System*. Cham, Switzerland: Springer.

Petit, V. (2021). *The Future Global Order. The Six Paradigm Changes That Will Define 2050*. London: World Scientific Publishing.

Ritchie, H., and Roser, M. (2019). "Air Pollution." Our World in Data. https://ourworldindata.org/air-pollution.

Ritchie, H., and Roser, M. (2020). "Fossil Fuels." Our World in Data. https://ourworldindata.org/fossil-fuels.

Roland Berger. (2016). *Think Act beyond Mainstream. The Industrie 4.0 Transition Quantified*. Munich, Germany: Roland Berger. https://www.rolandberger.com/en/Publications/The-Industrie-4.0-transition-quantified.html?country=WLD.

Sedac. (2020). *Percentage of Total Population Living in Coastal Areas*. Socioeconomic Data and Applications Center (Sedac). https://sedac.ciesin.columbia.edu/es/papers/Coastal_Zone_Pop_Method.pdf.

UN Environment Programme. (2019). *Global Resources Outlook. 2019: Natural Resources for the Future We Want*. Report of the International Resource Panel. Nairobi: United Nations Environment Programme. https://www.resourcepanel.org/reports/global-resources-outlook.

World Air Quality. (2020). "Air Pollution in Hong Kong: Real-time Air Quality Index Visual Map." https://aqicn.org/map/hongkong/.

World Health Organization. (2016). *WHO's Urban Ambient Air Pollution Database Update 2016*. Version 0.2. http://www.who.int/phe/health_topics/outdoorair/databases/AAP_database_summary_results_2016_v02.pdf?ua=1.

Yergin, D. (2009). *The Prize: The Epic Quest for Oil, Money and Power*. New York: Simon & Schuster.

Part 2
The "North Star"

CHAPTER 4

There Is a Stunning Potential to Do the Same Things ... Much Better

"Progress isn't made by early risers. It's made by lazy men trying to find easier ways to do something." (Robert Heinlein)

In the previous part, we have acquainted ourselves with a famous quote from Albert Einstein: "If you want to know the future, look at the past." The history of energy transitions has taught us that such transitions are always driven by social progress. In fact, it is the search for greater abundance that has been driving all innovation in the past and will continue to do so in the future. New technologies make such innovations possible. As they pervade the economy and society, they modify demand patterns. This in turn leads to transformations of the energy system. In short, energy supply chases demand, not the other way around. And while some of these new technological developments may come from the energy side, they by themselves do not suffice to trigger changes. What does trigger changes are innovations, and they often come as a combination of different technologies, including energy.

Innovations must also reach the right tipping point, when they all of a sudden make it possible to provide a given service in a better way and often at a fraction of its past cost, or provide a new service. Some of these changes may take decades to unfold, either because the combination of technologies is not mature enough or because the tipping points take time to be reached. But when this time comes, the transformation accelerates, and the energy system begins its transformation.

Since these innovations often tackle one specific issue or opportunity, they always change the energy system in part, as they deal with one demand pattern at a time. This is why the current energy system resembles a patchwork of multiple energy uses, with some people continuing to rely on ancestral technologies such as wood or coal that have not yet been removed from the system. Innovations for those have not thrived.

Like-for-like, predefined transitions that simply consist of switching one fuel for another in order to provide a similar service with no greater benefit do not exist, and I argued earlier that I see this approach, the current one in most debates on climate change, as fundamentally flawed. When I explain this in the inner specialized circles of energy experts, I often get genuine attention and at times a barrage of remarks. People tend to tell me that this time it is different, because climate change is upon us and the world needs to take a step forward in a coordinated manner that it has never experienced before. Their point is not to lose ourselves in such analyses, but rather to voice the imperative need to change our energy system for good by investing in it now and removing fossil fuels before it is too late. I appreciate the passion of the argument; I made it myself long ago when I started to educate myself on the topic. Yet, I finally realized that it was far from enough to move the needle forward.

The current energy transition, I argued above, has not really started because so far, it has essentially consisted of replicating the current system using new energy sources, without providing further benefits that would trigger mass adoption. As such, it has taken time for these resources to reach scale and cut costs (notwithstanding the massive subsidies required to kickstart them), and they have not provided any benefit to the final consumer of the services they are used for.

Instead, they have come at an increased cost and often with a variety of new problems, such as environmental damage — the precise opposite of their true purpose. Hence the skepticism! And consequently, the endless debates that agitate the energy and political spheres, and beyond that all of society, on what should be done to mitigate climate change once and for all and truly accelerate. Everyone seems to pass the buck to the next in line and we collectively fail to address the issue.

This is simply because we do not look at the problem from the right angle! Focusing on innovations in demand is the only way to actually foster change, and while climate change is among some of the most pressing issues we have to face (with the massive challenge of reaching a net-zero economy by 2050, not to say halve our greenhouse gas emissions by 2030), others must also be considered. Since only social progress, or greater abundance, drives rapid adoption, we should thus focus on outlining what constitutes those innovations that can contribute to it and then work backward from that point.

In such an exercise, we obviously cannot get it all right from the start, but at the very least we offer an inspiring and fresh perspective and a more plausible scenario for the future. Major energy agencies have continued today to focus on a traditional evaluation of potential fuel-switching strategies, based on government-driven (and subsidized) energy policies. This is probably why many of the changes that have happened in the last 20 years have gone unnoticed, until they suddenly emerge and throw all past scenarios out of the window.

The most striking example of this could be electric vehicles. I will come back to this in due time, but let's just say here that electric vehicles first emerged as a promising alternative to conventional vehicles in the late 2000s. Tesla was founded in 2003 and delivered its first cars to the market in 2012. Since then, the development of electric vehicles has accelerated in every country in the world. There are estimated to be 175 new models of electric vehicles in Europe at the end of 2020, and an expected 300 by 2025 (Jolly, 2019). Yet, the International Energy Agency (2019) continues to estimate in its scenarios that the demand for electricity in transport will remain below that for biofuels until 2040, even though biofuels have long proven that they mainly fitted a niche market (except maybe in Brazil) and even though most recent forecasts estimate that the purchasing price of electric vehicles will be lower (they are already less expensive to run) by 2025. Electric vehicles are (almost) here, yet they still fail to make it into the energy expert projections. What then should we say about emerging technological disruptions?

Let's focus on these future innovations in demand to unpack the upcoming realities that the energy system will have to face, forecasted or not. Several building blocks are already in place. I already identified renewable energy (notably solar), storage, computing and mobile connectivity, and atomic-scale technologies as key constituents of the upcoming innovations. How can these technologies create a new model for the way services are delivered to final consumers?

To do it right, we must explore some of the main issues and opportunities that we are confronted with. I have divided them into three main parts: the inefficiency of our economy, the fragility of our society, and the unsustainable use of our planet's long-term potential.

In this chapter, I set out to further explore the first aspect of the challenges we are facing: that of our economy. I already argued in the previous chapter that the way our current economy runs is extremely inefficient. We continue to increase our consumption of resources of all sorts at a rapid pace, with very limited productivity gains and significant waste overall throughout the extraction, transformation, manufacturing, and consumption value chain. And all these products and assets we depend on to maintain our lifestyle end up being significantly underutilized. In a way, our current economy has developed on building more while using less of it and trashing the old to acquire the new, in a permanent quest for more. There is nothing wrong with such abundance; the nineteenth and more importantly twentieth centuries have marked the world's history as a turning point in that regard. The problem is that the entire economic system is based on an ever-increasing consumption of goods, even if that comes with low utilization and major waste. But underutilization and waste fuel economic growth. The reason why our economy functions as it does also has to do with the innovations that prevailed during the previous cycle. Mass standardization has been the main paradigm, with the intent to provide goods that would otherwise not have been available to the general public at an affordable cost. Standardization was made possible because of centralized processes, based on the technologies available at the time. And because standardization moved along with scale, the larger the production, the lower the costs. And scale required markets to renew, so that the large infrastructure put in place could continue to operate in a profitable way.

I recognize that this quick description may be challenged and I also acknowledge the massive efforts to increase productivity in industrial activities. I work in one of such activity and can only testify to the attention to this. Yet, figures are striking, and I provided some above. Utilization rates of even optimized factories barely reach 60–70 percent. So do building occupancy rates, and what to say about private car utilization? When it comes to waste, there is no better example than the use we make of our energy resources, with over 60 percent of them wasted in the process of transforming, distributing, and consuming them. The bottom line is simple. There is a massive opportunity for efficiency in our current economic system, in various segments such as buildings, industries, the mobility sector, and infrastructure. Innovations based on the foundational technologies I described above will contribute to reaping more efficiency from the current system. This is a certainty.

Since these innovations will also build on the new patterns of technologies I mentioned — their infinite scalability, their highly decentralized aspect, and their ability to increase rates of return — they will change the system from the inside. Standardization might well be a thing of the past, and it is by removing it from our basic economic equations that the world might ultimately achieve greater levels of efficiency.

In fact, these transformations have already started.

Ultra-Efficient Buildings

The Edge

I will start with the construction industry and building use. The Edge building in Amsterdam is probably one of the smartest buildings in the world. At first glance, it looks like a typical modern office building. It is home to one of the headquarters of Deloitte in Europe. The spectacular atrium in the entrance, wrapped in an envelope of thin glass, and sophisticated air exchange systems give a feeling of still being outside. Ahead of the atrium, a 15-story tower, yet no office. There are 2,500 employees at Deloitte, but only 1,000 desks are available, and no one is assigned one. A smartphone app connects all workers to the building. The app uses each one's schedule and work habits to advise them on where best to sit when arriving at work, and for how much time, considering that a large part of working hours now takes place outside the office. The app also serves to find colleagues and schedule short meetings. Indeed, 25 percent of the building's space is dedicated to informal (or formal) meetings. When fewer people are expected at work on a given day (based on the aggregated schedule of work), the building even shuts down entire blocs to save on heating, cooling, and electricity. The entire energy supply of the building is of renewable origin. Radiant heating and cooling systems, circulating water from the aquifer 400 m below ground, help optimize the needs for power-based heating or cooling. Moreover, solar panels on the rooftop and facades produce more electricity than the building actually consumes (Randall, 2015). The building is virtually autonomous. It even collects rainwater to flush toilets and uses some of the energy produced by exercising machines in the open gym inside the premises to produce extra energy. Energy consumption is around 40 kWh/m^2 annually and can be zero at times when an excess of decentralized power is available (Buildup, 2017). In practice, it is thus much lower. A quick calculation, based on data from the International Energy Agency (International Energy Agency, 2019a, 2019c) shows that on average, the energy intensity of buildings is 150 kWh/m^2 per year globally. Interestingly enough, this number is higher in mature economies, around 200 kWh/m^2 per year (Davis, 2019; European Commission, 2013). This must be compared to best-in-class buildings, whose energy demand numbers way below these figures: on average 30–50 kWh/m^2 annually. An example is the Edge. Of course, the Edge is a new building that was constructed in the 2010s. However, this type of architecture redesign may also apply to retrofitting buildings. The Rocky Mountain Institute (2015, Mandel and Stone, 2019) has demonstrated that properly retrofitted buildings could reach closing performance, with energy savings around 50 percent. Hence, today, buildings can be designed for renewed purposes, enhanced interaction and productivity, and greater flexibility, with an energy footprint that is two to three times lower than the current average. The Edge thus exemplifies the future of office buildings: places dedicated to meeting and interacting rather than verticalized structures where the size of the individual office matches that of the paycheck.

The bottom line is a significant optimization of building space and energy use, and an environment that has been carefully thought out to optimize employees' productivity. This building also illustrates three main trends that modern technologies help realize.

Blended uses

First, a growing blend between different building types. Historically, office buildings were designed for work only. Nowadays, they increasingly encompass other services so that every employee can optimize their time during the day, whether they need to go to the gym, a restaurant, or shopping. Office and commercial buildings blend. Moreover, the Edge is based on the underlying assumption of significant home-office and flexible working hours. This is why the number of desks planned in the construction was fewer than half that of employees. Once more, the residential and office building types blend. More time spent at home doing work means more flexibility in the use of both residential and office premises.

Consumer-centricity

The second trend is that digital technologies enable a consumer-centric approach to using the building and its services. The Edge App helps direct the employee to their desk for the day, find people in the building they wish to meet with, organize meetings in private rooms for brainstorming sessions, charge their electric vehicle, etc. The building is designed around its user, and the app lifts the experience to a whole new level. In addition, the more services the building can offer, the easier it is to get access to it: only one new option in the app, and everyone can instantaneously benefit from it.

Space and energy optimization

A final trend is the optimization of space and energy. On the one hand, space occupancy and utilization are dramatically improved as a result of this renewed design. More importantly, since real-time information becomes available, the optimization of all building services becomes possible. This radically optimizes the resource intensity of the building, in particular energy demand. The remaining energy needs build to a large extent on the capacity of decentralized (and clean) energies, leading to a sharp drop of the average energy to be conveyed and distributed to the building, with critical impacts on infrastructure, which I will review below.

"Electronic orchestra"

These three trends (blend between types, consumer-centric approach, space and resource optimization) will ultimately apply to every single building application, beyond offices. Let's look at commercial centers for instance. Hong Kong, the place where I live, is home to one of the greatest densities of commercial centers in modern metropolitan areas. Given the high temperatures six months a year and a rather long rainy season, most of these shopping malls are indoor. On the weekend, giant buildings welcome cohorts of families and groups of young people hanging out, shopping and entertaining themselves in the numerous shops and venues at their disposal. These multistory buildings are filled with people during weekends and rather empty the rest of the week, when only a few people find time to hang out in the deserted corridors. What an efficient use of space! Beyond this, the traditional "consumerist" business model of these large retail centers is now threatened by emerging new purchasing habits. First, online shopping is on the rise, offering greater convenience and a broader ability to compare different product types. Online shopping is said to account for 30 percent of US retail sales by 2030, compared to a little over 10 percent in 2015 (Brown and Lubelczyk, 2020). China is probably already ahead of the curve, so impressive is the development of digital technologies in the consumer retail sector. Next, patterns of consumption are changing. The younger generation tends to attach less importance to ownership. Instead, their purchasing habits favor experience. Already nearly half of their discretionary spending is said to be related to experience spending, rather than to buying products per se, and this trend accelerates inexorably.

What is in it for commercial centers then, built with the mentality and tools of the twentieth century?

They will certainly not disappear, but they will have to transform and find a new purpose. Different generations may have different appetites and needs, and there could be a stronger blend between residential and commercial services; a trend that would definitely optimize the use of space and occupancy. Think of specific residential areas for the elderly with all proximity services for their own use as a very topical example. Think of a similar outfit for young students and what it could look like around university campuses. Beyond blending residential, work, and commercial services, these shopping malls will have to refocus on what consumers seek in terms of experience. As mentioned, that is expected to evolve depending on the generation, but a greater use of experience services, sharing, and online shopping is highly realistic. Finally, with the significant optimization of space occupancy, a renewed energy system is also probable, for a greater optimization of energy costs (which account for a sizable share of building lifetime costs) will be paramount.

A final example is the residential sector. Schmidt and Cohen (2013) describe the future of homes as an "electronic orchestra." They evoke a home where the central system, connected to one's personal calendar, would be able to prepare clothing suggestions, drive automatic cleaning (ahead of schedule), and take care of mobility through a combination of autonomous transportation, traffic management, etc. so that transportation becomes frictionless (and with no ownership involved). They also describe a home where all information (be it personal or more generic, such as environmental information) would be instantaneously available through a single entry point, which could serve as a virtual office when traveling to the office would no longer be required or could provide virtual entertainment right in front of the couch in the main room. Obviously, this would also be a home where one no longer has to clean, plan for and purchase provisions (the kitchen would do it), cook (the robots could do it) unless one wants to, etc. In short, an army of digital servants, and human beings would finally be kings. This "electronic orchestra" at the tip of one's finger strongly resembles the trends I discussed before. On the one hand, the house becomes a blend of home, entertainment, even tourism, work office, and shopping mall. Transportation from the home becomes entirely coordinated by the home mobility system, and extremely specific. Usage and occupancy are thus deemed to significantly evolve when this vision materializes at scale. On the other hand, this "electronic orchestra" is entirely centered around the user or household member, with the focus on providing them the best possible experience. And this becomes possible since real-time data about this person, collected over long periods, becomes available. In a way, Amazon's Alexa, the first virtual assistant in the world, is one of the primary steps toward this entirely personalized electronic orchestra.

With this mass of data on use, occupancy, and patterns available, it also becomes possible to optimize the actual use of energy in the household at a whole new level, and therefore, to provide a part of that needed energy, essentially electric, with decentralized power sources and storage. Solar rooftop panels or tiles are connected to the household electricity network and to various storage systems, either stationary storage systems or electric-vehicle battery systems, as well as variable loads that provide for flexibility, such as heat pumps or water boilers, in order to provide a permanent uptake of energy within the household at a cost that is increasingly becoming competitive with grid-retailed electricity (BloombergNEF, 2019). In many countries, this tipping point has already been reached, either because of the low cost of solar there, or simply because of the high retail electricity cost. For some households, it is not only about cost competitiveness, but often about resiliency as well. One striking example of this is California, home to the Silicon Valley. This is the heart of worldwide innovation, particularly in digital and new energy technologies. The region is prey to massive wildfires over the summer season, partly a result of climate change, which has excessively dried out land and vegetation. Some argue that the fires are also a consequence of the forest management policies that have been in place in the region for many decades. The bottom line is that this region of innovation is facing significant issues every summer, which put a strain on households. PG&E, the regional utility, whose cables cross the desertified lands, is forced to implement power cuts that can last up to 48 hours. In 2019, they cut power to nearly two million people, triggering outrage and sanctions from the public utility commission (Borunda, 2019; CNBC, 2019). In 2020, some of these power cuts have started as early as in April. With a dry season that could now last from April to late fall, the regional utility can no longer guarantee reliable power for nearly six months of the year, triggering a much greater recourse to decentralized energies, which become easier to control when digital technologies such as the ones described earlier come in to help.

And construction will also evolve

The last piece I have not discussed yet is that of construction itself. The construction industry has made virtually no progress in terms of productivity in the last 20 years (Economist, 2017). This has to do with the inherent fragmentation of the sector, hence the reluctance or inability to grasp more efficient ways of work at scale. Once again, digital technologies are a powerful enabler of change in that regard, as they help better synchronize the contribution of the workforce, simplifying design and procurement and hence removing all inefficiencies that come along when it comes to following a complex schedule of construction. But there is more! Atomic-scale technologies also offer the prospect of designing new materials that could replace traditional cement and steel, which form the bulk of construction and represent a significant share of overall demand: the construction industry represents over two-thirds of the demand for cement and one third of that of steel (Material Economics, 2019). Changes in demand for materials could therefore yield tectonic shifts in the upper value chain of materials' extraction and transformation. If these new materials ultimately come at a lower cost, then gigantic productivity gains are in sight.

Buildings are in for a significant change

To conclude, we must also realize that most of what has been described so far is already achievable with current technologies. What to say then about potential improvements, with technological advancements moving at rocket speed? For instance, further progress in third-generation photovoltaics (PV) or storage could enable the provision of energy directly into appliances, dramatically facilitating integration (and cutting the corresponding costs of installation). The same could be said about the infinite possibilities of advanced connectivity. 5G is already here and is ten times more efficient than traditional fixed cable connectivity. What to expect from upcoming further advancements such as 6G or more? Will our entire physical environment ultimately be connected?

As a last point, what also marks these innovations is greater human-centricity. In the end, the building stock evolution is steered toward a more granular approach to consumer needs, with new building types, greater virtual interaction with dwellers, and corresponding optimization of the asset and associated utilities. And this greater human-centricity lies at the heart of major efficiencies; a completely new paradigm.

Ultra-Efficient Industries

The same reasoning that I have just developed for buildings will also apply to the industry sector, with maybe even greater and quicker benefits. At the macrolevel, we can split industry into two subsectors: the manufacturing industry — which groups consumer goods (all the objects we use in our daily lives), capital goods (machines, heavy equipment), and transportation equipment (cars, planes, etc.) — and the food and beverage industries. The second subsector is primary (or heavy) industry, which includes petrochemicals and chemicals production, cement and other minerals production (e.g., copper, glass, etc.), and steel and other metals (aluminum, etc.). The primary industry provides refined materials, which are then used to manufacture the goods that we eventually consume. Tackling the topic of industry performance in a few pages is next to impossible because of the complexity and variety of different situations that apply. However, I will provide a glimpse of some of the most promising developments in the sector, and of how the technologies described earlier can have a fundamental impact on this competitive sector, where productivity plays a critical role.

The twentieth-century disruption

The industrial revolutions of the nineteenth and twentieth centuries have essentially consisted of leveraging the workforce with tools that helped perform better and faster operations at a lower cost. These tools and processes essentially do two things: they move, cut, and assemble things, or they provide heat to generate chemical reactions. While the craftsman of the eighteenth century essentially relied on his hands and sometimes on the support of an animal to lift or pull heavy loads, the operator of the twentieth century used these newly developed tools to do the same thing faster and more efficiently. Since the operator now had to rely more heavily on a machine that was able to do things only in a certain predesigned way, the industrialization of the economy became synonymous with standardization and repetitive processes. No example has better highlighted this move toward repetitive, fast, and cost-effective large-scale production than the Fordism of the 1920s, when Henry Ford showed the way by producing thousands of new automobiles in giant factories, shaping the modern twentieth-century industry.

This move to large-scale repetitive production yielded a sharp reduction in the costs of manufacturing, hence triggering new access to modern goods and services and new use patterns that have made the twentieth century that of a remarkable societal transformation. As French historian Francois Furet pointed out, people used to live in the same way for centuries, and there was little difference in their habits and patterns between the seventeenth century and the middle of the nineteenth century. The twentieth century, however, marked a significant transformation, unknown in history, which to a large extent was the product of these innovations in industry. These innovations were inherited from the original industrial revolutions and scientific discoveries of the nineteenth century.

Best available technologies

These tools and machines have been perfected over time, but not all factories around the world have adopted them just yet. It is generally acknowledged that a significant efficiency potential exists if the entire industry footprint would switch to "best available technologies" (BAT).

Motor systems for instance. They are generally used for motion, pumping, or fans, or as compressors. The motor is in general associated with an array of transmission systems, gears, flow management systems, etc., depending on its application. It has been widely recognized that such systems were very inefficient (with an energy waste of above 50 percent), and that 20–30 percent of increased efficiency was observed in "best available" systems (Petit, 2017). Moreover, using electric motors instead of traditional diesel engines also increases overall efficiency: today, they show energy yields in the range of 90 percent, compared to 20–30 percent for traditional combustion engines.

Next, heating systems. They take various forms depending on the segment of industry. At a macrolevel, industrial heat is used for drying (removing water from materials), driving chemical reactions (e.g., ammonia production), melting (e.g., producing glass or molded products), and food preparation (cooking, sterilizing, etc.). These different uses of heat lead to different requirements. Drying typically requires heat of around 100–300°C, chemical reactions from 100 to 1,500°C, and melting up to 1,800°C. Food processes however generally require less than 250°C (Beyond Zero Emissions, 2018). Yet again, it has been generally recognized that significant efficiency is within reach by simply adopting "best available" technologies, with efficiencies in the range of 30 percent (Petit, 2017). An example is the development of industrial heat pumps for low-temperature processes (drying, food production), which generate heat at an efficiency that is four to five times higher than that of traditional gas heaters. Another example could be the use of infrared electric heating for drying processes that require high-precision heating, such as in the automotive industry (drying the paint) or the paper industry (Beyond Zero Emissions, 2018).

Beyond traditional efficiency from the modernization of the industry footprint, the next opportunity is to modernize processes themselves. This essentially applies to the primary industry. Most processes operated today date back to the nineteenth century. Oil refining was first developed in the middle of the nineteenth century by Canadian Abraham Gesner. Industry-scale steelmaking became possible with the invention of the Bessemer process in the nineteenth century — later refined by Durrer in the middle of the twentieth century — that gave rise to modern blast furnaces (or basic oxygen furnaces). Mass-scale aluminum production became possible with the Hall-Heroult process, developed at the end of the nineteenth century by Paul Heroult and Charles Martin Hall and followed by alternative approaches from Austrian chemist Bayer. Ammonia production, which is used in a variety of applications, from detergents to pharmaceutical products, today follows the Haber-Bosch process, which was developed at the dawn of the twentieth century. Of course, some improvements have been made in some locations, but the foundations of the primary industry have largely remained unchanged for over a century. There are however exciting areas of innovation to follow.

Process intensification

First, process intensification (Westmoreland, 2014). Intensification consists of reducing the size of the process installations (to optimize capital and operating costs and reduce risk), use "extreme forces" (to drive a much higher efficiency in the transformation), or combine and reconfigure existing processes (new separation or distillation techniques). This could lead on average to an improvement of up to 20 percent of yields in the coming decades (Petit, 2017).

Electrification

Second, electrification. Electrified processes often show much higher yields. Direct reduction of iron with (electrically produced) hydrogen as a replacement of coal offers up to 20 percent of efficiency in energy use. Electrowinning (molten oxide electrolysis) is 30 percent more efficient. Using induction heating for casting is two times more efficient. Cracking electrification could save up to 60 percent of energy, and the list goes on (Energy Transitions Commission, 2018; Brolin, Fahnestock, and Rootzén, 2017; Banerjee *et al.*, 2010; Material Economics, 2018; International Energy Agency, 2009). Electrification thus also plays a critical role in boosting the efficiency of industrial processes, and with electrification comes the potential adoption of more decentralized power, as we have seen for buildings. However, some processes will continue to require significant power output, something that today, only large-scale installations are able to provide. As we have seen, a lot can already be done in terms of efficiency, and the adoption of best available technologies, process improvements and intensification, and electrification are among the main routes to increased efficiency.

Digital everywhere

Beyond these incremental improvements, digital technologies will also play a critical role. The first of these improvements is the significant increase in connected sensors being deployed throughout the process in machines and tools. These help develop a real-time perspective on the process's efficiency and on how to optimize it from a resource and energy standpoint. Most processes are already automated. The digital revolution brings another level of granularity to the management and control of those processes, and will to a large extent lead to a further level of labor productivity by possibly centralizing more systems controls.

Moreover, these technologies not only help improve the process itself but also enable the monitoring of the assets: the heavy machinery that constitutes the heart of these installations. These are the large compressors, gears, rotating machines, kilns and furnaces, etc. In doing this monitoring, they help optimize operations within the process and more importantly asset life, leading to further productivity of the plants.

More importantly, they create a new level of support for the workforce by providing real-time tools to augment workforce safety and capabilities. Augmented reality systems have the potential to help operators better run the process and safely realize critical interventions in the machinery: less mistakes, faster operations, and simplified procedures. A last benefit is that the digitization of the process also helps develop a real-time link to upstream and downstream channels to the logistics systems that supply raw materials to the actual production unit and to the customers and their "live" requirements.

The ultimate goal is to create a real-time "digital twin," which is a virtual real-time representation of the installation that improves the granularity of controls, assets operations and lifetime, workforce performance, and its integration into the overall value chain. Roland Berger (2016) has estimated that the deployment of such technologies, also referred to as the Industry 4.0 revolution, could help more than double the ROCE (return on capital employed) and the profitability of companies adopting it, while raising plants' utilization by more than a third; significant benefits in a highly competitive environment. Industry 4.0 has hit the headlines in recent years, and rightfully so. Indeed, industrial productivity has been slowing down dramatically for a decade or more (Immelt, 2016), and digital technologies are perceived to be one of the major enablers to restart this positive productivity cycle, which provides long-term economic growth.

Circularity at the core of the next wave of innovation

However, I would argue here that there is even a more disruptive transformation at play. Maybe the Industry 4.0 concept is not the alpha and omega of the future of industry and is in the end slightly overrated. The reason for such a provocative statement is that these efficiency gains — whether they are achieved through adopting best available technologies, optimizing processes, electrifying them, or deploying digital technologies at scale within facilities — are largely incremental improvements, which come on top of already largely optimized installations. The industry has made a living of productivity gains. Given this, they represent a reservoir of efficiency, albeit not a disruptive one, especially when taken separately. There is however a different approach that is beginning to emerge, and that could fundamentally change the game within the industry sector: circularity. The concept of circularity was first brought up by Kenneth Boulding in 1966 in his essay "The economics of the coming Spaceship Earth" (Boulding, 1966). Boulding did not refer to circularity specifically but was the first to mention the threats of a growing economy with no attention to optimizing the use of resources in a finite and naturally constrained environment. This concept was further reviewed in works by Walter R. Stahel and Geneviève Reday-Mulvey (1981), David Pearce and R. Kerry Turner (1990), and others. A research report by Stahel and Reday-Mulvey in 1976 (published as a book in 1981) was the first to introduce the concept of circular loops. The topic continued to gain steam during the first decade of the twenty-first century, and a report commissioned by the Ellen MacArthur Foundation (2013) analyzed the potential positive economic benefits of a transition toward a circular model.

The focus of circularity is on minimizing the waste of resources. It develops from five main approaches. The first one is to limit waste in production through efficiency improvements or resource conservation. The second aims at increasing the lifetime of products to minimize the need to manufacture new products and is based on lifetime monitoring and reuse, repair, or refurbish services. The third one seeks to increase the utilization of these products, which in turn limits the number of required products to generate a certain volume of economic activity. The fourth one looks at the economic development of recycling to effectively "close" the loop of material use. The last one is focused on transforming demand for products through a greater recourse to sharing services (part of what some have also coined a new breed of sobriety in use).

The actual implementation of such measures through regulation has been long-awaited. The European Union and China were the first regions in the world to mention the development of a circular economy. For Europe, it has become one of the core pillars of its Green New Deal in 2019. China had mentioned it as early as in its 2006 five-year plan. Yet, results are still to materialize at scale.

Improvements in efficiency, the lifetime of assets, and their utilization are all well served by current digital technologies, and to a certain extent the development of Industry 4.0 is a key enabler, even though a lot remains to be done in terms of modernizing industrial assets. However, the other two pillars of a full circular approach (recycling, sharing) have not yet fully developed, except in certain sectors. This is in part because it turns out that the cost of collecting and sorting waste is still prohibitive today, in the absence of a competitive and organized supply chain, while most products are still not designed to be easily recyclable (Covec, 2007; RDC Environment, 2003). This is also because, when it comes to sharing services, changes in consumers' spending habits will happen only when a compelling value proposition emerges. While great strides have been made in the transport sector, which I will come back to, it remains to be proven as a workable model in the consumer goods sector.

Despite these slow evolutions, there is a significant potential for digital technologies to accelerate these changes. I already talked at length about their potential to further improve the efficiency of production by reducing waste and optimizing operations, as well as their ability to better monitor the lifetime of assets in industrial facilities or increase their utilization. Digital technologies could also help set up platforms dedicated to sharing goods, particularly the ones reaching end of life. This is also what is referred to as collaborative consumption.

Let's think of it for a minute. What if you could access a resource or an asset at a fraction of its cost just when you need it (which is not all the time)?

Traditionally underutilized assets that end up standing idle for a large part of their lifetime could be mutualized to improve utilization. If access to the asset could be effectively organized (something digital technologies do very well), then the business case is very compelling. The asset becomes available at a fraction of its past cost, and with limited to no hurdles: a disruption by the book. Several examples exist in hospitality (Airbnb, Couchsurfing, etc.), office sharing (coworking), storage (Storemates, Spacer, etc.), goods (Fat Llama, etc.), and of course transport (Uber, BlaBlaCar, etc.), with many others to come.

Second, 99 percent of the goods we purchase on a daily basis end up trashed within six months (The World Counts, 2018). What if instead of trashing these products, these could be repaired, refurbished, and resold or redistributed as second-life products? Again, emerging platforms (MyTroc, etc.) show the way. A report from 2016 even established that "nearly 85 percent of Canadians have participated in some form of second-hand transactions" (Kijiji, 2016). Digital technologies are uniquely positioned to accelerate this trend, which — again — provides access to goods and services at a fraction of their original cost.

Finally, there is the recycling of materials. The main issue with recycling today is that it remains extremely expensive because of the lack of a structured supply chain and the complexity of recycling products that were not designed for it. Therefore, 50 percent of what is actually put in recycling ends up not being recycled, because it requires too much labor power to actually clean, sort, etc. And this quickly adds up when you realize that the world only recycles 9 percent of plastics, while producing 220 million tons every year (System IQ and the Pew Charitable Trust, 2020; Winter, 2015). Yet, once the product or material is available, recycling processes are considerably more efficient. In short, the amount of work (and energy) required to manufacture a new product based on an old one is lower than that required when you have to start from raw materials. Recycling steel, aluminum, or plastics is in general 80 percent more energy efficient than primary production; a giant leap forward in terms of efficiency, not to mention resources' utilization. Plastics for instance have a life expectancy of 500 years, and what to say of steel or aluminum? Second-life materials would then come at a fraction of the cost of virgin ones, and the more their lifetime increases, through multiple retrofits, the greater the returns, something some companies have termed "materials as a service".

Circularity is therefore the major disruption at play. On the one hand, the rise of digital technologies is a major enabler of the emergence of new sharing models that will reduce the demand for new goods, while creating new business opportunities for repair and refurbishment and new logistics systems. This decreased demand for new products is amplified by greater recourse to the recycling of products and materials, when supply chains (collection, sorting) are efficiently structured. This is a major challenge, however, and digital technologies will play a critical role in tackling it. With this, the actual demand for primary industry materials could drop to historical lows, as "circular loops" eventually close in on existing resources.

What then will the future of industrial production be?

As these innovations materialize, one of the main outcomes is probably a dramatic reduction of the traditional footprint of goods manufacturing, and more importantly of the primary industry sector as a whole, which sources and transforms raw materials. With the optimization of the full industrial value chains, major efficiency gains will obviously follow. This giant step toward a more efficient industrial setup will not happen overnight, but the building blocks are all here, and the prize is clear: less expensive goods.

And, as in the case of buildings, most of what has been described above is already achievable with current technologies. As a matter of fact, a number of organizations have already started the journey. And as the rest of the pack picks up the pace, technological improvements continue to flourish, further increasing the potential of these new applications to create increasing rates of return.

Ultra-Efficient Mobility

Multimodal mobility

We have looked at potential disruptions in the building and industry sectors. A similar paradigm can also be explored for the mobility sector. First, I need to unpack the topic. Transport can apply to people and goods, and these two categories follow different patterns. It can also take different forms: air travel, maritime transportation, rail transport, and road transport, either public or private.

Conceptually, the spatial organization of transport comprises hubs and networks. People or goods travel from one hub to another on a network. The price of transport on the network is defined by the mode of transport, but other important aspects come into play as well: the pace of transport, its convenience, etc. From the hub to the final destination, a distance always remains to be covered, essentially by road transport when walking is not possible (Rodrigue, 2020).

Air travel is dominant in long-range passenger transport and has displaced maritime transportation, which used to be the primary way of intercontinental travel before planes were invented at the dawn of the twentieth century. However, maritime transportation has remained the dominant form for transporting goods, since costs are lower and the pace of transport is often not a critical requirement. For shorter distances, rail and road transport are the dominants modes, for both passengers and goods.

Short-distance transportation represents the large majority, above 80 percent, of passenger travel. In energy terms, road and rail transport account for 80 percent of total transport, with rail representing a fraction of road travel. Air and sea travel account for 10 percent each (Petit, 2017). While long-distance travel represents a minority, it also often has well-structured value chains, organized and optimized, with very competitive costs. This does not mean that further progress and innovation will not kick in, but the bulk of efficiency is certainly to be gained by addressing short-distance travel challenges. Rail transport is a fantastic alternative to road transport. Since it is a public transport mode, costs are often very competitive, be it within cities as an alternative to road transport (metros), or across a region as an alternative to both road transport and very short-distance air transport (below 500 miles).

Finding the proper balance between hubs and networks in different modal offerings connected together is already a major challenge for municipalities and nations around the world. The steep changes in that area in the 1850s and later the early 1900s have dramatically transformed the overall landscape and economic productivity of (now) mature economies. The ability of governments to properly organize a rapid, efficient, cost-competitive set of transport infrastructures (hubs and networks) is therefore paramount.

Let's just think for instance of the hours spent in traffic jams in large cities such as Los Angeles, New Delhi, or Beijing to realize the economic rationale for a proper and varied transport infrastructure, and the impact it may have on overall economic productivity, notwithstanding health, safety, wellness, and other considerations. In the United States, people lose 100 hours in congestion per year on average. This figure tops 150 hours in most European cities, and the two most congested cities in 2019 were Bogota and Rio de Janeiro, with almost 190 hours lost in congestion per year and capita (Inrix, 2020). Alternatives are welcome! Rodrigue (2020) estimates that rail transport is two times less expensive, three times safer, and four times more energy efficient than trucking when it comes to transporting goods over relatively short distances. The right balance between modal solutions is hence critical. A decade ago, I lived in Moscow, Russia, and I remember vividly traveling by metro systematically within the city when I discovered the insane traffic jams. While it took me 45 minutes to reach my office by metro, the same trip by car would easily surpass two hours, or more, at commuting times.

One of the critical issues is to enable a smooth coordination between these different modal systems, something often referred to as multimodal transportation, or "the movements of passengers or freight from an origin to a destination relying on several modes of transportation using one ticket (passengers) or contract (freight)" (Rodrigue, 2020). This kind of coordination is a key success factor in enabling the optimized utilization of assets and removing congestion.

And, once again, digital technologies will play a critical role in facilitating this transition, both for passenger transport, notably within cities, and for logistics (Jemdahl, 2019). Their main benefit will be to remove friction between different modes of transport, making it possible to better schedule and ride various types of transport while optimizing overall costs and removing congestion and idle time. And when the usual friction, such as long waiting times and congestion during rush hours, is removed, much faster adoption becomes obvious. Imagine if you could plan your optimized route to work in the morning in advance, with a combination of bus-sharing, carpooling, metro transit, etc., no waiting time, no ticket to purchase, and a commute time decreased by say 30 percent? Some startups are already working on it and making great strides in this area (Door2Door, Transit, Migo, and others).

Electrification

The second major efficiency gain in transport is its electrification. Interestingly enough, the fate of transport was not defined in the early 1900s. In fact, steam, electric, and combustion engines competed until the development of the Ford T (1908) and the massive access to cheap refined oil pushed the balance in favor of current gasoline combustion engines. The emergence of gasoline-driven transport was then inexorable. However, a new wind is blowing in the sector with the reemergence of electrified transport solutions, notably electric vehicles. This is because one of the major limitations of the early 1900s has been overcome: that of electric storage capability.

The advent of powerful lithium-ion batteries has made it possible to actually store enough energy to have electric vehicles' ranges match those of traditional combustion engines vehicles. These lithium-ion batteries have emerged thanks to the mass deployment of smaller versions in modern smartphones. Without the iPhone in 2007 and the massive strain it placed on phones' batteries, fueling innovation in the area, it would not have been possible to eventually come up with larger versions applicable to vehicles. The rise of digital technologies fueled an electric revolution. Once the range of electric vehicles reaches that of traditional ones, a whole new set of benefits begins to emerge.

First, electric motors are four to five times more efficient than traditional ones. Modern electric motors enjoy a yield of nearly 90 percent, and with constant torque, they turn out to be much more convenient to drive.

Beyond this, electric vehicles are also much simpler to assemble. There are 100 times fewer moving parts in electric powertrains than there are in conventional ones (McMahon, 2019). Do the math! That means cheaper to assemble (much cheaper) and less maintenance over a lifetime. BloombergNEF (2019) estimates that the cost of new electric vehicles will reach parity with traditional combustion engines before 2025 and will then continue to fall. According to Tony Seba (2014), electric vehicles are also ten times cheaper to maintain. Electric vehicles are therefore "en route" to fully displace traditional combustion engines and revolutionize the automotive industry.

Going one step further, Seba also argues that electric vehicles are ten times cheaper to recharge (compared to filling the tank of a conventional vehicle). My own calculation reaches five times only, but this will probably depend on the projected performance of electric vehicles and costs of electricity. The conclusion still holds.

An important point to also note: electricity is one of the most ubiquitous sources of energy. Everywhere where there is human activity, there is always electricity available. This means that electric vehicles can be charged anywhere: at home, at work, in a commercial center — anywhere. There are even pilot projects using wireless charging for buses to recharge batteries at bus stops (Seba, 2014). And with significant progress made in batteries, with storage capacities potentially quintupling by 2030 (Bloch *et al.*, 2018), or disruptive new technologies emerging (such as virus-based batteries for instance, Hockfield, 2019), range anxiety and the imperative need to recharge EVs will soon be a problem of the past. In fact, electric vehicles will become much more than a mode of transport; they will become an energy asset, a battery on wheels, with significant potential to contribute to the overall new landscape of energy. I will come back to that.

Another unintended consequence is that the very large oil distribution system is expected to disappear more quickly than we think, and with it its associated costs. Electric vehicles are simply much more efficient and convenient.

Transport as a service

The next level of efficient disruption in short-distance transport will be the increase in transport as a service (TaaS). I have said it many times: I live in Hong Kong. When I first got here, I was offered two choices: either buy a car and take a parking spot at the office, or use the various transport services that existed in the city. I made a few calculations. The parking space's rent was nearly US$1,000 a month (Hong Kong is a very dense city), or US$12,000 a year! The car was expensive and so was the insurance. Accounting for depreciation, fuel, and maintenance costs, the acquisition of a mid-sized vehicle would have cost me around US$20,000 a year. The largest share of that was admittedly the actual parking spot. I spend at most a third of that in riding transport services, and that includes the numerous red cab drives I constantly use within the city. And Hong Kong is probably not even a best-in-class example of TaaS: Shenzhen, the high-tech hub of Southern China, 30 kilometers north of Hong Kong, is already almost fully electric, with a high level of TaaS. Crossing the Chinese border to go visit Shenzhen is always a fulfilling experience. The city appears to already live in a distant future.

The think tank RethinkX, cofounded by Tony Seba, has pulled the numbers. TaaS, which includes taxis, ridesharing, carpooling, etc., is a true disruption in the cost of mobility. According to RethinkX's analysis, using a modern version of transport a service (not the one I use in Hong Kong!), powered by digital technologies, could cost four to five times less (in dollars per kilometer) than driving a traditional car, and up to ten times less if using what the think tank refers to as TaaS-pool, or a combination of public and private mobility services (multimodal transportation), and all of this within the coming decade (Arbib and Seba, 2017).

The report goes on and lists the benefits: a 90 percent decrease in financial costs, 80 percent in maintenance costs, 90 percent in insurance costs, 70 percent in fuel costs, and cars that could drive up to one million miles in their lifetime.

The conclusion, according to RethinkX, is plain and simple: by 2030, 95 percent of passenger miles in the United States (the focus of their study) will be made by TaaS, and the actual number of vehicles will be divided by five in the meantime. We can either question the timeline or choose to believe in it. But one thing is for sure: if the numbers are right, and they are pretty detailed, this is only a matter of time. Provided that the service experience is frictionless, there will no longer be an interest in driving one's own vehicle. And for all the services that will potentially not be available by 2030, such as longer distance or intercity or rural transportation, there is still the option to actually rent a car rather than buy one. The automotive industry is definitely up for a big disruption.

Autonomous vehicles

The last of the critical steps toward a more efficient transport system is the appearance of autonomous vehicles. There are five levels of driving automation systems (SAE, 2018). The first level is about driving assistance, with one action performed by the system and monitored by the driver, such as for instance cruise control. The second level includes several functions that are performed at the same time, but the driver is still expected to monitor the environment.

This can be both cruise control and lane-keeping assist for instance. From the third level upward, the system monitors the environment and performs all driving functions. These differ in terms of the level of engagement of the human person onboard. At the third level, the system may request a human (driver) to intervene and actually take control of the driving functions. There is still a person seated in the driving seat, but they are doing something else than driving. The fourth level differs slightly from the third in that the system must be designed to operate safely, even without the intervention of the human (driver). It may be programmed not to operate in specific environments; thus, you still have a human driver in there, but they are asleep most of the time. In the fifth and last level, there is simply no human driver, and the car is completely autonomous. The human is only a passenger and there is no longer a driving seat.

There are still many questions about when autonomous vehicles will be truly available, and forecasts differ greatly on this, from a few years ahead to over a decade and a half (Anderson, 2020; Faggella, 2020; O'Donnell, 2020). This also has a lot to do with the level of autonomy, and while it could take more than a decade to reach true level 5, lower levels may be available sooner. Most automotive companies are focusing their efforts on levels 3 and 4, and some simple applications (e.g., airport shuttles, university campus rides, etc.) are already functional.

Yet, the question is not so much when. There is no debate on autonomous vehicles being the next wave of innovation to hit the automotive industry and reshaping the entire transport sector, particularly the section that is devoted to short-distance, point-to-point transport. The latter constitutes the largest and most fragmented part of kilometers effectively traveled over a year. And again, figures are impressive. Keeney (2017) estimates that the cost of autonomous TaaS (autonomous taxis) could be ten times lower than that of riding a conventional cab: as low as US$0.35/mile (compared to a traditional cab in the United States at around US$3.5/mile). Let's rerun the simulation I made earlier for my personal trips in Hong Kong. It would cost me US$20,000 a year to own a car in the city. It costs me a third of that, around US$7,000 a year, to ride a mix of public transport and many taxis. With autonomous taxis at a tenth of current costs, my bill for the year falls down to less than US$1,000 a year, or US$3 per day on average. In other words, almost free transport, and without the hassle of hailing taxis in the street. Once more, the service becomes available at a fraction of its previous cost; hence its fast adoption. It is very likely that all these transformations will eventually occur through numerous waves of innovation, but the potential for economic and travel efficiency is unmatched. It is only a question of time.

Future of transport

The combination of multimodal mobility and TaaS, electrification, and autonomous vehicles will trigger a revolution in the transport industry in the coming decade or so because of the significant optimization of costs and convenience that these new innovations bring. In the end, this revolution of mobility will lead to greater human-centricity by removing the hassles associated with traditional transportation while cutting costs.

That being said, and with the exception of autonomous mobility, technologies to enable these innovations to emerge are mostly already here. Future developments, notably in native connectivity and computing power, are expected to help accelerate these transformations. Going forward, new energy harvesting solutions, such as third-generation PV, could help cars recharge while driving, while further enhancements of storage batteries will keep improving the performance and range of electric vehicles. Even wireless charging (directly from underneath the road surface) for buses has been tested already. This is only the beginning.

Ultra-Efficient Infrastructure

Huge energy productivity potential

The potential for a giant leap forward in terms of efficiency for buildings, industry, and transport is here. And this will obviously have ripple effects on infrastructure as well.

Building environments will radically transform through the combined impact of more efficient envelopes, a new blend of building uses, a more customer-centric approach, massive space and resource optimization, and decentralized energies' penetration. Factories and the entire industry system will also transform through the progressive modernization of industrial processes (best available technologies), increased processes' intensification, the electrification of new processes, more digitally enabled optimization, and a growing circular footprint with an extended lifetime and utilization of machines, materials' recycling, and more sharing services. Transport will also significantly evolve through digitally enabled multimodal transport, electrification, TaaS, and eventually autonomous vehicles.

Each one of these transformations, powered by new energy, digital, and atomic-scale technologies combined, holds the potential for radical changes in the way the economy is driven. They will happen because each one of them entails a significant increase in efficiency in terms of what we build and how we run things. The inevitable consequence will be that services will become cheaper over time, propelling mass adoption. As these transformations unfold, impacts on the energy system and its infrastructure will be massive.

The first impact will of course be the actual demand for energy, what is often referred to as energy productivity or the volume of energy required to generate US$1 of GDP. Existing buildings could be 50–60 percent less energy-intensive with current technologies, and new buildings are approaching net-zero energy, with a baseline consumption two-thirds below current averages.

The recourse to circularity in industry could further reduce the demand for manufactured goods on the one hand (sharing, lifetime services, increased utilization), and the need for primary materials on the other (recycling). If 20 percent of the demand for goods could be cut (for the same service), half of materials used recycled, and 20 percent efficiency in plant operations realized, the impact of circularity would yield around 50 percent drop in energy demand.

The rise of electric fleets operated as a service in cities (70 percent of the world population by 2050, UN, 2014) could reduce the number of cars by over 80 percent. Assuming more limited change in rural areas, that would again be a reduction in energy demand (80 percent of total transportation energy) of around 50 percent.

There is thus a magic number that keeps emerging from one sector to another: the potential of a 50 percent reduction in energy demand, or, if we prefer, a twofold increase in energy productivity. Admittedly, the figures are raw. But the size of the opportunity is unquestionable.

Systemic efficiency

The question could then be: at what pace would this occur and what key enablers would unleash such a positive transformation? I will come back to that. Nowadays, the world consumes around 120,000 TWh of final energy on a yearly basis (International Energy Agency, 2019c). What if it could live and prosper on half that volume? The world also invests around US$2,000 billion per year in its energy infrastructure. You can at least double that figure to account for maintenance and associated operating costs.

What would the economic consequences of a 50 percent reduction in energy demand be?

A massive productivity impact on the economy — and of course a significant reduction in the actual "cost" of energy for a given service. Things are not so simple, however, because energy still requires distribution. Today, the cost of distributing energy pretty much corresponds to that of producing it. Electric grid costs represent half of retail electricity cost (without taxes). Gas grid costs represent a higher percentage of total gas costs. Oil distribution is slightly less expensive than oil production. As a whole though, we can take 50 percent as a proxy for this discussion.

If the volume of energy required drops by 50 percent, the world still needs to pay for the distribution of its energy. Assuming a 50–50 split between production and distribution costs, that would mean (all other things being equal) that a 50 percent reduction in the volume of energy would yield a 25 percent drop in costs (still a good bargain). More importantly, the share of energy distribution would increase to two-thirds of total energy costs, compared to 50 percent today.

In an ultra-efficient economy, the main costs of energy would no longer be its production but its distribution, a radical change of paradigm. This natural evolution would logically lead to a further penetration of decentralized energies, which will increasingly become cost-competitive with a grid-driven cost paradigm for centralized energy supply. The tipping point has already been passed in several regions of the world, and this quick exercise just shows that this trend is here to stay and gain strength (and in fact it could accelerate if regulation begins to differentiate the price of distribution depending on real costs, notably through locational pricing schemes). It is therefore all the more surprising to see that so little importance is given to the penetration of decentralized energies (notably rooftop solar) in most existing energy forecasts, despite a technical potential that is evaluated at one and a half times the current global electricity demand (Deng *et al.*, 2015; International Energy Agency, 2019b, 2019c).

An inevitable increase in decentralized energies thus lies ahead of us. This does not mean a full displacement of large energy (grid) distribution systems, however. The Edge building in Amsterdam is a net-positive energy building. Its final demand is 40 kWh/m^2 annually on average. Yet, there are times of the day when the building produces more energy than it needs. In such cases, the building does not pull any energy from the grid. There are also other times when the building draws its entire final demand, or 40 kWh/m^2 per year, from the grid.

There are thus times when the building operates virtually autonomously from the grid, and others when it does not. The grid remains essential to providing continuity of service, notably when rooftop solar panels do not produce enough energy to meet demand. Yet, grids are dramatically underutilized. We can estimate that electric grids typically operate below 70 percent of their capacity over the course of a year, even though detailed studies are missing (Petit, 2018). This makes complete sense when one realizes that grid systems are designed for peak demand, which is typically one and a half to two times higher than baseload demand (with obvious differences across regions) (Petit, 2018).

What applies to electric grids also applies to gas grids. Gas grids' bulk demand is for heating purposes, and this materializes only in winter, at best half of the year. On top of that, demand for heat is tightly linked to occupancy.

It therefore flares when people reach the office or get back home after a long day at work and the building or home is heated, and drops significantly when the inner temperature has to be kept constant only.

The bottom line is pretty clear. All gas and electric grids are underutilized because of their partial utilization during the year and their design for peak demand. And these grids are expected to eventually represent up to two-thirds of energy costs! Once again, emerging decentralized technologies offer a powerful answer to the issue. This is a concept that has recently been introduced for buildings as "grid interactive" (Rocky Mountain Institute, 2020). In a nutshell, the concept takes stock of this significant underutilization and promotes a combination of decentralized energy, storage, and digital technologies applied to flexible sources (such as heating systems or electric-vehicle charging, etc.) to dynamically manage the load profile of the building in real time. Instead of having a load profile that peaks at up to one and a half to two times its baseload power, the building energy infrastructure manages to maintain an equal level of demand throughout the day and the year, or one that dynamically adapts to constraints on the grid system. Decentralized energies produce energy intermittently, which is stored in decentralized storage systems and dynamically redistributed to the building to maintain an equal draw of energy from the grid (or to adjust to grid constraints). Digital systems use the significant level of flexibility in demand of some loads to balance the grid. With grid-driven demand becoming dynamic, the overall utilization of the infrastructure is maximized and its size optimized, reducing the actual cost of the infrastructure to the final consumer. This is a very similar concept than that of a "supply following" system I introduced earlier.

This promising development is not years away. It has already been piloted in many installations. An interesting example is that of the Smart Neighborhood in Birmingham, Alabama, which combines "high-performance homes, energy efficient systems and appliances, connected devices, and a microgrid (…) with PV panels, battery storage, and a backup natural gas generator" for a 62-home residential area, leading to cost savings and optimized grid efficiency (Department of Energy, 2019). And this trend toward flattening load profiles is all the more enhanced by the redefinition of building use described above, with a greater blend in buildings use that could optimize overall assets' occupancy.

This type of application does not apply to buildings only, even though these have been the primary focus to date. It can to a large extent also apply to industrial processes, with perhaps even greater feasibility. Industrial processes have traditionally been part of demand-response programs, the historical (and nondigitized) version of grid-interactive assets. In such programs, the industrial plant contracts with the utility to reduce its load when called on to do so. With greater flexibility available on the industrial plant (from the combination of decentralized energies, storage, and digital technologies), industries are also a key part of infrastructure optimization.

Smart sector integration

Beyond load profile adjustment, another important topic will be to optimize grid infrastructures with the electrification of end use. Part of the reason that distribution infrastructure is underutilized is also related to the fact that different energy vehicles supply different loads within a given asset (be it a building or a factory). The convergence toward one source of energy (electricity) is a crucial enabler of optimization. Most gas distribution provides heat. Yet, heat pumps bring massive efficiency in energy use, in the range of three to five times more heat per unit of energy consumed. They are also electric. The transition of heat demand to electric heat pumps hence provides both increased efficiency and a larger base of flexibility for the infrastructure. In addition, heat demand is among the most versatile and flexible energy uses and therefore provides a significant potential for flexibility on the grid if it is electric, while it has no impact on gas grids, which are almost solely designed for that specific use. Energy distribution infrastructure could represent up to two-thirds of total costs of energy that is centrally distributed over time. There is however a significant potential to tame those infrastructure costs and maintain them or even lower them from their current baseline, though the combination of more decentralized energies, mass storage, and digital technologies applied to electric loads (including heating).

Infrastructure is in for a big disruption

In a world where a significant share of daily energy demand can be locally produced (and consumed), the remaining centralized energy system will thus have to cope with disruptions and potential seasonal deficits. It will increasingly play the role of a collective insurance and build on large renewable farms, but also on alternative technologies that are capable of being dispatched at will. This could take the form of large-scale storage systems (hydropower is one of the oldest of those), nuclear power plants, or highly flexible fossil-fuel-based plants. If the aggregated load profile is as stable as possible, the level of utilization of such systems could also be optimized. Digital technologies on grids will also play a critical role in optimizing the use and reliability of the distribution system.

Thus, energy infrastructure is also facing a significant transformation into optimization and increased efficiency. And since a complete transition toward more decentralized energy ultimately entails a reduction in energy costs for the consumer, it is probable that these necessary evolutions are inevitable.

The Next Stage of Economic Development Will Be Human-Centricity

Let's wrap up. The world runs an extremely inefficient economy. Since 1970, resource consumption (including energy) per capita has grown twofold, and most of these resources are actually wasted, be it at the time of extraction or production of a good or asset, or when that good or asset reaches end of life. Most economic projections focus on traditional indicators such as the labor force or economic productivity, but none have actually looked into how the final demand for products and resources will evolve over time. The argument I developed in this chapter is that this is actually the key to understanding upcoming evolutions, and that an ultra-efficient economy is within reach.

This vision is far from wishful thinking; it is already a reality in many cases and a transition that is just beginning to climb the famous S-curve of mass adoption. New energy, digital, and atomic-scale technologies will be the main constituents of this evolution.

Buildings will evolve toward a greater blend of uses, higher and dynamic customer-centricity, and space and resource optimization. This will have a considerable impact on buildings' energy demand, which — combined with a 50 percent energy efficiency potential and increased penetration of decentralized solar and storage — will lead to a new energy paradigm in the existing built environment.

Industries will also transform massively. The progressive modernization of industrial footprints with the deployment of best available technologies, process intensification and electrification, and granular controls with digital technologies will lead to significant productivity gains. Beyond this, digitally enabled circularity will further enhance the lifetime of assets and goods and a greater recourse to sharing services and recycling of materials, with a 50 percent potential for reduced demand.

Transport is next in line, with a transition toward multimodal transport systems, electrification of vehicles, TaaS, and autonomous vehicles already well on its way, with again a 50 percent potential of reduced demand.

These significant transformations of our working and living environment will also transform energy infrastructures, whose mission will have to evolve. The significant efficiency gains on demand will mean that centralized infrastructure costs will be almost entirely driven by distribution. The distribution infrastructure has however significant potential for optimization, with a greater use of "interactive" (or "supply following") demand, which could help tame and optimize load profiles during a given day or season.

What it means for energy

These innovations hold the keys to a major reduction in demand and hence a significant rise in energy productivity, and a much-improved utilization of building, industrial, transport, and energy assets. This ultra-efficient economy will have one direct consequence: it will reduce prices for pretty much everything we do: the energy we consume, the goods we purchase, the mobility services we use. In other words, the cost for end-consumers will decrease dramatically, and with this will come mass adoption, in a self-reinforcing loop that will make this transition inevitable.

Of course, it will not necessarily happen overnight, and the roadblocks are many. These transitions may also not happen at the same pace across sectors and regions. Yet, the path toward modernity and social progress is clear, and one can only hope that the sooner it becomes a reality, the better. It has already started. For the energy transition, which is the topic of this book, this quick review also stands as a call for action to better model these evolutions and truly capture the actual transformations at play and the dramatic (yet positive) impact they will have on our current energy system. There are many issues and questions associated with it. How costly will it be to maintain a centralized infrastructure in that highly distributed energy system? Will that be possible at a reasonable cost? What will happen if we cannot rely on large capacities of intermittent renewable energies for a prolonged period of time? These are just a few examples, and I do not discard them. Some elements of an answer have already been provided by specific studies, and the sum of knowledge around the topic continues to increase.

However, this does not change the initial bias that this book is determined to challenge. The energy transition conversation has long revolved around the imperative need to replace our current energy system with one alike yet decarbonized. I argue here that the transition to come will lead us to a different energy system than the one we have known, driven by social progress and innovation, decarbonized by design, and that is the one we need to prepare for.

Drivers of and challenges to adoption

Cost and productivity will be essential drivers of all these transitions. These are what will first drive adoption in commercial building upgrades, industry, and private mobility. Cost stands for the cost of acquisition of the solution or the upgrade. Productivity is the benefit that the solution brings to the adopter. The quest for productivity in commercial and industrial operations is a major driver of adoption, and probably an easier case than solutions dedicated to consumers directly, for which productivity is seldom a key driver. The combination of both cost and productivity provides a rate of return, which can be expressed in months or years. As I discussed already, these technologies all provide increasing rates of return over time. The greater the technology progress, the higher the rate of return, hence the faster the adoption.

However, there will be other drivers of adoption as well. The primary intent of Schmidt and Cohen's (2013) "electronic orchestra" is to bring greater convenience to all the little things in life that need to be organized. In a way, the primary goal of "human-centricity" is to bring greater convenience. This will apply to the residential context, but also to large retail markets' experience. Do you remember coming back from the supermarket and realizing you forgot half of what you needed to purchase, and having to go back again? Do you remember spending hours traversing the corridors of a retail center looking for a specific shop? All these little inconveniences could disappear in the coming few years. The same will apply to industrial operations. Operator-centricity could play a critical role in increasing safety and efficiency in operations while providing greater productivity through remote controls. In the mobility sector, too, TaaS could simply become more convenient over time. Provided it is easily available, it removes the stress of driving and parking while freeing up time. In the end, convenience will prove vital, as long as it comes at the right cost.

Progressivity will also play a critical role, notably in buildings (commercial, residential) and industries. The ability of these technologies to scale up progressively to pervade every aspect of operations will be essential in facilitating adoption: start small and then expand. Human-centricity in buildings or factories, building repurposing with a stronger blend of uses, space and energy optimization, modernization of industrial footprints with proven or new technologies, upgrading supply chains with digital technologies, and a digitally enabled transport revolution do not need to happen all at once. They can start from a specific application, or a specific subset of a building or factory, and then progressively expand. To a large extent, these technologies also build on open protocols and open access, enabling networking effects and hence scalability.

There will however be challenges to adoption. Technological advancement will be the first. Beyond the actual cost that follows well-known learning curves, the inherent capability of some technologies will be of the utmost importance. For instance, battery density and storage capacities are instrumental in removing range anxiety for electric vehicle adoption. Beyond this, compatibility across various applications will prove a central topic to enable progressivity and hence scalable adoption. This will be particularly important for all digital technologies but is also the case for the electrification of transport, with standardized charging plugs for instance. It would enable platform effects and thus the accelerated deployment of an ubiquitous charging infrastructure. Compatibility would also help develop integrated offerings over time and thus generate constantly improved experiences and results, thanks to the increasing rates of return that form the nature of these technologies, provided they are able to do so. At the same time, the reality of deployment has also demonstrated that their potential is often not realized, due to the way solutions are developed around these properties. My own professional experience suggests that this is almost always related to the way these technologies are actually being implemented, failing to factor in the design of these solutions the inherent scalability of modern technologies. The ability to design solutions based on inherent progressivity will thus be a key challenge to adoption. Simplicity will also play a critical role, notably in sectors where the acumen for such technologies is relatively low: buildings, mass transport, small industries. In those sectors, the simpler the system, the easier the adoption. If any deployment requires weeks or months of dedicated specialists' on-site intervention, first the cost will not be right, and second the willingness to switch will not be there. But, the potential ability to deploy these technologies (notably connectivity and energy, such as third-generation PV or batteries) directly into appliances could also be a major adoption booster, dramatically simplifying deployment. Nevertheless, further progress in technology is still needed to really make it a compelling case.

Business models could be another barrier to adoption. This will especially be crucial in buildings and industries. While new construction standards are expected to quickly switch to these new technologies when it makes sense, the challenge will lie in the stock of existing build, which represents and will continue for long to represent the majority. Hence, adoption within the existing stock is key. There is a need to reinvent a retrofit market that facilitates the adoption of these technologies — most importantly energy technologies, which require extensive hardware work. While direct integration of energy or digital provisions into appliances could be a major accelerator, the development of specialized channels to provide integration services, at cost, will be compulsory as well. And the cost of these will probably require significant optimization to become acceptable. Let me give a simple example: solar panel modules represent a fraction of total costs of a new installation. The rest — system costs — stands for project design and installation expenses. While the cost of solar modules has been steadily dropping with mass manufacturing (and is expected to continue to do so), that of project and installation follows a different trend. This has to do with learning experience and repetitive design and procedures. The National Renewable Energy Laboratory (2018) has shown that for a solar-module cost of around US$0.5/W in 2018, total costs of installation vary between US$1/W for large utility-scale farms and US$2.7/W for rooftop residential solar systems. Over two-thirds of the costs of a rooftop solar installation are what NREL calls soft costs, including labor, origination, overheads, etc. The main barrier to mass-scale adoption is therefore not related to the technology itself, but rather to the ability of established commercial channels to diffuse and deploy these new technologies.

These costs are obviously much lower in new building construction, since a lot of the overheads or origination costs are not required anymore, but they become increasingly important in building renovations. My estimate is that costs of retrofitting an installation with new energy technologies average around €400 per square meter (based on data from Elliot, 2019 and Kato, 2018). What this means is that it takes €60,000 to retrofit a 150-square-meter home, a price likely to be way beyond any acceptable budget, and very little of that is related to actual hardware. Digital technologies could thus be a powerful enabler of new business models dedicated to retrofit, by simplifying the origination of projects and systematizing the design and installation procedures, to the point where it will become much less expensive to deploy such solutions, accelerating the tipping point and adoption. New commercial channels of local companies would also have to come up with the required toolset and capabilities to handle these projects at scale. If the existing ones are today still struggling to make money, this will not last. We are obviously in the middle of a transitional period where the technology is struggling to deploy at scale. Back to the €400 calculation I made above, a good target would probably be to cut this in five or ten to enable mass adoption.

Beyond retrofit, the adoption of circularity will require a complete reboot of existing supply chains. Finding a way to transition from well-established and optimized materials supply chains to completely new ones will prove a significant roadblock to adoption. Suppose you want to manufacture products with plastic. You know well where to purchase and procure plastic today, and you never faced any shortage or quality issue that could have endangered your operations. Now you want to move to recycled plastic. Provided your usual supplier is able to provide you with it, you might be able to go with this solution. But you have only passed the burden to your Tier 1 supplier. In fact, your supplier now needs to procure the plastic somewhere else. It might come at an extra cost, and quality might also be questionable. In the end, even you find it, it will first come with extra cost, and potential quality issues you will have to deal with. This is a big barrier to adoption! This is why circular supply chains will need to be supported by new and specialized operations that will deal with the complete supply chain of recycled materials in an efficient way: collection, sorting, reprocessing, etc. Digital technologies will be a powerful way to help them do the necessary "tracing" and optimize their cost. Not all materials may come up first, nor in all sectors. The easiest materials to recycle (or the ones that provide the best productivity compared to raw material production) will come first (a good example would be aluminum). The sectors that are least dependent on quality degradation could also be prime targets for recycled materials (a good example could be packaging) in order to ramp up the market, before more complicated applications are considered. Last, there has been lots of excitement about service business models, another way to ensure end-to-end circular loops. A growing appetite for asset-light industries, with some capital owners willing to invest in new infrastructure, has been built on the inherent capabilities of the technologies I described above, particularly digital technologies. These new models will be key enablers of adoption as well.

Finally, competency and culture could be a significant barrier to adoption, too. Most of these technologies are indeed new, hence will require specific competencies. This will be particularly acute in areas where there is hardware involved and thus installation works. Typically, the deployment of solar and storage technologies at scale in the existing building market could stumble on the lack of channels available to provide that service at cost, efficiently. Beyond this, culture could also prove critical. Conservative stances are the norm in energy sectors, which have developed on safety and reliability principles. Often, the average age in such sectors is also disproportionately high. In the United States for instance, energy workers are on average 50 years old (Cantwell, 2016). The training and competency-building effort should not be underestimated. Without competency, there will be no channel available to deploy these technologies. The same holds true, in part, for digital technologies. The gap in competencies in this field could threaten 25 to 30 percent of job holders in some countries (Petit, 2021) (Figure 1).

A human-centric economy

A significant potential thus exists to do things a lot better. Technologies are already largely available, and innovations have begun to emerge. Some challenges

Toward an ultra-efficient economy

Innovations	Drivers of adoption	Challenges to adoption
Buildings - blend - human-centric - autonomy	Buildings - convenience - productivity - cost - progressivity	Buildings - competency - business models - technology
Industry - BAT - process intensification - electrification - digital controls - circularity	Industry - productivity - cost - progressivity	Industry - policies - business models - technology
Mobility - multimodal - EV - TaaS - AV	Mobility - cost	Mobility - technology
Infrastructure - decentralized infrastructures	Infrastructure - productivity - cost	Infrastructure - competency

Toward an ultra-resilient society

Innovations	Drivers of adoption	Challenges to adoption
Resources	Resources	Resources
Trade	Trade	Trade
Social	Social	Social

Toward an ultra-clean civilization

Innovations	Drivers of adoption	Challenges to adoption
Agriculture	Agriculture	Agriculture
Industry waste	Industry waste	Industry waste
Energy	Energy	Energy
Water	Water	Water

Human-centricity @ the core

Figure 1   Demand-driven innovations

still need to be removed for adoption to accelerate, and current progress and development in technologies (notably digital ones) are promising in that regard.

Going further though, what also emerges from this short review of innovations is an economy that is based less and less on mass standardization and scale effects and is evolving toward greater human-centricity. This applies to buildings and mobility as well as manufacturing. And this is a significant paradigm shift compared to what the world has experienced in the twentieth century. A new frontier for economic growth? And, also, a renewed sentiment of greater abundance?

References

Anderson, M. (2020). "Surprise! 2020 Is Not the Year for Self-Driving Cars." *IEEE Spectrum*, April 22. https://spectrum.ieee.org/transportation/self-driving/surprise-2020-is-not-the-year-for-selfdriving-cars.

Arbib, J., Seba T. (2017). *Rethinking Transportation 2020–2030. The Disruption of Transportation and the Collapse of the Internal-Combustion Vehicle and Oil Industries.* RethinkX, May. https://www.rethinkx.com/transportation.

Arbib, J., and Seba, T. (2020). *Rethinking Humanity: Five Foundational Sector Disruptions, the Lifecycle of Civilizations, and the Coming Age of Freedom.* RethinkX, June. https://www.rethinkx.com/humanity.

Banerjee, R., Cong, Y., Gielen, D., Jannuzzi, G., Maréchal, F., McKane, A. T., Rosen, M. A. *et al.* (2012). "Energy End-Use: Industry." In *Global Energy Assessment: Toward a Sustainable Future*, 513–74. Cambridge: Cambridge University Press. http://www.iiasa.ac.at/web/home/research/Flagship-Projects/Global-Energy-Assessment/GEA_Chapter8_industry_lowres.pdf.

Beyond Zero Emissions. (2018). *Zero Carbon Industry Plan. Electrifying Industry.* Melbourne: Beyond Zero Emissions. https://apo.org.au/sites/default/files/resource-files/2018-12/apo-nid270186.pdf.

Bloch, C., Newcomb, J., Shiledar, S., and Tyson M. (2019). *Breakthrough Batteries: Powering the Era of Clean Electrification.* Report, Rocky Mountain Institute. https://rmi.org/insight/breakthrough-batteries/.

BloombergNEF. (2019). *New Energy Outlook.* Report, Bloomberg New Energy Finance. https://about.bnef.com/new-energy-outlook/.

Borunda, A. (2019). "Climate Change Is Contributing to California's Fires." *National Geographic*, October 25. https://www.nationalgeographic.com/science/2019/10/climate-change-california-power-outage/.

Boulding, K. (1966). "The Economics of the Coming Spaceship Earth." In *Environmental Quality in a Growing Economy*, edited by H. Jarrett, 3–14. Baltimore, MD: Resources for the Future/Johns Hopkins University Press. http://www.ub.edu/prometheus21/articulos/obsprometheus/BOULDING.pdf.

Brolin, F., Fahnestock, J., and Rootzén, J. (2017). *Industry's Electrification and Role in the Future Electricity System: A Strategic Innovation Agenda.* SP Technical Research Institute of Sweden and Chalmers University of Technology, February. 10.13140/RG.2.2.34794.88003.

Brown, M., and Lubelczyk, M. (2020). "The Future of Shopping Centers." Kearney. https://www.kearney.com/consumer-retail/article/?/a/the-future-of-shopping-centers-article.

Build Up. (2017). "The Edge: Amsterdam Office Building with Highest BREEAM Score To Date." Build Up: the European Portal for Energy Efficiency in Buildings, January 11. https://www.buildup.eu/en/practices/cases/edge-amsterdam-office-building-highest-breeam-score-date.

Cantwell, M. (2016). *Building an Energy Workforce for the 21st Century.* Prepared by Democratic Staff of the US Senate Committee on Energy & Natural Resources, August. https://www.eenews.net/assets/2016/08/17/document_gw_07.pdf.

CNBC. (2019). "California Regulator Sanctions PG&E over Power Outages." *CNBC*, October 14. https://www.cnbc.com/2019/10/14/california-regulator-sanctions-pge-over-power-outages.html.

Covec. (2007). *Recycling: Cost Benefit Analysis.* Report prepared for the Ministry of Environment of New Zealand, April. https://www.mfe.govt.nz/sites/default/files/recycling-cost-benefit-analysis-apr07.pdf.

Deng, Y., Haigh M., Pouwels W., Ramaekers L., Brandsma R., Schimschar S., Grozinger J., de Jager D. (2015). *Quantifying a Realistic, Worldwide Wind and Solar Electricity Supply.* Global Environment Change 31, 239–52, Elsevier. https://www.sciencedirect.com/science/article/pii/S0959378015000072.

Department of Energy. (2019). *Grid-Interactive Efficient Buildings, Overview.* US Department of Energy, Office of Energy efficiency and Renewable efficiency, April. https://www.energy.gov/sites/prod/files/2019/04/f61/bto-geb_overview-4.15.19.pdf.

The Economist. (2017). "The Construction Industry's Productivity Problem." *Economist*, August 17. https://www.economist.com/leaders/2017/08/17/the-construction-industrys-productivity-problem.

Ellen MacArthur Foundation. (2013). *Towards the Circular Economy. Economic and Business Rationale for an Accelerated Transition.* https://www.ellenmacarthurfoundation.org/assets/downloads/publications/Ellen-MacArthur-Foundation-Towards-the-Circular-Economy-vol.1.pdf.

Elliott, J. (2019). "Can You Go Off the Grid with a 10 kW Solar System Plus Battery Storage?" *Solar Choice*, September 9. https://www.solarchoice.net.au/blog/off-grid-with-10kW-solar-and-battery-storage.

Energy Transitions Commission. (2018). *Mission Possible: Reaching Net-Zero Carbon Emissions from Harder-to-Abate Sectors.* November. http://www.energy-transitions.org/mission-possible.

European Commission. (2013). "Energy Use in Buildings." https://ec.europa.eu/energy/eu-buildings-factsheets-topics-tree/energy-use-buildings_en.

Faggella, D. (2020). "The Self-Driving Car Timeline — Predictions from the Top 11 Global Automakers." *Emerji*, March 14. https://emerj.com/ai-adoption-timelines/self-driving-car-timeline-themselves-top-11-automakers/.

Hockfield, S. (2019). *The Age of Living Machines: How Biology Will Build the Next Technology Revolution.* New York: W. W. Norton & Company.

Immelt, J. (2016). "Digital Industrial Transformation." Presentation at the GE Oil & Gas annual meeting of 2016. https://annualmeeting.bakerhughes.com/sites/g/files/cozyhq381/files/2018-09/GEAM2016_Jeff_Immelt_GE.pdf.

Inrix. (2020). "INRIX 2019 Global Traffic Scorecard." https://inrix.com/scorecard/.

International Energy Agency ©. (2009). Chemical and Petrochemical Sector. Potential of Best Practice Technology and Other Measures for Improving Energy Efficiency. September. https://webstore.iea.org/chemical-and-petrochemical-sector.

International Energy Agency ©. (2019a). Perspectives for the Clean Energy Transition. The Critical Role of Buildings. April. https://webstore.iea.org/perspectives-for-the-clean-energy-transition.

International Energy Agency ©. (2019b). *Renewables 2019. Analysis and Forecast to 2024.* October. https://www.iea.org/reports/renewables-2019.

International Energy Agency ©. (2019c). *World Energy Outlook.* November. Paris: IEA. https://www.iea.org/reports/world-energy-outlook-2019.

Jemdahl, J. (2019). "7 Global Future Logistics Trends." *Greencarrier* (blog), January 15. https://blog.greencarrier.com/7-global-future-logistics-trends/.

Jolly, J. (2019). "2020 Set to Be Year of the Electric Car, Say Industry Analysts." *Guardian*, December 25. https://www.theguardian.com/environment/2019/dec/25/2020-set-to-be-year-of-the-electric-car-say-industry-analysts.

Kato, Y. (2018). The Real Costs of Building a Home, in One Graphic. *Fixr* (blog), July 26. https://www.fixr.com/blog/2018/07/26/the-real-costs-of-building-a-home-in-one-graphic/.

Keeney, T. (2017). "The Future of Transport is Autonomous Mobility-as-a-Service." *Ark Invest*, November 30. https://ark-invest.com/analyst-research/autonomous-mobility-as-a-service/.

Kijiji. (2016). *The Kijiji Second Hand Economy Index.* 2016 Report. https://www.kijiji.ca/kijijicentral/app/uploads/2016/08/Kijiji-Index-Report-2016-1.pdf.

Mandel, J., and Stone, L. (2019). "Making Our Existing Buildings Zero Carbon: A Three-Pronged Approach." Rocky Mountain Institute, December 4. https://rmi.org/making-our-existing-buildings-zero-carbon-a-three-pronged-approach/.

Material Economics. (2019). *Industrial Transformation 2050 — Pathways to Net-Zero Emissions from EU Heavy Industry.* Cambridge: CISL. https://materialeconomics.com/latest-updates/industrial-transformation-2050.

McMahon, J. (2019). "More Electric Cars Mean Fewer Mechanical Jobs." *Forbes*, May 30. https://www.forbes.com/sites/jeffmcmahon/2019/05/30/more-electric-cars-fewer-manufacturing-jobs/#6542746a3378.

National Renewable Energy Laboratory. (2018). "Costs Continue to Decline for Residential and Commercial Photovoltaics in 2018." NREL, December 17. https://www.nrel.gov/news/program/2018/costs-continue-to-decline-for-residential-and-commercial-photovoltaics-in-2018.html.

O'Donnell, B. (2020). "How the Race to Autonomous Cars Got Sidetracked by Human Nature." *Fast Company*, February 17. https://www.fastcompany.com/90459114/how-the-race-to-autonomous-cars-got-sidetracked-by-words.

Pearce, D. W., and Turner, K. R. (190). Economics of Natural Resources and the Environment. Harlow, England: Pearson Education Limited.

Petit, V. (2017). *The Energy Transition: An Overview of the True Challenge of the 21st Century.* Cham, Switzerland: Springer.

Petit, V. (2018). *The New World of Utilities: A Historical Transition toward a New Energy System.* Cham, Switzerland: Springer.

Petit, V. (2021). *The Future Global Order. The Six Paradigm Changes That Will Define 2050.* London: World Scientific Publishing.

Randall, T. (2015). "The Smartest Building in the World." Bloomberg, September 23. https://www.bloomberg.com/features/2015-the-edge-the-worlds-greenest-building/.

RDC Environment. (2003). *Evaluation of Costs and Benefits for the Achievement of Reuse and Recycling Targets for the Different Packaging Materials in the Frame of the Packaging and Packaging Waste Directive 94/62/EC.* March. https://ec.europa.eu/environment/waste/studies/packaging/costsbenefits.pdf.

Rocky Mountain Institute. (2015). "Historic Building Performs Equal to or Better Than New Buildings." Blog post, September 23. https://rmi.org/blog_2015_09_23_historic_building_performs_equal_to_or_better_than_new_buildings/.

Rocky Mountain Institute. (2020). "Grid-Integrated Energy Efficient Buildings." Rocky Mountain Institute. https://rmi.org/our-work/buildings/pathways-to-zero/grid-integrated-energy-efficient-buildings/.

Rodrigue, J.-P. (2020). *The Geography of Transport Systems*, 5th ed. New York: Routledge.

Roland Berger. (2016). *Think Act beyond Mainstream. The Industrie 4.0 Transition Quantified.* Munich, Germany: Roland Berger. https://www.rolandberger.com/en/Publications/The-Industrie-4.0-transition-quantified.html?country=WLD.

Schmidt, E., and Cohen, J. (2013). *The New Digital Age: Reshaping the Future of People, Nations and Business.* London: John Murray.

Seba, T. (2014). *Clean Disruption of Energy and Transportation.* Clean Planet Ventures.

Society of Automotive Engineers. (2018). *Taxonomy and Definitions for Terms Related to Driving Automation Systems for On-Road Motor Vehicles. Society of Automotive Engineers.* Revised June 15. https://www.sae.org/standards/content/j3016_201806/.

Stahel, W., and Reday-Mulvey, G. (1981). *Jobs for Tomorrow: The Potential for Substituting Manpower for Energy.* New York: Vantage Press.

System IQ & The Pew Charitable Trust. (2020). "Breaking the Plastic Wave." https://www.systemiq.earth/wp-content/uploads/2020/07/BreakingThePlasticWave_MainReport.pdf.

Westmoreland, P. (2014). "Process Intensification: Concepts and Applications." NSF Workshop, AICHe Academy, September 30–October 1. https://www.aiche.org/system/files/aiche-proceedings/203056/papers/-553/P-553.pdf.

Winter, D. (2015). "The Violent Afterlife of a Recycled Plastic Bottle. What Happens After You Toss It Into the Bin?" *Atlantic*, December 4. https://www.theatlantic.com/technology/archive/2015/12/what-actually-happens-to-a-recycled-plastic-bottle/418326/.

The World Counts. (2018). "A World of Waste." https://www.theworldcounts.com/challenges/planet-earth/state-of-the-planet/world-waste-facts.

CHAPTER 5

Are We Too Big to Fail, or Is It the Opposite?

"Decentralized systems are the quintessential patrons of simplicity. They allow complexity to rise to a level at which it is sustainable, and no higher." (L.K. Samuels)

My argument for this book has been all along that energy transitions are byproducts of innovations in demand, founded on technological developments that may include energy but are not limited to it. This is a very significant change in the way we collectively look at energy transitions. These innovations can take several forms. They may provide new services that were unthinkable before, but most of the time they will first provide existing services in a better way, and often at a fraction of their past cost. There may be barriers to adoption at first. Yet, when the conditions for a successful deployment of these innovations are here, adoption accelerates and the innovation climbs the S-curve. As it does so, the underlying foundations of the "current" energy system evolve to follow these new or transformed usages. Energy supply chases demand, not the other way around.

This is what has been happening in the past, and what will happen again, in constant repetition and a suite of social developments. The technologies for these changes to happen are here: decentralized renewable (solar) technologies, mass energy storage technologies, computing and mobile connectivity technologies, and atomic-scale technologies. They all follow exponential improvements and cost-reduction curves. They also all have common patterns: infinitely scalable and highly decentralized, they tend to provide increasing rates of return over time, a significant change of paradigm compared to twentieth-century technologies. The question then is, how will these technologies combine into practical innovations, and what will be the tipping points of adoption?

One way to explore these potential transformations is to review the critical issues and opportunities our world is currently facing, as these will be the natural playground for all upcoming innovations. I have divided these into three main arguments. I argue that our economy is inefficient, our society fragile, and our civilization unsustainable.

In the previous chapter, I explored the first of these arguments. We have discovered that a massive potential for waste reduction and assets utilization optimization exists across all sectors of activity: buildings, industry, and mobility. We also realized that this potential had dramatic impacts on energy infrastructure, with up to 50 percent of energy productivity accessible. This would lead to a significant increase of the share of distribution costs in total energy costs, putting in check the way the traditional model has been designed. The consequences of such an optimization of energy use and of the infrastructure to deliver it (centralized and decentralized) could be a significant reduction of the actual cost of energy use, a significant new source of economic productivity, and a major reallocation of capital toward consumers (while heavily supporting the climate change agenda). All these innovations toward further efficiency share a common pattern: they build on greater human-centricity, a paradigm shift compared to the twentieth-century economic model, which was largely based on standardization.

Fragile societies

In this chapter, I look into the second argument. Our societies are fragile. I already explained the roots of this. As our world is growing larger and more interconnected, our dependency on critical and distant resources has massively increased. Trade dependencies have also been growing, at times creating power struggles between nations that depend on one another. Finally, the inner structure of modern capitalism has increased social inequalities, within and across nations. To a large extent, the twentieth century has been an exception to the rule, which most likely can be explained by the two World Wars that reset capital distribution across social classes.

The central question we can now ask is whether longer-term trends will further aggravate these fragilities. Arbib and Seba (2020) believe we have reached the end of our current social system. They define the new era to come as the "Age of Freedom," as opposed to the "Age of Extraction," which they believe we are about to leave. They give the instructive example of the rise and fall of Rome to draw similarities with our current times. Rome was built on the ashes of the fallen Babylonian and Egyptian civilizations, as a continuation of the rise of the Greeks and Phoenicians. At its peak, it controlled over five million square kilometers, but could never surpass that number. They estimate that the social structure made it impossible to expand it further. More relevant for our argument is their description of the inherent fragilities of the "command and control" organization of Rome, which had to expand its geographic control to "feed the center," up to the point that single points of failure converged and precipitated its collapse: "climate change (...), regular pandemics, political infighting, and increasing inequality." Sounds familiar? We can certainly build on these findings.

Today's global economy is largely interconnected and, as recent history has shown, a single issue in one country can incapacitate the economic machine. Pandemics, but also unexpected geopolitical tensions or confrontations, dramatically expose dependencies across regions of the world, can endanger long-term sustainable development, and put the world on a track toward derailment. As recent as 2020, the world realized that a single virus could bring the entire world's economy to its knees, and it is still unclear, at the time of the writing, how the global economy will bounce back and what the social and political implications of this crisis are. At the same time, a confrontation about oil prices between Russia and Saudi Arabia has turned the entire energy system upside down, triggering spectacular wealth transfers from one region to another in a matter of weeks and thus new imbalances, with devastating consequences.

Increased demand for more resources is also creating a strain on mature economies, which need to secure a growing amount of resources to run their economies. The latest report from UN Environment Programme (2019) shows that by 2050, provided current trends continue, humanity is set to consume twice as many resources as today: a doubling in less than 30 years. This is based on the assumption of a continued imbalance between low- and high-income countries, with low-income countries' GDP per capita not exceeding a sixth of that of high-income countries by then. What would be the equivalent resource consumption of a world where everyone would consume as much material as high-income countries currently do? The analysis has not been done. Let's just note that the people of Africa consume nearly four times fewer resources per capita than people in the United States. And some of our identified reserves are already sharply depleted, with less than 30 years of production available at the current pace (Petit, 2021). This does not mean that we will run out of materials, but that an intense competition for new deposits is expected to emerge, with new frontiers such as ocean exploration gaining ground. The geopolitics of raw materials will evolve and intensify in the coming decades. Though a fascinating subject of research, this well illustrates the growing fragility of the current construct. What has already become apparent for fossil fuels will expand to all resources necessary for an "extraction" economy.

Finally, social inequalities are also set to rise. Let's build up on the report from UNEP I mentioned above. Current trends show continued unequal development of low-income and high-income countries. While average GDP per capita in low- and middle-income countries averages around US$5,000 per capita today, compared to US$45,000 per capita in high-income countries, by 2060 these low- and middle-income countries would triple their activity to around US$15,000 per capita, compared to a whopping US$80,000 per capita for high-income countries (UN Environment Programme, 2019; World Bank Group, 2020a). In fact, the difference in wealth creation in absolute value would be higher than today's gap!

High-income countries house a population that today is roughly equivalent to one billion people, out of nearly eight billion people on the planet. By 2060, the gap will widen, with low- and middle-income countries accounting for over 90 percent of the global population. A lot of growth will happen in Africa, whose population is set to double in the coming decades (Petit, 2021). How will these massive and increasing inequalities play out in a world where demographic pressure increases way beyond what we have seen to date?

Can recipes from the past still work?

As Arbib and Seba (2020) put it, can the current organizational structure in place continue to operate with such massive inequalities? The same question applies within nations themselves, as it has been demonstrated that today's top 1 percent of the population owns nearly 50 percent of global wealth, while 8 percent owns 85 percent of the wealth (Petit, 2021).

And this could get worse. GDP is on a slowing course. In the last 50 years, GDP growth has averaged 3.5 percent per year, with half coming from labor growth and the rest from economic productivity (McKinsey, 2017). Economic productivity is clearly decelerating today (Immelt, 2016), while labor growth has been slowing too, with a lower increase in population. Total population should eventually reach eleven to twelve billion people and peak before the end of the century (Petit, 2021). What will happen then to a social construct which is — like the Roman Empire — based on expansion?

Finally, climate change could also play its part, and I will review it in the next chapter in more detail. Given all this, it should be no surprise that the appetite for a new form of living or governance begins to emerge among the young generations, and these will to a large extent define the coming decades as they reach maturity. In short, the theory of Arbib and Seba (2020) might hold the test of time. Long-term trends are here to stay and will exacerbate the inherent fragilities of our current social system and economy, which is based on resources extraction, continued expansion, verticalized societies, and capital intensification.

The bottom line of this introduction is that our current economic system (and its underlying blood system, energy) is a fragile construct. Trade, resources, and social structures have grown increasingly fragile over time. This is not because they were weak points from the start, but rather because demand has grown so large, and the world so interconnected, that these dependencies and entanglements have become single points of failure in the system. And these fragilities, which were very much exposed during the 2020 crisis, are bound to continue to amplify. The question then is whether the world as we have known it is on the verge of collapse or of reinventing itself as something new, or both! The theory of Arbib and Seba is that our economy will rapidly evolve from a resource-based economy to a creation-based economy, fueled by the massive potential of technology. They believe that technology has the potential to enable humankind to reinvent a new social and economic construct, becoming less dependent on increasingly scarce resources while providing equal opportunity and accelerated wealth convergence.

One thing is for sure: resiliency will increasingly become a key question. It will revolve around sustainable resource use, sustainable trade, and sustainable social systems. It will not be about protecting the ancient world as much as it will be about finding a new wind for inclusive social progress, one that delivers increasing returns to society over time and helps it take a leap forward toward the next stage of civilization. Our economy and society will undergo an inevitable paradigm shift, for better or worse. And I concur with Arbib and Seba that technology (or innovation) is where we can find the answer. As I have argued all along, social progress drives transitions, and technology adoption drives social progress. It also becomes clear that when it comes to building an ultra-resilient society, we need to look at technologies enabling greater decentralization.

Resilient Resources

Let's start exploring what these new technologies I described above could do to build sustainable resource systems with increasing returns.

Circularity

We can start from the description of circularity I made in the previous chapter. I explored circularity's significant potential for increased efficiency and digital technologies' crucial role in enabling circularity at scale.

Yet, there is more to it. Material Economics (2018) has focused its research on Europe and demonstrated that enough steel is already in use and scrapped every year in Europe (from the built environment for instance) to fulfill the needs for new steel on a yearly basis. In other words, recycled steel from local waste could be enough to supply the entire demand of steel. That will obviously not work if the steel is contaminated with other types of metal and requires specific design rules to be enforced. Provided these would be put in place, however, a fully recycling steel industry could be set up, with no further need for virgin primary steel production and hence no more dependency on iron ore extraction. The case of Europe is quite specific, as the demand for new steel remains limited on a year-to-year basis and the actual stock of steel in the European built environment is already extremely large. The same cannot apply to other economies as they continue to develop and catch up with modern living standards. Several studies have elaborated on this and come to the conclusion that as the economy keeps growing, the stock of existing materials cannot fully compensate for the rise in materials demand (Grosse, 2010; Labbé, 2016). However, the Energy Transitions Commission (2019) has reached similar conclusions for China in 2050, and the same is probably already applicable to other developed economies, such as the United States. Over time, it is thus likely that circularity can help tame the increase in raw resources demand. What is applicable to steel can also be relevant for other materials, such as plastics, copper, aluminum, etc. Detailed studies lag on the opportunity, but Material Economics (2018) has built a similar case for plastics, though as stated, transformations in how plastics are designed are required to enable full recycling capacity, particularly for mechanical recycling.

The other big outcome of the potential for large-scale circularity development is resource independence. Indeed, with a full stock of existing steel (or other materials) being enough to address new needs as the economy develops, the materials economy decentralizes, with a significant reduction in dependencies on raw materials extraction from other economies. Moreover, since the cost of recycling existing materials (if properly designed) sharply contrasts with that of producing virgin material, the actual return on using the recycled material improves over time. We see another increasing return for the economy here, one that can boost economic productivity as a result, with materials coming at a fraction of their cost and dropping over time. Circularity of materials thus makes it possible to create a less dependent economy that is more decentralized, with rising productivity levels. The challenges are numerous, and such deployment is complex as it involves multiple stakeholders, but the theoretical value is clear.

A new periodic table of new materials

Another area of innovation, powered by new technologies, will actually be the design of new materials. Arbib and Seba (2020) once again expect a flurry of new materials to emerge, based on the convergence of digital technologies (and massive computing power), biotechnologies, and nanotechnologies. According to them, these new materials would put an end to the dependence on extracted raw materials, enabling the industrial ecosystem to fully rely on better, cheaper, and abundant new material sources. They even predict that the cost of solar photovoltaics will become so low that they will ultimately disrupt and replace traditional construction materials. Actually, this could already be the case (IronMatrix, 2020). With building shells made entirely of ultra-resistant photovoltaic materials, "the effective cost of electricity [would] (…) be zero or even negative" (Arbib and Seba, 2020). The famous President Emerita of MIT, Susan Hockfield, says nothing less in her fascinating book *The Age of Living Machines: How Biology Will Build the Next Technology Revolution* (2019), in which she describes some of the disruptive innovations she has come across in her years at MIT. In effect, the true disruption in materials and resources comes from today's ability to work at an atomic scale and rebuild the well-known periodic table through new combinations that the power of computing helps test in almost real time.

And once again, with these renewed abilities, dependencies on traditional materials vanish. This is to the benefit of local communities, who are able to redesign the materials they need at a fraction of the past cost of extracting, shipping, and transforming Earth's resources. In short, a more decentralized and highly productive economy.

One could argue of course that despite significant research and a score of new material innovations reaching the market every year, only a handful of them actually reach maturity, and that the world continues to build on existing systems and resources. This is true, but it fails to take into account two major facts. First, the world is at the beginning of its digital disruption, and the massive potential of computing power and design have yet to be grasped. Second, we look at long timelines of change. Most scenarios I mentioned early on project the future to 2050 and beyond, 30 years down the line. Who would have imagined in 1990 that today, half of the world's population would have at its fingertips 100,000 times the equivalent computing power of the system that guided Apollo to the moon in 1969?

Food and water revolution

What applies to materials also applies to food and water. Let's first look at quick facts. Worldwide demand is expected to have grown by 70 percent by 2050, and to have doubled in new economies. Many regions are dependent on food imports: over 160 countries are said to be dependent on imported food today.

And this number could grow, as these are also the places that are expected to see the highest growth in demand. In these regions, considerable gaps in agricultural yields persist (notably compared to mature economies), with most of them (particularly in Africa, India, and Central Asia) running at less than half of their theoretical potential. This is obviously primarily due to a lack of equipment and access to modern farming techniques. In most countries of the world, agriculture remains first and foremost an economy of subsistence. But this is also related to the lack of suitable arable land in several regions, notably in Asia, due to a lack of space or sometimes polluted soil. In China, for instance, 40 percent of arable land is said to be polluted (Petit, 2021).

This increase also has an impact on water demand. Indeed, 70 percent of water withdrawals are associated with agriculture (with another 10 percent with energy production). With this growth in demand for both food and energy, the actual supply of freshwater could be 40 percent short on demand by 2030 (International Renewable Energy Agency, 2015; Petit, 2021). Many water basins have already been depleted and are under significant pressure from growing demand, particularly in North Africa, the Middle East, Central Asia, and India.

The future of food and water is thus at stake, and the outlook for several new economies is pretty bleak. This could rapidly deteriorate with climate change. Again, despite uncertainties, climate change could reduce yields by as much as 20 percent in some of these regions (Petit, 2021).

Will we thus see cohorts of people leaving their country of birth and set out for more productive and clement areas? Or will we see an intensification of food and water trade across countries, beyond what we have seen already?

Global food trade today represents around US$500 billion per year, which is 3–4 percent of the global goods trade (Petit, 2021; University of Minnesota, 2015). Agriculture is still mainly a local activity. One thing is for sure: something will have to change in the coming decades, as demographics continue to expand, and most probably in these economies that have the greatest problems with ensuring food and water access security. The Food and Land Use Coalition (2019) estimates that out of an estimated market value of US$10,000 billion, the sector generates hidden costs of around US$12,000 billion, or a net loss for the world. Health issues account for half of that cost, while environmental and economic losses account for the rest.

The organization has therefore identified ten critical transitions to ensure the development of a resilient and sustainable food supply for generations to come. First, adopting healthy diets, ensuring a productive ocean for seafood, reducing waste, protecting and restoring nature, and accelerating the demographic transition in most economies is a way to limit the impact of agriculture's needs on nature's endowments. Second, the Food and Land Use Coalition advocates for supporting the development of productive and regenerative agriculture everywhere, particularly in new economies. This would be a mix of traditional techniques, such as crop rotation or local livestock grazing control, but also a further penetration of precision farming. This would be combined with reinforcing local loops and developing stronger rural livelihoods, which would in effect help millions exit a life of subsistence. It is striking to see that the agriculture sector represents only 3 percent of the workforce in mature economies, but around 60 percent in low-income countries (World Bank Group, 2020b). This says a lot about the potential improvements that are up for grabs in new economies. Finally, the organization recommends a stronger focus on technology capabilities, particularly through diversifying protein supply sources (including laboratory-grown proteins) and using digital technologies as a tool to boost the sector's productivity, notably through the use of gene-editing but also through precision farming or improved logistics in supply chains.

Tubb and Seba (2019) go one step further. They predict a disruption of the sector by 2030. They claim that a modern food industry is within reach, building on the massive potential of digital and atomic-scale technologies. This modern food industry essentially consists of rebuilding the nutrients and micro-organisms that we need, as a substitute for growing them from nature. They notably focus on proteins (meat, seafood) and estimate that modern food production could be ten times more efficient and need ten times less water, five times less energy, and 100 times less land. The consequences, according to them, would be spectacular. Live feedstock could be reduced by up to 25 times, and the overall industry value could shrink by a factor of ten.

This transition would also have ripple effects on other sectors, freeing massive land areas for other purposes, dramatically reducing the cost of land, while driving a significant energy transition toward more electric energy (in essence, electrically powered processes would replace natural livestock growth).

Time will tell to what extent these new technologies will materialize, but one thing seems for sure. The industrialization of agriculture holds significantly more potential for rapid deployment than a slow conversion of millions to more progressive traditional farming techniques, in a context of rapid population expansion and urbanization. And, as said, it provides increasing rates of return. The cost of technology is dropping at pace with increased adoption, using far fewer resources than the previous model. At the same time, new designs, models, and genetic combinations are expected to improve over time, providing greater benefits. Therefore, a sustainable food industry is possible, which will be ultra-localized yet reliant on modern biotechnologies and digital technologies, with adjacent benefits to health, the environment, and living standards. As the pressure on demand and supply imbalances mounts in the system, these modern developments could make significant strides in the coming decades.

Harvesting free, locally available energy

The last theme on resources is that of energy itself. According to REN21 (2017), the technical potential of renewable energies stands at around 11,940 exajoules per year (a fraction of the total amount of renewable energy available which I mentioned above, yet one that is deemed retrievable with current technologies), with around 80 percent of the potential in solar energy and 10 percent in geothermal energy. Wind and other renewable energies (hydropower, tidal waves, and bioenergy) account for the rest. This is to be compared to a global final energy demand of around 450 exajoules per year, or around 25 times less. The picture obviously varies per region. Some regions, such as the Middle East, Africa, or the Pacific, are blessed with vast quantities of solar irradiation but consume only a fraction of the energy they could harness. This is particularly true for Africa, which is endowed with a renewable potential 200 times its current energy demand, or the Middle East (50 times). Others have scarcer resources to count on, notably Europe and China, whose resources are only three times greater than their current energy demand. Yet, the conclusion is clear. The technical renewable potential that can be harnessed with today's technologies by any region in the world largely exceeds current consumption, and solar energy alone could fuel all our needs and also our needs to come, and this for centuries.

And this does not even account for the potential improvements in technology. Current solar photovoltaic panels convert only 10–20 percent of solar irradiation, but much more energy is actually hitting the surface of Earth. New technologies could in theory increase this potential threefold, at a fraction of the cost of current cells!

The other critical aspect of these momentous endowments that the world has just begun to harness is that they are available to anyone. Early on, I made the case of the fragility of the current energy system due to long global supply chains. These renewable energies are available to all, prefiguring a fully decentralized energy system in which one of the major weaknesses of the current energy system would eventually be addressed. Moreover, since renewable energy is freely available, it does not cost anything to harness it once the capital-intensive investments have been realized. As an example, a current source of solar energy (say your home), generates electricity for free when solar panels are deployed. As the installation reaches its end of life (25 years after the spend), a new installation can be put in place, with upgraded technologies that are likely more efficient. The supply of solar energy is enlarged. This runs opposite to traditional mining. In a mine, people extract resources, and the more extraction occurs, the higher the cost of further extracting resources. With solar energies, the more we use them, the cheaper they get, generating increasing returns over time and providing more energy at a fraction of past costs.

Electrons to replace molecules

The last point on sustainable energy resources is the upcoming domination of electricity as the main energy vehicle. Indeed, the most efficient and cost-effective way to use these gigantic renewable energy resources is to convert them directly into electricity, notably for solar through the now well-known photovoltaic effect. As I discussed already, the world is at the beginning of innovations in this field, thanks to massive advancements of computing power, biotechnology, and nanotechnology, which could help design much more efficient solutions. Solar technology, distributed by nature, is also notably endowed with almost infinite scale effects, which could bring its costs to a fraction of what they are now, even though they have already dropped by considerable amounts and are reaching parity with current conventional technologies. All this while further increasing its performance. This is just the beginning.

And electricity offers a clear set of benefits compared to other forms of energy. Electrical energy is already here, in use in most appliances in our daily lives, and widely available. It therefore dramatically outcompetes any other form of energy, which would require a complete infrastructure buildup.

Moreover, it is at the heart of electronic (digital) systems, which have invaded our daily lives in recent decades, and this for a good reason: electronics (digital) outperform physical machinery in every way (Barnard, 2017). Wherever large physical processes exist, there is always an opportunity to do better, simpler, and cheaper with electricity and electronics. It is true that some existing processes have not yet been made electric, because the solutions available have not proven to be competitive, but this is more the result of a lack of innovation in the field than of the true physical potential of electric energy and electronics. Electricity and electronics enable granular and ultra-fast controls, at time scales and precision scales unmatched by traditional systems. On the one hand, digital technologies and electronics are further enabled by the spread of electric processes, while on the other hand, they support this spread. It is simply about doing better, faster, and cheaper with a new array of available technologies.

Currently, many processes are already turning electric. When it comes to controls and motion, all processes are electric. Some remote machinery in oil fields still runs on gasoline, but this is not for long. The vast majority of motion applications have already switched. Drying processes are often electric because of the precision and flexibility of electrical infrared heating. Many other heating processes are also progressively migrating away from coal or natural gas toward electricity, simply because it makes more sense. When low-temperature heating is required, heat pumps — as we have seen already — offer significant efficiency gains. For higher-temperature heating, electric furnaces have made their way to certain industries (aluminum, secondary steel, etc.) but have not yet managed to pervade beyond these. However, there are multiple initiatives that look into this today, particularly in cement and petrochemicals, sectors especially hard to transform (Wilhemsson *et al.*, 2018; Scott, 2019).

Electricity is also highly versatile. There is nothing as similar to one electron as another electron, wherever it comes from. It is a tradeable currency, very similar to banknotes (Barnard, 2017). This means that electric energy can be shared and exchanged in a variety of ways that have not yet been designed, and this across all its users. It is true that there are technical issues related to balancing power grids with multidirectional flows of energy, be it in terms of frequency or voltage control of the system, ensuring the safe, coordinated operation of decentralized sources. This has been widely discussed in many reports. But again, we have only just begun to explore the potential of electronics. Already, embedded electronic systems in solar farms have been able to recreate the physical inertia of the large rotating machines that power our lives today and contribute to frequency control, ensuring the proper functioning of all appliances we connect to the grid.

With ubiquitous, digitally enabled and versatile electricity, the decentralized potential of renewable and particularly solar technologies could thus be magnified. It would then become possible to decentralize production wherever solar hits Earth, no longer having to rely only on large (centralized) facilities, which limit its potential. Solar panels can be installed on rooftops or even replace building walls as previously discussed, capturing every fragment of light available and providing momentous amounts of energy.

The combination of solar energy and electricity thus has the potential to enable a massive decentralization of energy production, down to the last mile of use. Solar energy obviously runs only during daytime, so some will say that we do not know what to do with all that energy available and that most of it will eventually be wasted, as there will be no demand to consume it when it is available. Again, this topic is heavily debated in most energy organizations and at conferences.

I already mentioned how Dorr and Seba (2020) see it rather as an opportunity to provide access to near-zero cost energy, in a new "supply following" energy system. This is also where the large innovations in mass storage come into play. The technological potential of affordable, mass-scale storage is only years away from being realized, and with it will come the ability to store these vast amounts of renewable energy and reuse them at times of production scarcity. Storage energies have followed a learning curve similar to that of solar technologies, since they essentially follow the same paradigm: infinitely scalable, with costs that keep dropping as demand increases. Again, we have seen only the beginning of its development. With infinitely scalable solar and storage technologies, developing on a ubiquitous, digitally enabled, and versatile electricity network, energy will become much more decentralized, reducing dependencies at every level; a complete paradigm shift with increasing levels of return.

Pushing the envelope even further, can we imagine the emergence of mass-distributed storage and third-generation PV directly into appliances in the coming decades, effectively transforming each of them into near-autonomous devices? How far are we from such a feat?

Resilient resources system

To sum up, a sustainable resources system is achievable, powered by new technologies. First, digitally enabled circularity could help generate materials independence, a more decentralized materials market, and increasing returns (as resources are reused across several lifetimes). Also, the combination of digital technologies, biotechnologies, and nanotechnologies will offer a whole variety of new materials designs, which will effectively reduce dependencies on scarce resources. This will have a significant impact on the actual energy devoted to sourcing and transforming these elements in terms of what energy will be used and for which purpose. Then, biotechnology-engineered food components have the potential to dramatically increase access to food locally, reduce its environmental impact, and optimize health — again with increasing returns over time — while significantly reducing the need for water (hence mitigating scarcity) in a context of growing stress on the food and water supply chains. This will also transform the energy system as a result, with a much greater reliance on electricity. Finally, energy itself will change, building on the growing potential of infinitely scalable renewable (solar) and storage technologies, developing on a ubiquitous, digitally enabled, and versatile electricity backbone. This means cheaper and localized energy resources, which are hence more resilient. The landscape of resources will thus dramatically change over time and move toward a more decentralized, more resilient, and more sustainable one.

Resilient Trade

The same approach can be taken to trade, our second theme. Trade is essential for a thriving economy. It allows for sustained competition, increased economies of scale and specialization, and, ultimately, lower prices. And trade has been around for millennia. Today, it represents around 35–40 percent of global GDP, and it has significantly expanded in the last decades.

Global but fragile

There is logic in this. First, a relatively long period of peace, with the last geographic frontier collapsing with the Soviet Union in the early 1990s. Second, the search for cheaper labor costs in order to gain competitive advantage, notably for basic goods. This led to the significant development and optimization of logistic systems, whose costs plummeted. This is not to say that these costs have gone down to zero, but transportation costs barely represent 5 percent of total costs of goods sold in well-handled systems (Alicke and Losch, 2010; Snowdale, 2009). With logistics costs being a fraction of labor costs, the globalization of goods trade has significantly expanded. With new economies opening up, flows of capital have also soared in a quest for higher returns on investment. The three decades that have just passed have thus witnessed an increasing entanglement of economies, with growing dependencies of all kinds. This has been essentially for the better, since it helped many countries around the world improve their standard of living and helped wealthy countries get even wealthier (Petit, 2021). The global logistics system, in a quest for higher efficiency, also evolved toward lower levels of stock, in lean, agile, and almost on-demand supply chains.

More efficient, more productive, yet more fragile. The Covid-19 crisis of 2020 brutally exposed the fragility of the trade system based on "close to zero" stock levels, revealing major dependencies of one country on another, and essentially of most of the world's economy on China. This prompted, in the fury of the moment, many to argue for the relocalization of industries, without considering the extraordinary burden that this would place on the cost of goods and the consequential impact on inflation and economic development. At the time of writing, this problem is far from being resolved. In fact, political posturing seems to have taken center stage in the competition for votes from those who have just lost their jobs. Yet, beyond the speeches, no one has really pulled the numbers. And they will probably be disastrous, when considering like-for-like relocalizations.

Circularity, again

Yet, reshoring may well happen, but probably not in the way some have thought it out, and certainly not in such a short time frame. Technology could — again — play a critical role. First, circularity is a powerful enabler of reducing dependencies on resources. We have seen that. In addition, circularity is also (and maybe essentially so) about extending the lifetime of products to reduce the need for new goods. Circularity services such as repair, refurbishment, or retro-fitting services have the potential to give products a second life. Let's remember that 99 percent of goods purchased are put to waste in less than six months. A proper, decentralized service sector could thus significantly enable the reduc-tion of dependencies on trade and improve access to goods. Local services are a significant source of jobs, but they will only work provided the right supply chains are put in place. This is where digital technologies are likely to play a sig-nificant role going forward. I already discussed the emergence of such platforms, which trade goods in a peer-to-peer fashion. Associated with circularity services, this is an entire second-hand economy that could be developed, one where the accumulated stock of acquired goods becomes a major economic asset.

Decentralized manufacturing

Yet, as massive as this could potentially be, this is only the tip of the iceberg in terms of what technologies can do. First and foremost, centralized companies enjoy economies of scale, which can reach a significant percentage compared to decentralized factory setups but are also less flexible and reliant on complex and international supply chains. Decentralized setups are more agile, closer to their customer base. They deliver more quickly and can often support their customers more efficiently with local services, significant benefits that often justify a price premium. This is something that the Covid-19 supply shock exposed in 2020. The complexity of handling decentralized operations grows with the level of decentralization, however. This is where digital technologies play a critical role, optimizing flows of resources across factories and directly connecting those to evolving demand, in a permanent attempt to minimize stock levels and optimize the costs of goods sold. Enterprise Resource Planning (ERP) systems have been around for a long time, but it is always surprising to see how little they have pen-etrated the markets, with the exception of large corporations (Garrehy, 2014). I remember an interesting experience I had about ten years ago, when I worked in Russia. Russia is the largest country in the world, covering about one-eighth of its inhabitable land area. Any business operating in this country has to face significant supply chain issues. The customer we supported at the time struggled with this. A leader in the food and beverage industry, the company was losing millions per year due to poor logistics planning, with inventories running too high or too low, difficulties shipping from one place to another and planning accordingly, and, more importantly, often an inability to supply demand effectively as a result, yielding poor utilization of its assets. In a country the size of Russia, every single hiccup could take gigantic proportions and was hard to resolve. The company managed to overcome this unfortunate situation through the deployment of a number of digital technologies that helped it control almost all its operations remotely. The benefits were significant, and the company has been thriving since.

Going beyond, we have already seen that the digitization of factories also leads to significant improvements in the efficiency of running industrial operations. However, the industry of the future will be largely unstaffed and operated remotely. As manufacturing processes have standardized, a growing number of tasks can actually be performed by machines. With progress, the role of the operator in many factories is already to simply monitor the proper operation of the facility and perform maintenance activities on the machines. With growing remote connectivity and predictive maintenance operations, factories could soon find themselves deserted and monitored from a distant office location. This would also improve workforce safety, as many incidents in industrial operations often proceed from human errors.

With these evolutions, it is clear that the primary root of centralization and globalization, the search for cheap labor, has vanished. With an increasingly capital-intensive industrial setup, factories can now be relocated much closer to customers, the benefits largely outweighing the constraints. Unstaffed factories will progressively become the new norm. Fully digitized, they will be connected to their supply chain and customers' demand, and the flows across the enterprise will be available to the production manager in real time, from a distant location.

Additive manufacturing

But that is not all; traditional industry could transform even more radically. Additive manufacturing was first brought to the public in a 1974 article by David Jones in the *New Scientist Journal*. In the decades that followed, it slowly developed, essentially as an instrument to rapidly deploy product prototypes. The progress of these technologies, and that of digital design tools, has however been significant, and some believe that additive manufacturing could be on the verge of displacing many traditional subtractive manufacturing processes in the coming decade or so.

Subtractive manufacturing is extremely inefficient for mainly two reasons. First, the traditional process of constructing shapes with machines that cut and remold materials can waste up to 50 percent of the original material. Second, these shapes are by design fairly simple, thereby needing to be assembled (welded and screwed) together in later stages of the process to form more complex structures. Additive manufacturing does not operate like this. It adds layers of materials in stages, with limited to no waste, and since it operates in 3D based on a digital design, can execute fairly complex shapes. It has been found that additive manufacturing could help build lighter parts, with fewer materials and fewer needs for extra assembly afterward, and therefore greater robustness and an extended lifetime. The GE Catalyst aircraft engine was developed using this technique, and the results were outstanding: the engine had only 12 parts (against 885 parts in the initial design), with a reduction in the cost of production as a result (undisclosed), and a reduction in weight, hence fuel demand (AMFG, 2020).

Additive manufacturing also applies to many other sectors. Jezard (2018) believes that 25 percent of Dubai's buildings will be "3D-printed" by 2025. He has described best-in-class pilot projects that reached a 50 percent reduction in labor costs. The company ICON is one step further, as it says it is capable of "printing" a 60 m^2 home in less than one day at a cost of US\$10,000, soon to be US\$4,000 (Warren, 2018). This is 10–20 times lower than traditional costs of construction.

What makes additive manufacturing stand out is the complexity of the shapes it can produce. Digital technologies play a critical role, as design tools and computing power enable the design of these complex forms and then run them through the manufacturing process. Next, additive manufacturing is all about precision manufacturing, relying on advanced automation and electrical energy (precision heating and precision motion). Additive manufacturing is thus much more efficient from a material standpoint and also more precise. More importantly, it helps reduce the overall number of parts in assembly, increasing competitiveness and robustness and extending lifetime.

It is also more energy efficient, at least for a number of applications. Several studies have identified savings of above 50 percent in energy demand (AMFG, 2020; Kreiger and Pearce, 2013; Renzenbrink, 2013). Others are more cautious. In like-for-like process comparisons, certain processes have proven to be more energy-intensive with additive manufacturing, because they are slower to run (AMFG, 2020). The truth is that we lack a global study across all sorts of use cases to fully understand the exact state of play. It is highly probable though that, as with many innovations, the new applications of additive manufacturing will primarily replace extremely inefficient processes and industrial systems that they can disrupt, and not the others, at least not at first.

In short, additive manufacturing has the potential to reduce reliance on resources and make entirely automated operations possible (no labor). But, more importantly, it is decentralized in nature and could be scaled infinitely. Indeed, when it becomes democratized, one can imagine major disruptions in basic commoditized goods. Another key driver of a more resilient, decentralized society.

Software supersedes hardware

Another point is worth adding as well. Since the cost of manufacturing is expected to drop because of the combined effect of digitization, automation, and potentially additive manufacturing toward complete commoditization, the value of the product in the future will be less a function of the cost of goods sold and more of the cost of the design. It will shift away from physical reality (which will become a fraction of product cost) to a virtual one. Industry will become truly digitized, and production commoditized. With this move, again, increasing returns are to be expected, since the design of a product could be reutilized millions of times, while costing money only once. Goods will come at a fraction of their cost.

Happy deglobalization in an interconnected world?

To conclude, the future of trade is bound to evolve. Globalization has been the defining factor of the last few decades, especially after the collapse of the Soviet Union. It fostered a significant acceleration of global trade and more entanglements across nations. The new motto, after decades of chasing efficiency and cost reduction, is that of increased resiliency of nations, a probably populist claim when considering the inherent cost impacts of a "return" to the *ex ante* situation. However, technology holds significant promises and these will to a large extent unfold, at least for the most basic consumer goods. Circularity, digitally enabled and optimized decentralized manufacturing, and additive manufacturing are likely to come in at some point and restructure these segments. To a large extent, they have already made strides in different applications, but they still lack scale. Yet, as the progress in additive manufacturing continues — and on digital technologies and computing power — the landscape of industrial footprints will also evolve toward much greater localization and cheaper and more customized goods. Is there a better example to illustrate this than the vision of Erick Sprunk in 2018 (Nike Chief Operating Officer)? "One day, consumers will be able to buy a shoe design file from Nike and 3D print the shoe themselves"; a complete change in business model (Groot, 2018).

Obviously, all these changes in materials and goods trade across borders will have a significant impact on the energy system. We can picture flows of goods as transfers of energy "packets" across the world: they have their embodied energy (the energy required to manufacture them, including that of extracting the necessary materials to do so) and the energy required to carry them around. With decentralized, fully digitized production and potentially additive manufacturing, the impacts on the entire industrial value chain would probably be systemic. A lower need for goods (circularity) would reduce the footprint of manufacturing demand. A greater recourse to decentralized manufacturing would reduce the need to transport goods around the world. A greater use of novel additive manufacturing techniques could significantly impact the need for raw or refined materials (which could be partly or fully recycled). All this would add up and displace the entire primary industry sector, which happens to be the most energy-intensive (and polluting) sector of all. Thus, the future of trade will mainly be defined by technology, and that will significantly impact the future of the energy system as a result.

Resilient Society

The third of the key topics I want to look at here is that of the social system. Dunbar showed that a normal human being could not manage to maintain relations with more than 150 people at the same time. Yet, our societies have evolved into much larger groups. The invention of farming fueled this expansion. It coincided (possibly) with slight changes in climate, which made the transition to farming more favorable. What is interesting is that it emerged in several and distant regions of the world at pretty much the same time. The big discovery was that of securing food supplies for an entire year. However, this required a centralized form of organization with specialized duties for all. Farmers were supported by carpenters, millers, plowmen, bakers, etc. Land control was of the essence, alongside command of resources such as wood, water, etc. These emerging societies were dependent on controlling larger areas of land as their population expanded. And they did expand rapidly, supported by secured food resources. Our modern societies inherited these principles and are largely centralized. Empires but also nations emerged, which confronted each other in a permanent ballet of rising and falling. In doing so, they developed their own principles of organization and their own cultures, which were built on their heritage and marked them as different from those on the other side of the *limes*.

Also, the nature of these societies has been to expand themselves beyond their boundaries, to stretch their control in order to fuel the center. The more the center grows, the more land it needs to control, and the larger and more verticalized the society structure becomes. This is maybe because of the following principle: empires have been rising and collapsing in recent history because they tend to grow inexorably until their inner structures collapse under the weight of what they are actually trying to support. Arbib and Seba (2020), for instance, have shown that the Roman Empire was never able to control more than five million square kilometers. Their argument is that the social structures (and the capacities of technology at the time) did not make it possible to expand beyond this area without facing a risk of collapse. Every time the Roman generals tried, they faced defeat.

Another aspect of these modern society principles is that of inequalities. Despite modern outcries over the problem of inequalities, these lie at the heart of our societies. People tend to forget this, but inequalities have been around for as long as history can trace them. Slavery (and related forms, such as serfdom in Europe) has been a truly global trade for millennia, in every region of the world. Even ancient democratic structures such as the Greek or Roman societies were actually closer to oligarchies than to modern democracies. Looking at more recent history, Piketty (2014) has shown that inequalities were larger in the early 1900s than they are today. What is striking in his demonstration is that the two World Wars of the twentieth century and their devastations actually disrupted the permanent process of capital concentration. With the significant wealth redistribution that occurred when societies rebuilt themselves, some believed that modern democracies and modern social structures were at the heart of a more distributive system that enabled all to rise. But Piketty showed that slowly but surely, wealth inequalities began increasing again immediately after the war was over toward the levels of the early 1900s, which they have not fully met yet today. Currently, 8 percent of the global population owns 85 percent of global wealth, and 1 percent alone owns more than 50 percent. The current social construct, founded on the concentration of power and resources, leads to major inequalities in societies. The revolt of the populace is as old as history and a permanent threat to the powers in place. Everyone (in Europe at least) has learned about the jacqueries of the fourteenth century led by Jack Goodfellow (he was actually not the leader, but he gave his name to the revolts). It is textbook. The current social construct is fragile, always at the mercy of revolts and overthrows. These inequalities do not only form within societies but also across them. In the modern and interconnected global economy, wealth and capital transfers tend to benefit the rich. In the last 15 years, mature economies (the rich) captured over 56 percent of global wealth creation, despite representing 15 percent of the global population (Petit, 2021). And 30 percent of the world population still lacks access to convenient forms of energy today, notably in Africa, the last area of global population growth in the coming century.

Should we thus expect this situation to continue? And with significant demographic pressure from new economies, or the growing impact of climate change, will the balance across nations endure or will it be put in check?

Again, technologies can help change the paradigm, for better or for worse. They will do it on several fronts. I identify four of them.

Information

The first one is that of information. Some people believe that the distributed press of the fifteenth century gave rise to the religious wars of the sixteenth and seventeenth centuries and ultimately to the democratic revolutions of the eighteenth century. True enough, this invention revolutionized information, giving access to knowledge and hence informed opinions across the entire world. It also did so at a fraction of past costs, and as a result enabled the transmission of that information to the multitude. The information system then barely changed for four centuries. It just kept improving with the invention of the press, the radio, and then the TV.

The Internet is another invention, but this time very different. Again, we have seen only a tiny bit of it. The Internet is a step similar to what the distributed press represented in the fifteenth century. This time, information is free and available to all, at any time and in real time. Information has been a luxury for a long time. The Internet put an end to that. Information is not a luxury anymore; it is free. Google — Alphabet, the company that reinvented information — has the fifth-largest market capitalization in the world, with a net worth close to US$1,000 billion in 2020 (Statista, 2020). With the rise of free information, anyone now has equal access to any piece of information and has the capacity (theoretically at least) to make sense of it and form an opinion of their own.

Of course, this tsunami of information also leads to fake news and misinterpretations. What is now becoming a luxury is the ability to make sense of this deluge. Yet, the infinite potentialities of this revolution remain to be discovered. Information — when not manipulated — is a powerful equalizer.

Education

A second front is that of education. Quality access to education is one of the 17 Sustainable Development Goals of the United Nations. It is widely recognized that access to proper education is paramount to creating opportunities for development. There are currently around one billion children attending school, but there are also around 600 million who are unable to reach minimum proficiency levels in reading and mathematics (UNESCO, 2017). This learning crisis is a true global challenge in terms of inequality.

Access to higher education is even more difficult. Recent history in the United States has demonstrated that college students tend to come from society's upper classes and benefit from a scandalous system of cooptation (*New York Times*, 2020). But even without corruption at the highest levels of prestigious colleges, access to higher education in the United States and across the world is extremely restricted. I studied in the United States for two years 20 years ago and remember the extremely high tuition fees. I was fortunate enough to arrive with an advanced degree, which provided me with the right qualifications for taking a job there and get tuition for free. However, when you have no such luck, there is little option but to get your family to support you or take out expensive loans, which will take a toll on your budget for years to come. Hence, access to education remains reserved to those who are able to pay for it. The United States is probably a critical example of this, but other countries are not all that different. Despite "free" education in France, my own country, studies keep demonstrating that the vast majority of graduate students come from wealthy families. Why is that? Simply because they have had the chance to live in more educated surroundings and often to attend better high schools. Highly educated people tend to pass their luck on the next generation, and they fill prestigious universities around the world. Those are many seats that are not available to others. Inequalities start almost at birth, and too little can and has been done to change this unfortunate reality.

Again, however, technologies could change this to a certain extent. The arrival of Massive Open Online Courses has been spectacular. Progress made in this new form of online learning, which gives anyone access to remote teaching of the best quality, has been impressive. At the end of 2018, there were over 100 million students enrolled in at least one of the over 12,000 online courses available, from 900 universities (Shah, 2018). It still costs money (around US$20,000 to get a master's degree), but this is already cheaper than traditional programs, which are one and a half to five times more expensive. More importantly, these courses provide access to a form of education that would otherwise not be available. Of course, this concerns higher education, but one can imagine that it will spread and become widely available to lower levels of education, and that these technologies, deployed at scale, are a way to further erase differences and inequalities among people. The Covid-19 crisis, which is still in full swing at the time of writing, has demonstrated that it was in fact possible to educate children from a distance. I have seen it firsthand in Hong Kong: all schools were closed for nearly six months, but education went on. Why would this not progressively become more of the norm?

Future of work

The third front to consider here is access to work opportunities. In their essay "The New Digital Age," Eric Schmidt (previous CEO of Alphabet) and Jared Cohen (2013) describe a world of opportunities, where companies could contract with anyone from anywhere for specific jobs. They explain that this would create a lot of opportunities for work in regions where branches of large companies are not necessarily present and where the economy is not as developed. And indeed, a lack of integration into the global economy remains an important barrier, which nurtures inequalities. Access to global opportunities would represent a fantastic accelerator of opportunities.

This is already happening, by the way. Take the example of a previous book I wrote (or any other for that matter): it was written in Hong Kong, edited in Germany, and prepared for production in India. And it has been sold in the United States, among other countries. Remote work and structures are the new norm, but the further penetration of digital technologies could take it a step further. If the German publishing company that is editing the book today is contracting with a separate organization in India to drive production work, a standard process has been defined between these two companies. A specific company needs to be set up in India, with the right qualifications to drive the process.

What Schmidt and Cohen are talking about is going one step further and using more self-employed contractors to do specific work for a given company. As we have seen, more liquidity and flexibility in the system would exist to drive more opportunities to all by removing barriers to entry. Schmidt and Cohen acknowledge that significant issues, such as different social contract regulations (and overall social protection), would have to be resolved for this type of model to actually emerge. But this kind of nonfixed and possibly part-time, on-the-task job could attract people who are looking to complement their revenue, grow their skills, or manage their work-life balance.

Digital technologies bring opportunities. The question is to what extent regulatory authorities will let them do so. Very recently, the fast deployment of the Uber platform (an alternative to taxis) has raised a lot of questions on actual working conditions of Uber operators and the extent of their social protection, forcing Uber into updating its practices. The platform has continued to thrive, however, proving that these issues can probably be resolved.

This renewed access to work opportunities could be further fueled by the progressive penetration of distributed manufacturing solutions, such as additive manufacturing. Because such solutions can be built at scale, nothing prevents us from imagining that within a decade or so, it will become possible and rather affordable to actually build one's own manufacturing operations. I have a friend who has already made that decision. He purchased one of these machines and found himself able to actually manufacture a variety of (traditionally commoditized) pieces, which he then does not need to go out and purchase anymore, and which in addition he can finetune at will. However, this is still an expensive hobby. But, as for all these technologies, if development picks up eventually, then costs will probably follow the learning curves of mass production, significantly reducing prices. A substantial share of industry could then end up being displaced, as predicted (and mentioned above) by Eric Sprunk in 2018.

Today, around 10 percent of the workforce is self-employed. The figure is fairly consistent across all countries, except for India. Could it be that the future of work is that of a few corporations acting as platforms for running projects and a large majority of the workforce contributing to collaborative projects through networks in a more decentralized and autonomous economy?

Financing

The last front of social inequalities relates to access to financing. Again, this is a major barrier to development. Current wisdom is that capital is extremely cheap, and indeed it is. Only not for everyone! In fact, in most countries, people live without a bank account, simply because there is no bank around. In 2017, this applied to 30 percent of the global population (if we exclude children under 15) (Ritchie and Roser, 2019; Demirgüç-Kunt *et al.*, 2017).

Access to finance is a critical condition for development and investment, and hence for moving beyond an economy of subsistence only. New digital technologies bring new opportunities, notably microfinancing, exemplified by Dr. Muhammad Yunus (Microworld, 2020), or peer-to-peer financing. Blockchain could also make it possible to secure transactions between two individuals over time (including across countries), fulfilling a critical condition for driving such transactions and thus doing business.

More equal, more fragmented, yet interconnected?

There are thus four fronts on which digital technologies can potentially bring significant benefits and make the economy more inclusive: information, education, work, and access to finance. Now, what are the patterns common to these innovations I just described? All are, once again, infinitely scalable, highly decentralized, and bringing increasing rates of return. They are infinitely scalable, which means their costs plummet over time as adoption kicks in and expands. The cheaper they get, the faster the adoption, the greater the benefits. They are highly decentralized: they do not rely on complex development schemes, which are the norm in traditional industry and business today. Adoption is faster and potentially exponential, and the ease with which these technologies can be brought to the individual makes them even more relevant. Finally, they provide increasing rates of return. Most are platforms and, as for every platform, the more people are connected to it, the greater the benefits. For instance, the more contractors and companies join a network, the greater the choice and the greater the opportunities for work.

It is because of these patterns that these technologies are expected to pervade the economy in one form or another. In doing so, they will bring greater opportunities for more people. At the same time, they could lead to a more "equalized" world, where traditional social structures (particularly related to work, culture, etc.) are put under considerable pressure.

If these technologies hold the potential for greater equality in and thus resilience of societies, they could indeed shake them at what has been their core for centuries. The initial dream of the Internet was that of a "global village," where information and opportunities traveling around the world at light speed would help "equalize" and "uniformize" the globe. After 30 years, nations have picked up on digital technologies to try to control them within their own borders, at least to a certain extent. The current rivalry between China and the United States also (and maybe specifically so) applies to the digital world (Petit, 2021). Far from creating a "global village," the development of digital technologies has so far resembled a new competitive stake for nations.

However, there are other underlying trends that should not be discarded, such as the development of even more local bonds within nations themselves, be it regional movements or local communities. Against all initial ideas, rather than uniformizing the world, digital technologies may end up being better suited to reconnecting local communities. Facebook is emblematic of this. The overwhelming majority of Facebook connections are between traditional and close friends. Facebook recreates and fluidifies existing relations. It helps rebuild the small community of 150 people described by Dunbar. Could it thus be that, against the initial vision of a globalized world, digital technologies will ultimately help build a more decentralized world at a level that is ever more granular than that of nations, yet interconnected? What would it mean to these nations? Would it bring peace or conflict? Notwithstanding these developments' critical potential for good, the jury is still out on their long-term implications.

The Next Stage of Our Social Construct Will Be Decentralization

Let's wrap up. I made the argument that our economy is fragile. On the one hand, our extractive economy depends on an ever-growing amount of resources. Because these are unevenly distributed, this creates dependencies across nations that get amplified over time. Since resource extraction also follows decreasing rates of return, the cost of materials grows over time. This will be accelerated by the actual growth in demand, which is projected to nearly double by 2050.

Our economy is also global, and with that come significant dependencies and potential imbalances between nations. The current US/China trade war, which is raging at the time of writing, is an example of such issues: imbalances have piled up over time, creating instability and uncertainty in global trade. Another example is the Covid-19 crisis, which basically put the economy to a stop for a significant part of 2020.

Finally, the foundations of social cohesion are fragile: there are significant inequalities — within and between societies — in a world where demographic pressure (from the poor) intensifies, wealthy populations age, and information is made available in real-time. How long can the historical paradigm of verticalization, hierarchization, and differentiation prevail?

Technology to the rescue

Because these issues are quite acute right now and are intensifying, one can expect that changes will occur in the coming decades. And technology, as is my argument, will be one powerful force of change among others; a positive force that will bring significant benefits.

First, the world economy's extreme reliance on resources could be mitigated. Circularity developments could significantly tame the demand for materials, while research on new materials could remove dependencies. Biotechnology and precision farming could redefine agriculture, in a context of growing demand and limited suitable available land in some regions. Renewable energy has the potential to supply (with current technologies) 25 times the global final energy demand, with endowments in every region that largely exceed their needs. A new paradigm of less reliance on finite and distant resources is thus on its way.

The same applies to trade. Circularity can significantly help reduce trade dependencies, notably through the greater recourse to lifetime extension and associated services. The automation of manufacturing is also a powerful enabler of a more decentralized manufacturing setup. Over time, manufacturing tended to delocalize to cheap labor countries, because labor was an important part of the cost of goods sold and largely exceeded the additional cost of logistics. With automation, this trend can now be reversed, and technology will probably bring industrial setups closer to their demand because of the inherent advantages of producing in proximity to customers. Finally, additive manufacturing is likely to expand, help further distribute manufacturing, and commoditize the production of specific goods. This will probably start with basic goods (that are already largely commoditized) as well as with repair, but it could possibly extend beyond these sectors and displace more traditional ones, such as construction.

Technologies could also help reshape social relations toward less inequalities. There are four main drivers of inequalities, or barriers to personal development: the lack of access to information, education, work opportunities, and financing. Technologies offer the potential to change the current paradigm. The Internet already provides real-time, free information to all, in a way that was simply unimaginable years ago, and we are just two decades into the Internet transition. Access to education is also on the cusp of being revolutionized with the mass deployment of online open courses, a major driver of equality across social groups: costs of education are going down and the reliance on historical networks is losing its importance. Challenges are still massive, but online education could boost the average level of education and transform societies more radically than anything else. Access to work could also be significantly improved, particularly for those living in countries that still lack integration into global economic trade. This could further redefine the future of work toward more task-based contractor jobs within project-based organizations. There are fears that this would level work down and create precariousness, but it does not need to end that way. These technologies also have the potential to bring more "fluidity" to work and thus remove barriers and create further opportunities. Access to finance is the last of these, with technologies expected to make it possible to replace (or leapfrog) inadequate financing systems in specific countries and offer a development alternative to the many who are still unbanked.

More decentralization

The patterns common to all these innovations described in this and previous chapters are that they are infinitely scalable and highly decentralized, and that they bring increasing rates of return over time. In other words, they will roll out at a rapid pace because their costs will plummet over time. They will also create positively reinforcing loops of innovation, since they tend to provide increasing rates of return over time. The more the technology develops, the greater the benefits. Finally, they are highly decentralized, to a point where they can redefine some of our current notions of granularity in control and understanding. To take just a few examples from the above: could we imagine that materials extraction will become a thing of the past if scientists are able to rebuild the periodic table with new elements designed in labs, thanks to the ability to now work effectively (and affordably!) at an atomic scale? What would happen to the entire industry footprint as a result? What about additive manufacturing? Could we imagine that all our basic goods (furniture, toys, clothes, equipment parts) become available at a fraction of their past cost?

The bottom line of all this is that the world, fueled by inexorable and positive technology development, is moving toward a more decentralized setup, which should be encouraged because of the increased resilience it brings to the fragile construct of living together. Moreover, this more decentralized society will return resources and opportunities to people at a fraction of their cost. In short, this decentralized society is about progress, and with it, greater abundance for all will come.

Major impact on the energy system

This kind of transition will obviously have a large impact on the energy system, which will follow these evolutions in demand (as it always did).

First, some parts of the energy system will get stranded. As we have seen in the previous chapter, circularity could bring systemic efficiency to the industrial sector. This could be accelerated by the development of additive manufacturing, which would further displace some commoditized manufacturing applications. Additionally, one can think of global trade and logistics across regions as gigantic moves of energy "packets" (embodied energy). The decentralization of the economy would thus also, beyond efficiency, redefine where energy is actually consumed and where it is not, while significantly reducing demand for freight transport overall.

Demand in mature economies that have been mainly dependent on imports for decades would certainly pick up in such a context, while the expected growth of certain new economies could eventually be altered; expectations that are at odds with current wisdom.

Finally, most of these new technologies will depend on the electricity backbone. Consequently, electricity will probably become the bloodline of the energy system, simply because it is much better at end-use. Electricity is ubiquitous (already here, everywhere, and available) and versatile (allowing loose coupling across all applications), and electric processes (and electronics) outperform all alternatives because they can be applied in a much more granular way and show time responses that are unmatched.

Of course, one of the big issues with electricity is that of its production and transport. It is inefficient (with fossil fuels) and thus expensive. However, the new technologies considered in this book can take up part of that demand, particularly for low-density needs, at costs that could never be matched by any other alternative. Near-free energy! Let's take the example of autonomous devices. With the costs of third-generation PV and storage plummeting to ridiculous levels over time, the cost impact of an "autonomous" appliance would become negligible. This negligible impact would translate into almost free energy for 25 years to come.

To which extent can such technologies scale up? And how does that impact the centralized energy infrastructure we have been living with for a century or so?

It will probably be a significant disruption. Vaclav Smil (2015) does not agree with this. In his book on power densities, he reaches the conclusion that renewable energies would have a hard time coping with modern energy demand, because most uses are high density, while renewable energies are typically low density. Despite Smil's very commendable effort, I would argue once more that granularity matters here. For instance, Smil argues that decentralized renewable energies will never be able to pick up the load demand of a large office building, so their penetration will remain limited. However, the load demand of a large office building consists of various elements, and some of them can be powered by decentralized energies, while others cannot. On top of that, the study does not account for potential technological advances in the coming decades.

I can try to map this out in order to come up with an average figure of what could be at stake. I use the 2018 final energy demand mix and break it down into its various usages, grouped by density level (Andrae and Edler, 2015; Energy Information Administration, 2018, 2020; Gaglia *et al.*, 2019; Mills, 2013; International Energy Agency, 2017; International Energy Agency, 2018; Petit, 2017). This is an estimate that can obviously be challenged, but that has not been made in detail so far.

Low-density needs (IT appliances, lighting) represent around 5 percent of final energy demand, and they are clearly eligible for disruption in the short run. Medium-density needs include traditional appliances, low-temperature heating (in buildings or factories), and light-duty transport. These range from 1 kW to around 100 kW. These medium-density applications can already be powered by batteries (or any other energy storage solution), though only intermittently as they require charging. This can work for specific uses, such as transport, or within the built environment. These specific uses add up to around 60 percent of total energy demand. The remaining energy needs require larger amounts of power output and must operate continuously, making them currently unfit for such decentralized provisions.

The outcome of this though is that around two-thirds of current energy demand could, over time, become eligible for such low-density provisions of energy; a massive number! This is a sizable transition, even if it happens only partly, and should consequently not be dismissed. At this level, it would deeply transform the energy system and, as I have argued throughout, we better be prepared, because most ongoing debates will probably make little sense if in the end, the new footprint of the energy system strongly diverges from what we expected it to be!

Drivers of and challenges to adoption

This transition is likely inevitable, at least in part, because of the key drivers that will push adoption. Resiliency will of course be one such key driver. The ability to prevent resource shortages — whether in terms of materials, food, water, and energy — plays a critical role. However, the concept also extends to other domains of activity. Security of supply in an interconnected world becomes a crucial element of the discussion. This has long been the case for energy supply, particularly following the two oil crises of the 1970s, but it is expected to pervade other areas of economic activity as well, notably food, materials, industrial supply chains, and health- and safety-related products. In this regard, the Covid-19 crisis has exposed some of the gaps. Obviously, if resiliency is accompanied by increased productivity, as we have seen in the previous chapter, this will only accelerate adoption; a multi-benefit switch to modern technologies.

Progressivity will also prove to be a key driver of adoption (if done right), as mentioned in the previous chapter. Paramount in enabling adoption will be the ability to scale adoption progressively and gradually reinforce resiliency over time, while generating increasing rates of return or increased benefits thanks to network effects.

A last driver of adoption will be inclusion. Building a more decentralized society is also a way of increasing the inclusion of disadvantaged populations. In other words, create a vibrant local ecosystem that provides job, learning, and financing opportunities, and contribute to reducing social inequalities. This has always been a critical priority in local policies, and these innovations will likely make great strides if they are able to demonstrate their ability to improve inclusion, notably by providing low-skilled jobs. I experienced this firsthand in several conversations I had during the Covid-19 stimulus package discussions in 2020. In most of these conversations, which obviously had different flavors across different regions, the main question was always: how many jobs? Digital technologies have been heavily challenged in this process, as there is significant concern about their potential impact on local job markets. Some believe that more than half of current job types could be partially at risk with the widespread deployment of these new technologies. So far, there has been a lack of consensus on how many jobs would be created in return, and how easy it would be for the workforce to switch from one job to another (Petit, 2021). Yet, as we have seen, the deployment of these technologies could also provide significant benefits to the work environment, and more importantly to workforce training and upskilling.

Beyond these drivers, key challenges may however derail their unfolding. As in the previous chapter, progress in technology will prove crucial. Apart from what has already been described, the rise of decentralized industries is dependent on advancements of digital technologies, particularly the scaling up of additive manufacturing. Time will tell to what extent this new industry can find a starting point, scale, and cost reduction that is significant enough to enable new models to emerge. This will also have to be confirmed for larger corporations to adopt a more decentralized footprint for their manufacturing while remaining competitive.

Business models will also play a critical role. I have discussed the topic of circular value chains at length, and the imperative to competitively retrofit the existing building stock for the fast adoption of new technologies, so I will not elaborate on this topic. Yet, without those, deployment will probably be significantly slowed down. This will also be true for other areas of development, such as education or finance.

Policies will be of the utmost importance as well. Above, I described a more decentralized society, but with a specific flavor to it. The world that these technologies create is not entirely "localized," nor will it be entirely "globalized." It will in reality operate as a network of decentralized activities. For these innovations to thrive, free trade and exchange across regions will be paramount. This is how massive network effects can be created, leading to scalability and increasing rates of return over time. Without this, the pace of development will very probably slow down significantly, and potentially be halted in regions that do not have the capacity to fully control the end-to-end value chain. This will notably be true for developing the right competencies, with major discrepancies across regions (Petit, 2021). Education policies will therefore play a critical role. Beyond these, environmental and energy policies will also be needed to ramp up circular value chains and facilitate the adoption of new energy technologies.

Figure 1   Demand-driven innovations

Even if benefits are clear, it may take a significant time for industries to scale up if proper policies are not in place. More importantly, these environmental and energy policies will require the necessary balance between forceful transformation and a positive distribution of its effects across society. Without this, consensus across different parts of the society is unlikely to emerge (Figure 1).

A decentralized society

One of the most striking outcomes of this quick review is the potential impact that these innovations could have on the traditional way in which we look at infrastructures and value chains. These infinitely scalable, highly decentralized technologies that bring increasing rates of return over time have the potential to steer our societies toward greater decentralization, at a level that could challenge current social structures, for better and possibly worse. For millennia, the paradigm has been one of centralization and the concentration of power. The innovations described above do just the opposite. They lead toward fewer dependencies and a greater distribution of opportunities; in short, a world that is more decentralized, yet interconnected. And decentralization is likely to come with a feeling of greater abundance, whether in terms of accessing services or opportunities.

References

Alicke, K., and Lösch, M. (2010). *Lean and Mean: How Does Your Supply Chain Shape Up?* McKinsey & Company. https://www.mckinsey.com/~/media/mckinsey/dotcom/client_service/operations/pdfs/lean_and_mean-how_does_your_supply_chain_shape_up.pdf.

AMFG. (2020). "How Sustainable is Industrial 3D Printing?" March 10. https://amfg.ai/2020/03/10/how-sustainable-is-industrial-3d-printing/.

Andrae, A., and Edler, T. (2015). "On Global Electricity Usage of Communication Technology: Trends to 2030." *Challenges* 6: 117–57. https://doi.org/10.3390/challe6010117.

Arbib, J., and Seba, T. (2020). *Rethinking Humanity: Five Foundational Sector Disruptions, the Lifecycle of Civilizations, and the Coming Age of Freedom.* RethinkX, June. https://www.rethinkx.com/humanity.

Barnard, M. (2017). "7 Reasons The Future Is Electric." *Clean Technica*, November 12. https://cleantechnica.com/2017/11/12/7-reasons-future-electric/.

Demirgüç-Kunt, A., Klapper, L., Singer, D., Ansar, S., and Hess, J. (2017). "The Unbanked." In *Global Findex Database 2017: Measuring Financial Inclusion and the Fintech*

Revolution, 35–41. Washington, DC: International Bank for Reconstruction and Development/The World Bank. https://documents.worldbank.org/en/publication/documents-reports/documentdetail/332881525873182837/the-global-findex-database-2017-measuring-financial-inclusion-and-the-fintech-revolution.

Dorr A., Seba T. (2020). *Rethinking Energy 2020–2030*, RethinkX. https://www.rethinkx.com/energy.

Energy Information Administration. (2018). "Space Heating and Water Heating Account for Nearly Two Thirds of U.S. Home Energy Use." November 7. https://www.eia.gov/todayinenergy/detail.php?id=37433.

Energy Information Administration. (2020). "Electricity Consumption in the United States Was About 3.9 Trillion Kilowatthours (kWh) in 2019." December 22. https://www.eia.gov/energyexplained/electricity/use-of-electricity.php.

Energy Transitions Commission. (2019). *China 2050: A Fully Developed Rich Zero Carbon Economy.* Rocky Mountain Institute, November. https://www.energy-transitions.org/wp-content/uploads/2020/07/CHINA_2050_A_FULLY_DEVELOPED_RICH_ZERO_CARBON_ECONOMY_ENGLISH.pdf.

Food and Land Use Coalition. (2019). *Growing Better: Ten Critical Transitions to Transform Food and Land Use.* Global Consultation Report, September. https://www.foodandlandusecoalition.org/wp-content/uploads/2019/09/FOLU-GrowingBetter-GlobalReport.pdf.

Frankopan, P. (2016). *The Silk Roads: A New History of the World.* London: Bloomsbury Publishing.

Gaglia, A, Dialynas, E, Argiriou, A., Kostopoulo, E., Tsiamitros, D., Stimoniaris, D., and Laskos, K. (2019). "Energy Performance of European Residential Buildings: Energy Use, Technical and Environmental Characteristics of the Greek Residential Sector — Energy Conservation and CO_2 Reduction." *Energy & Buildings* 183 (January): 86–104. https://doi.org/10.1016/j.enbuild.2018.10.042.

Garrehy, P. (2014). "Centralized vs. Decentralized Manufacturing." *Industry Today* 17, no. 10. https://industrytoday.com/centralized-vs-decentralized-manufacturing/.

Groot, A. (2018). "The Future At Nike: 3D Printing Customized Shoes At Home." Digital Initiative, last updated November 14. https://digital.hbs.edu/platform-rctom/submission/the-future-at-nike-3d-printing-customized-shoes-at-home/.

Grosse, F. (2010). "Le découplage croissance/matières premières. De l'économie circulaire à l'économie de la fonctionnalité: vertus et limites du recyclage." *Revue Futuribles* 365, July 1. https://www.futuribles.com/fr/revue/365/le-decouplage-croissance-matieres-premieres-de-lec/.

Hariri, Y. N. (2014). *Sapiens: A Brief History of Humankind.* London: Harvill Secker.

Hockfield, S. (2019). *The Age of Living Machines: How Biology Will Build the Next Technology Revolution.* New York: W. W. Norton & Company.

Immelt, J. (2016). "Digital Industrial Transformation." Presentation at the GE Oil & Gas annual meeting of 2016. https://annualmeeting.bakerhughes.com/sites/g/files/cozyhq381/files/2018-09/GEAM2016_Jeff_Immelt_GE.pdf.

International Energy Agency ©. (2017). *Digitalisation and Energy.* November. https://www.iea.org/reports/digitalisation-and-energy.

International Energy Agency ©. (2018). *World Energy Outlook 2018.* November. Paris: IEA Publishing. https://www.iea.org/reports/world-energy-outlook-2018.

International Renewable Energy Agency ©. (2015). *Renewable Energy in the Water, Energy and Food Nexus.* January. https://www.irena.org/documentdownloads/publications/irena_water_energy_food_nexus_2015.pdf.

IronMatrix. (2020). "Iron Matrix. Clean Energy Structures." http://www.ironmatrix.com/.

Jezard, A. (2018). "One-Quarter of Dubai's Buildings Will Be 3D Printed by 2025." World Economic Forum, May 15. https://www.weforum.org/agenda/2018/05/25-of-dubai-s-buildings-will-be-3d-printed-by-2025.

Kreiger, M., and Pearce, J. (2013). "Environmental Life Cycle Analysis of Distributed Three-Dimensional Printing and Conventional Manufacturing of Polymer Products." *ACS Sustainable Chemical Engineering* 1, no. 12: 1511–19. https://doi.org/10.1021/sc400093k.

Labbé, J.-F. (2016). "Les limites physiques de la contribution du recyclage à l'approvisionnement en métaux." *Responsabilité et Environnement* 82 (April): 45–56. http://www.annales.org/site/re/2016/re82/RE-82-Article-LABBE.pdf.

Material Economics. (2019). *Industrial Transformation 2050 — Pathways to Net-Zero Emissions from EU Heavy Industry.* Cambridge: CISL. https://materialeconomics.com/latest-updates/industrial-transformation-2050.

McKinsey & Company. (2017). *A Future That Works: Automation, Employment and Productivity.* McKinsey Global Institute, January. https://www.mckinsey.com/~/media/mckinsey/featured%20insights/Digital%20Disruption/Harnessing%20automation%20for%20a%20future%20that%20works/MGI-A-future-that-works-Executive-summary.ashx.

Microworld. (2020). "About Microcredit." https://www.microworld.org/en/about-microworld/about-microcredit.

Mills, M. (2013). *The Cloud Begins with Coal. Big Data, Big Networks, Big Infrastructure, and Big Power.* National Mining Association and American Coalition for Clean Coal Electricity, August. https://www.tech-pundit.com/wp-content/uploads/2013/07/Cloud_Begins_With_Coal.pdf.

New York Times. (2020). *College Admissions Scandal.* Dossier. https://www.nytimes.com/news-event/college-admissions-scandal.

Petit, V. (2017). *The Energy Transition: An Overview of the True Challenge of the 21st Century.* Cham, Switzerland: Springer.

Petit, V. (2018). *The New World of Utilities: A Historical Transition toward a New Energy System*. Cham, Switzerland: Springer.

Petit, V. (2021). *The Future Global Order. The Six Paradigm Changes That Will Define 2050*. London: World Scientific Publishing.

Piketty, T. (2014). *Capital in the Twenty-First Century*, translated by A. Goldhammer. Cambridge, MA: Belknap Press.

REN21. (2017). *2017 Renewables Global Futures Report: Great Debates towards 100% Renewable Energy*. Paris: REN21 Secretariat. https://www.ren21.net/wp-content/uploads/2019/06/GFR-Full-Report-2017_webversion_3.pdf.

Renzenbrink, T. (2013). "3D Printing Beats Mass Production in Energy Efficiency." *Elektor Magazine*, October 11. https://www.elektormagazine.com/articles/3d-printing-beats-mass-production-in-energy-efficiency.

Ritchie, H., and Roser, M. (2020). "Fossil Fuels." Our World in Data. https://ourworldindata.org/fossil-fuels.

Rodrigue, J.-P. (2020). *The Geography of Transport Systems*, 5th ed. New York: Routledge.

Scott, A. (2019). "European Chemical Makers Plan 'Cracker of the Future.'" *Chemical and Engineering News*, September 4. https://cen.acs.org/business/petrochemicals/European-chemical-makers-plan-cracker/97/i35.

Shah, D. (2018). "By The Numbers: MOOCs in 2018." *The* Report by Class Central, December 11. https://www.classcentral.com/report/mooc-stats-2018/.

Smil, V. (2015). *Power Density: A Key to Understanding Energy Sources and Uses*. Cambridge, MA: MIT Press.

Snowdale, R. (2009). "The Impact of Transportation Services & Logistics Costs on Corporate Profitability." Freight Shipping Blog, DSI, February 17. http://www.dsi-tms.com/freight-shipping-blog/bid/8479/The-Impact-of-Transportation-Services-Logistics-Costs-on-Corporate-Profitability.

Statista. (2020). "The 100 Largest Companies in the World by Market Value in 2019." https://www.statista.com/statistics/263264/top-companies-in-the-world-by-market-value/.

Suman, S. (2020). The Ricardian Theory of Rent (With Diagram). Economics Discussions. December 21. https://www.economicsdiscussion.net/rent/ricardian-theory-of-rent/the-ricardian-theory-of-rent-with-diagram/12612.

Tubb, C., and Seba T. (2019). *Rethinking Food and Agriculture 2020–2030*. RethinkX, September. https://www.rethinkx.com/food-and-agriculture.

UN Environment Programme. (2019). *Global Resources Outlook. 2019: Natural Resources for the Future We Want*. Report of the International Resource Panel. Nairobi: United Nations Environment Programme. https://www.resourcepanel.org/reports/global-resources-outlook.

UNESCO (2017). "6 Out of 10 Children and Adolescents Are Not Learning a Minimum in Reading and Math." April 15. http://uis.unesco.org/en/

news/6-out-10-children-and-adolescents-are-not-learning-minimum-reading-and-math.

University of Minnesota. (2015). "Unraveling the Complex Web of Global Food Trade." *Phys.org*, February 11. https://phys.org/news/2015-02-unraveling-complex-web-global-food.html.

Warren, T. (2018). "This Cheap 3D-Printed Home Is a Start for the 1 Billion Who Lack Shelter." *The Verge*, March 12. https://www.theverge.com/2018/3/12/17101856/3d-printed-housing-icon-shelter-housing-crisis.

Wilhelmsson, B., Kollberg, C., Larsson, J., Eriksson, J., and Eriksson, M. (2018). CemZero. A Feasibility Study Evaluating Ways to Reach Sustainable Cement Production via the Use of Electricity. Vattenfall and Cementa, December 17. https://www.cementa.se/sites/default/files/assets/document/65/de/final_cemzero_2018_public_version_2.0.pdf.pdf.

World Bank Group. (2020a). "GDP per Capita (Current US$)." https://data.worldbank.org/indicator/NY.GDP.PCAP.CD.

World Bank Group (2020b). "Employment in Agriculture (% of Total Employment) (Modeled ILO Estimate)." June 21. https://data.worldbank.org/indicator/SL.AGR.EMPL.ZS.

Yergin, D. (2009). *The Prize: The Epic Quest for Oil, Money and Power*. New York: Simon & Schuster.

CHAPTER 6

When We Reconcile with Our Original Beliefs

"I think the environment should be put in the category of our national security. Defense of our resources is just as important as defense abroad. Otherwise what is there to defend?" (R. Redford)

Renewable energy, digital, and atomic-scale technologies will be the bedrock of upcoming innovations. These innovations will primarily tackle existing issues and opportunities. They will be aimed at solving problems and providing better services, and possibly develop new services that have not yet been invented, driven by the goal of making social progress and providing greater abundance. And with these innovations, new demand patterns will emerge, which will ultimately transform the energy system and drive the upcoming energy transition.

I have divided these issues and opportunities into three arguments. I already explored the potential of running our economy more efficiently and making our societies more resilient. I now explore our third argument, that of how our civilization threatens its own existence by how little consideration it has for the planet's resources.

This unsustainable use of resources mainly revolves around two issues: pollution and climate change. These two are entangled but are slightly different. First, our civilization generates significant amounts of pollution of the air, water, and soil, all critical resources for maintaining sustainable life on Earth. Around 40 percent of rivers in the United States are said to be too polluted for fishing or swimming, while one-third of the world's topsoil is said to be already degraded (and most of it could be by 2080). Marshall (2011) also mentions that 40 percent of arable land in China is already polluted, a national security issue. Pollution comes in various forms and from various causes.

Part of this pollution, because of its sheer size, has also triggered irreversible modifications of the climate balance, something we refer to as climate change. The name of the game in the coming decades will be to avert the effects of both pollution and climate change, even though the damage cannot be entirely repaired. At the very least, however, the trend can be reversed.

I gave a brief introduction of the issue in the first part of this book. Now, it is time to dig into it further in order to understand fully how upcoming innovations could help tackle these issues.

Three Revolutions Must Take Place

Air pollution

Air pollution can be both indoor and outdoor. Indoor air pollution is easier to understand. It accounts for all traditional solid fuels that are burned to provide cooking facilities (or light and heat). This includes wood, crops, dung, or waste, and particularly applies to low-income, rural economies. Today, 40 percent of the global population is estimated to rely on such traditional fuels for cooking. This number was above 55 percent 30 years ago. It dropped in most regions of the world, but some still rely heavily on such fuels. About 80 percent of the population in Africa and 60 percent of that in South and Southeast Asia still have no access to clean cooking facilities. As a result, this type of pollution is directly responsible for 1.6 million deaths per year (Ritchie and Roser, 2019). 70 percent of these deaths are concentrated in Asia, with India being one of the key regions. Africa comes second. Other regions are much less impacted.

These numbers have considerably improved in the last decades. The number of deaths surpassed 2.7 million 30 years ago. Yet, while these numbers have decreased everywhere, we should take into account that half of this decrease has come from modernizing China. Other regions have not necessarily experienced major breakthroughs, particularly Africa, South and Southeast Asia. Indoor air pollution is thus a major and contemporary driver of pollution.

The second source of air pollution is outdoor air pollution. Outdoor air pollution comes from various pollutants that are released in the atmosphere and combine into toxic gases. They are generally emitted by gas exhaust pipes from cars, by industrial processes surrounding cities, or by thermal electricity production. They include sulfur dioxide, nitrogen oxide, volatile organic compounds, ammonia, ozone, and, more importantly, particle matters, which often stem from a combination of dust and hydrocarbons (Ritchie and Roser, 2019).

What is striking is the little progress that has been made globally in 30 years. True, emissions in mature economies have improved. During the last 30 years, sulfur dioxide emissions have been slashed tenfold on average, and nitrogen oxide and volatile organic compounds twofold in the United States and fivefold in the United Kingdom. Particle matters have decreased by 80 percent for those that are 10 micrometers or less (PM10) and by respectively 25 and 50 percent for the United States and the United Kingdom for those measuring 2.5 micrometers or less (PM2.5, the most dangerous ones, as they can penetrate the lungs). Yet, the situation in new economies is far from bright and has worsened in a number of regions. If we concentrate on PM2.5, 50 percent of the world's population (30 percent in China and India alone) lives in areas with very low air quality or concentrations above 35 micrograms per cubic meter. While average concentration in mature economies is now around 10–15 micrograms per cubic meter, it ranges from 40 to 50 in Africa, the Middle East, and East and Southeast Asia, and tops 80 in India. The situation of ozone concentration, which stems from a reaction between the sun and some of the chemicals emitted from fossil fuel burning, has virtually not improved, with concentrations in the atmosphere that are globally equivalent to what they were 30 years ago. The same can be said about ammonia, which is essentially used as a fertilizer in agriculture (Ecavo, 2016; Health Effects Institute, 2019; Pirlea and Huang, 2019; State of Global Air, 2020). Outdoor air pollution is still a major global issue.

While some improvements have been made in mature economies and the smog has radically diminished in some of the major cities of Europe and the US, outdoor air pollution is turning into a global health issue in most new economies of the world, particularly in India. The consequence is that globally, the number of deaths from pollution has virtually not decreased in 30 years. In regions such as the Middle East, India, or China, this number represents up to 10 percent of total deaths, and it surpasses 3.5 million deaths a year globally. All this is caused by the extensive use (and concentration) of fossil fuels, as well as traditional industrial production techniques, and a significant recourse to fertilizers (also driven by fossil fuels) in agriculture.

Yet, there is another source of even more insidious air pollution. One that might not impact health in the short run as much but one that could have dramatic consequences going forward: greenhouse gas (GHG) emissions. GHG emissions are composed of a variety of gases that contribute to modifying the constitution of the atmosphere and increasing the level of heat trapped in it, hence increasing global temperatures. The Intergovernmental Panel on Climate Change (2007, 2014) has long made the case for the impact of human activities on climate change. While the reality of global warming has also long been unanimously acknowledged by most scientists around the world, it took decades to make the case for its root causes. The Earth cycle is indeed a highly complex system, and there is a multitude of factors that can explain why the climate is changing, from astronomic evolutions and sun irradiation changes to volcanic activity evolutions and transformations in oceans and vegetation (Petit, 2021).

However, with the significant progress made in climate modeling, the IPCC has progressively refined the science and has indubitably concluded that human activities have a negative effect on the climate. "Anthropogenic"

GHG emissions have been building up in the atmosphere to concentrations that would now be enough to alter the way global heat exchanges take place, leading to more heat from sun irradiation being trapped.

If we exclude water vapor (which is by large the first greenhouse gas), these GHG emissions mainly come in the form of carbon dioxide (75 percent) and methane (15 percent). They are not intrinsically bad for people. It is the buildup of their concentrations in the atmosphere that can potentially alter the climate. CO_2 emissions now top 400ppm, about 50 percent above preindustrial levels, and anthropogenic emissions are the main cause of this increase, according to the IPCC. There are also other gases within the GHG mix. Fluorinated gases, nitrogen oxide, and aerosols based on ozone mixed with other chemical substances in the air come into the equation as well. Of around 50 $GtCO_2$ equivalent per year of emissions, nearly 75 percent comes from energy production derived from fossil fuels, 20 percent comes from agriculture (notably methane), waste, and land management, and the remaining 5 percent from industrial processes (also based on fossil fuels). Carbon dioxide and methane have a significant warming impact. Yet, aerosols, which are mainly derived from ozone and particles in the air, partly negate those effects and cool the atmosphere (the smog prevents irradiation from sun and thus heating). It thus turns out that averting the significant negative health effects of pollution could in fact have a negative impact on mitigating global warming.

This is the sheer contribution of energy-related emissions which has triggered the current conversation on a necessary energy transition. According to the IPCC, emissions must be zeroed by 2050, and halved by 2030, an unprecedented challenge in history. Failure to achieve this would lead to rising temperatures above 1.5 degrees, triggering ecosystem transformations that we could find ourselves unable to adapt to.

Water pollution

A second form of pollution is that of water. I am lucky to live in the surroundings of Hong Kong, in a small estate called "Clear Water Bay." Every true Hong Konger would tell you it is one of the best places to be. It is quiet, full of nice houses on the hills, and endowed with a beautiful view of a magnificent bay. Indeed, I just need to go down the hill from where my home is located to reach the beaches, a few hundred meters away. At first, I was truly excited by the prospect of living so close to the South China Sea, and exhilarated by its smells when I moved there. Imagine my surprise when I reached the beach the first time! The beach had not been cleaned for some reason, and the tide had thrown an awful lot of garbage back onto the shore: plastic bottles, dressings, bandages, etc. Even a washing machine had run aground. I turned my back to the beach and never came back. However, an army of servants secretly cleans up the place every early morning. They pick up all this garbage, put it in plastic bags, and then dump it into landfills. Some of it ultimately finds its way back to the sea, and the process starts again. At least, beaches are more or less clean from 9 a.m. onward, for the swimmers and families to meet up and enjoy the apparent pleasure of swimming in the "Clear Water" bay area. However, while the beach is artificially cleaned, the waters are not. The situation is no better in other places in the world. The sad reality is that water is the best dissolvent and the easiest way of getting rid of waste. Because of this, humanity continues to pollute its waters to very worrying levels, and the example of the beach I just mentioned is sadly only the tip of the iceberg and certainly not the worst case.

Water comes in different forms. There is freshwater and ocean water. Freshwater can be found on the surface (we talk about surface water: rivers, lakes, etc.) or deep in the ground (groundwater or aquifers). All these "deposits" relate to one another within the water cycle. 2.5 percent of the planet's water is freshwater, and in fact only 1 percent is up for grabs (Denchak, 2018; Berkey, 2020).

With this, a significant part of the population lacks proper water access. Around 2.5 billion people worldwide (25–30 percent of the global population) are said to be living without proper access to sanitation (Pacific Institute, 2010).

There are two reasons for this. The first one is water stress. Most of Asia's population today, alongside that of North Africa and parts of the Middle East, lives in already stressed areas. People draw water resources largely in excess of what is renewable, leading to a significant depletion of surface water and aquifers. As an example, the Arabian aquifer system is estimated to be 80 percent depleted already (Petit, 2021), and it will not take long before it is fully exhausted, leading to a significant water crisis in the region. Estimates show that 50 percent of the global population will end up living in such areas by 2025. Since demand keeps growing (it should increase by 50 percent by 2050), these people could struggle to find available drinking water in their region by 2050, a major humanitarian issue (Denchak, 2018; Globe Water, 2020; World Health Organization, 2019). And climate change, which I discussed above, will be a significant aggravating factor.

The second reason for the lack of access to drinking water is pollution: 70 percent of water today is used for agriculture. The remaining 30 percent is split equally between energy production, industrial use, and domestic use. And pollution follows the same division. Agriculture is the biggest source of pollution, through the dissolution of chemicals and pesticides in both surface water and groundwater. Fertilizers based on ammonia and phosphorus are at the origin of algae formations in rivers and shores. The use of pesticides has increased five-fold since the 1960s (Citi, 2017). When polluted, groundwater may take thousands of years to be (naturally) depolluted (Denchak, 2018). Energy is also a cause of pollution. Energy production is highly dependent on water. For the extraction of primary energy resources such as coal, natural gas, or oil, water is used for fracking rocks or for purifying the resources extracted. The used water mixes up with chemicals and a variety of particles that contaminate it. Running and abandoned mines in the United States have been one of the root causes of surface water pollution in the last century. Water can also be used to cool thermal processes of electricity generation. Lots of water is required to do this — 1,000 to 10,000 liters for a ton of oil-equivalent energy (Citi, 2020). Water is also used in industry and in domestic contexts. Again, used water gets contaminated.

And the volumes of wastewater are staggering. The annual volume of wastewater represents six times that of all rivers in the world (Pacific Institute, 2010). It would be acceptable if wastewater could be treated before it is transferred back into the water cycle, rivers, aquifers, and oceans. However, 80 percent of wastewater in the world is disposed of untreated. That figure is much lower in mature economies, around 30 percent (but still!), and close to 100 percent in many new economies (Denchak, 2018; Globe Water, 2020). This is further aggravated by random waste. Back to my example of Hong Kong's beaches above, 8-10 million tons of plastics are dumped into the ocean every year, leading to the creation of plastic islands, also called the Great Pacific Garbage Patch (National Geographic, 2020; System IQ & The Pew Charitable Trust, 2020). And 70 percent of industrial waste in new economies goes directly into the water as well, untreated (Pacific Institute, 2010).

All this obviously has major consequences. First, for people: 25–30 percent of the global population is estimated to drink contaminated water on a regular basis, which would translate into 1.5 million deaths per year. That figure tops 50 percent in China (Denchak, 2018; Globe Water, 2020; World Health Organization, 2019); a major health and social issue in the making. Similarly, 70 percent of surface water in India is said to be unfit for consumption, and India is one of the most dynamic regions in terms of demographics in the coming decades (Hirani and Dimble, 2019). The other obvious impact is biodiversity. Excessive concentrations of nitrogen and phosphate tend to deplete oxygen in waters, reducing species' fertility, while concentrations of metals and chemicals lead to genetic modifications and health issues, which travel up the food chain as well. To conclude, water is an increasingly scarce resource that becomes even more depleted with climate change, and humanity is further reducing access to freshwater through a criminal handling of waste that results in a dramatic level of pollution of what could well become the most precious resource of the planet by 2050.

Soil pollution

The last form of pollution is that of soil. Pollution of soil is both direct and indirect (coming from water pollution or even air pollution, which deposits onto soil). The sources of pollution are the same. Agriculture and its waste, notably pesticides, and fertilizers contribute to contaminating soil. Overintensive agriculture also drains soil from its nutrients. Industrial and municipal waste is the other major source of soil pollution. Although 80 percent of waste is unharmful, nearly 20 percent is dangerous to the environment. This includes plastics, composite and synthetic materials, as well as chemicals that nature does not know how to break down quickly. The result is that these substances remain in the ground for longer and contaminate the environment (Bradford, 2018; Woodford, 2020). It takes 500 years to break down plastics. Other dangerous forms of waste are textiles (with plenty of chemicals and synthetic materials in them) and electronics, which are made of a variety of composite materials. Another source of soil pollution is mining, which removes fertile topsoil from the ground, in effect transforming possible arable lands into a moon-like desert. All these different forms of waste lead to soil contamination, depletion, and erosion, durable impacts that may take hundreds to thousands of years to recover from.

Not all countries perform in the same way when it comes to pollution management. OECD countries for instance generate up to five times more waste than sub-Saharan African countries, or around 2 kg of waste per person per day. Yet, they also manage it better. On average, these countries only landfill around 40–50 percent of their waste. Landfilling is also more regulated. The rest is incinerated or recycled. Sweden, for instance, recovers nearly 100 percent of used materials and recycles 30 percent of them. In comparison, Turkey only recovers 10 percent (FAO, 2018; Organisation for Economic Co-operation and Development, 2020), and this percentage is the same or lower in most new economies. In those regions, open landfills or dumps are the norm, and without oversight, they aggravate soil pollution.

The consequences of this kind of pollution are severe. There are an estimated 10 million hectares lost to erosion or salination every year, and another 20 million abandoned because of already degraded soil, no longer fit for agriculture (Everything connects, 2013). And this depletion of land resources takes a dramatic turn in economies facing increased food demand, as they need more arable land. Since 1960, food demand has grown three times, and it is expected to grow another 70 percent by 2050 (and to double in new economies). However, many regions are already running out of suitable land for agriculture, notably North Africa, the Middle East, and most of Asia (Petit, 2021). Moreover, 40 percent of arable land in China is said to already be polluted and unfit for agriculture. In addition, and for several of these regions, the effects of climate change could further decrease existing agricultural yields that are already low. Food supply will therefore become another major global challenge in the coming decades. There are already 160 countries that depend on other regions for food imports. This number will probably increase, as is the level of their dependency, triggering a global food crisis. Improving agricultural performance based on traditional techniques will also prove complex, as it is now widely acknowledged that these techniques heavily contribute to soil pollution.

It can only get worse

There are thus three main types of pollution: air, water, and soil. These different forms of pollution always come from the same sources. First, the way we use fuels for energy leads to massive air pollution (both indoor and outdoor) as well as climate change. This concerns industrial heating, electricity generation, gasoline use for transport, or the use of solid fuels in cooking. Second, modern industry has come up with a variety of processes that manufacture nondegradable materials such as plastics and composite or synthetic materials (textile, electronics, etc.), and in doing so, they also generate massive waste and emissions of chemical pollutants that are poorly handled. Finally, twentieth-century agriculture is one of the main sources of pollution. It relies on artificial fertilizers and pesticides that contribute heavily to water, soil, and even air pollution.

The consequences are already significant, with over six million deaths per year, 25–30 percent of the global population having access to contaminated water only, and 20 million hectares of land abandoned annually due to soil degradation. An important point though is that this can only get worse, and we have not seen it all. If nothing changes, these trends will probably accelerate significantly indeed and change the world for good, fostered by three main realities: population expansion, urbanization, and industrialization. The global population today is around 7.8 billion people. It is expected to hit the 9–10 billion mark by 2050 and stabilize around 11–12 billion by the end of the century. It was only 2.5 billion in 1950. Within a century, the global population will thus have increased fourfold. In the last decades, most population growth occurred in Asia. The future will be more balanced, with significant growth expected in Africa as well, which is expected to be the last location of population growth after 2050 (Petit, 2021). This significant demographic expansion will also lead to increased demand for food, and thus higher agricultural needs. And as we have seen, there is a major food problem building up in these regions that are going to be the hotspots of population growth (India, Africa). Then comes urbanization. In 1950, the urban population was only 29 percent. That ratio today is around 50 percent and should reach 67 percent by 2050, or 2.7 billion additional urban dwellers (Petit, 2021). This migration, unique in history (because of its pace), will significantly impact energy demand but also demand for transport, housing, and other goods. While it is an accelerator of development, enabling populations to reach modern living standards, this important evolution will probably lead to much greater energy use, which again will impact the same regions, together with the Middle East, Central Asia, parts of Southeast Asia, and China. Finally, and for the same reason, industrial demand is likely to pick up significantly as economic development and the historical catch-up of new economies continues. And with modern industrial use, the associated release of gases, chemical substances, and other hazardous waste are expected to increase significantly. In a do-nothing scenario, emissions will increase by nearly 50 percent by 2050, while waste would double (International Energy Agency, 2018; Petit, 2021). And this is not even based on scenarios where new economies would catch up to modern living standards by that date. What happens if economic development goes faster than expected? All this would come at a tremendous cost for humankind. Two questions then come up: how much of a cost? And who will pay?

The true cost of pollution

Modeling the cost of pollution is certainly not an easy exercise, because so many factors can and should be included in it. The cost of health is one obvious factor and is generally integrated into the models. It is rather easy to monitor. Then come the costs of environmental impacts and what they take away in terms of opportunities. Here, estimates are harder to build. How to relate soil pollution to economic development? Is there a direct correlation, or should it be measured in terms of lost economic opportunity, hence GDP? Finally, the topic of climate change presents itself. The economic impact of climate change has been debated for over a decade since Nicholas Stern (2006) issued his first conclusions on the economics of climate change. While the issues are not necessarily significant yet, the question is how large they could become in the foreseeable future, what the tipping point — when it makes sense to start doing something about it — will be, and how to model this tipping point.

If we focus first on the costs of pollution, an analysis by *The Lancet* estimates these to be around US$4,600 billion per year, or around 6 percent of global economic output (Cohen, 2017). This is already a sizable figure, which is backed up by a study from the Organisation for Economic Co-operation and Development (2016), which finds that costs of air pollution alone (*The Lancet* looked at all types of pollution) amount to around US$3,000 billion per year. In the end, and despite differences in the analysis, the ballpark figure gives an idea of the current impact of pollution on global economic activity.

It is also important to recognize that these costs are not accounted for in the same way across geographies, and this adds to the complexity of understanding impacts. Actually, the OECD analysis shows that air pollution costs are currently shared equally between high-income countries (OECD) and others, despite new economies representing nearly 90 percent of the global population (and being the regions with the most pollution). In short, these costs are unevenly distributed. They could and should be much higher in new economies if these had the same capabilities to mitigate pollution and deal with its aftermath, which they have not. The true cost that they face is actually invisible. The OECD says this in so many words when estimating the evolution of these costs going forward, yet again for air pollution alone. Their perspective for 2060 is a doubling of costs for mature economies, from US$1,500 billion per year to around US$3,000 billion per year, which is likely to remain a constant in terms of cost per GDP unit. The costs for new economies would however multiply by ten, from US$1,700 billion per year to between US$15,000 and US$22,000 billion per year. In GDP terms, and accounting for forecasted evolutions (European Environment Agency, 2017), this would mean that the costs of air pollution alone would multiply fourfold (per unit of GDP) and could reach up to 15–16 percent of GDP of new economies by 2060, a major burden on their markets and probably inconsistent with the GDP forecasts I used in the first place.

Hence, instead of showing up on the balance sheet, these costs are likely turned into a reduction in economic growth, thus GDP. This is what another study by the World Bank has estimated for water pollution, considering that above a certain level of water contamination (by fertilizers and pesticides), the economic impact could be as high as one-third of GDP growth in concerned geographies (Phys, 2019). When all forms of pollution (air, water, and soil) are combined, it becomes clear that the costs of pollution can become truly significant as time goes on. The other conclusion is that mature economies would probably better cope with increased costs, while such a turn of event in new economies (primarily concerned with such issues) would be catastrophic for economic development.

And this conclusion also holds when looking at further effects of pollution, such as climate change. Obviously, the economic impacts of climate change can be challenged in many ways. They first depend on the extent of the issues and on economic development, which are highly uncertain. I compared several of those, and they all tell a similar story up to a certain point. The economic impact of climate change tends to increase significantly with global warming; on this, everyone agrees. Impacts remain minimal below 2 degrees of warming, however, which explains why a temperate increase of 1.5 to 2 degrees is considered a safety line that we should not cross. Beyond this level, forecasts begin to diverge. For a 4-degree increase, forecasts vary from 4 to 50 percent of annual economic output fractional loss. At 50 percent fractional loss, annual economic growth is massively hampered, likely leading to no improvement in living standards, increased polarization, and significant issues (Amadeo, 2019; Burke *et al.*, 2015; KPMG, 2014; Wade and Jennings, 2016). The extent of the impact is expected to remain uncertain for a period of time, as is what should be directly associated with climate change (heatwave-related mortality, extreme weather events, economic opportunity loss, etc.). But it is quite evident that beyond a certain level, these impacts will have more importance, at least in certain sectors of the economy, and more importantly in certain geographies.

All these forecasts recognize that around 80 percent of associated economic impacts will be borne by new economies. Hence, one should be careful when talking about global annual fractional loss of economic output. While some of these figures may look small (and they are not necessarily small!), when globally aggregated, they end up being potentially massive for certain geographies. And they turn out to be the same countries as those facing pollution issues and massive demographic demand for economic growth. No matter what we think of forecasts and figures, it is loud and clear that pollution in all its forms (air, water, soil, climate change) will generate daunting issues for the world going forward, particularly as the demand for economic growth intensifies. This will primarily concern a subset of new economies, in which unfortunately all issues come together. However, one should not be complacent. The magnitude of the issue (possibly billions of people crammed together in city slums, lacking access to food and water, suffering from pollution, climate change, and a lack of economic opportunities) means that it will turn into a global crisis if it is not averted (Petit, 2021).

Reverse innovation

These issues appear to be so daunting that some Western activists are now preaching a new contract based on sustained economic decline. In short, they choose the mitigation of pollution and climate change over economic development in what they present as an impossible bargain. If it is impossible for the human species to survive and bloom with ten billion of us (or more) and the modern economy we enjoy, then it is better to come to terms with nature, reinvent frugality, and maybe control birthrates. To a certain extent, this argument reminds me of Rousseau's "Noble Savage." Life was better before, let's return to it then. Traces of that reasoning have also appeared in Hariri's momentous *Sapiens: A Brief History of Mankind* (2011), in which he describes the terrible psychological and physical burden that people began to carry the day they adopted a more sedentary lifestyle in an agriculture economy. As much as it may revive some subconscious dreams from past education in Western minds, let's not forget that any economic decline would be totally unacceptable for close to 90 percent of the global population, i.e., many new economies that have just begun to exit centuries of misery. This selfish position is more outrageous when one thinks of what Western countries did purposely to obtain, and then retain, their advantage over such a long period of time. You will have understood that I am not very supportive of economic decline. Instead, I would rather look for alternatives.

And so will the world, or at least a subset of it. New economies, particularly from India, Southeast Asia, and Africa, will be fronting all challenges and opportunities. Historically, patronizing Western thought leaders have considered that the natural path to economic development for new economies was to basically follow in the footsteps of mature ones. Their GDP would grow, and they would pollute more. When living standards would improve beyond a certain tipping point, they would take the necessary measures to mitigate their impact on the environment. More recently, a new line of thought has emerged, already more rational according to me, stating that new economies have the choice to make it right the first time, i.e., to develop sustainable economies, or urbanization and industrialization that are not accompanied by environmental pollution. This is because technology exists and is often already competitive. The debate is between these two approaches. I would introduce a third one here, which some may find provocative. These massive issues will impact booming populations in new economies, and the above has clearly shown that things will have to change to cope with these. In other words, "If you have always done it that way, it is probably wrong" (Kettering). The undisputable evidence on innovation is that it is always driven by the young generation. It is true that today, most innovation happens at the expensive universities of America or Europe, but these are actually filled with young people from everywhere. These universities already recruit worldwide cohorts of young students from new economies, and these students are the ones who drive innovation. Why wouldn't it be then that, in the face of such challenges, this youth from new economies mobilizes to develop the solutions of tomorrow; solutions that will not make Western economies richer but rather will help new economies make their way toward development, despite these issues? This is what is often referred to as "reverse innovation," or innovations that emerge in new economies and then develop in mature ones.

What if the solution to the problem was coming from India or Africa? And what would it look like?

Three revolutions must take place

In the end, there are three revolutions that need to happen: in agriculture, industry (and particularly its waste), and energy. I am using the term revolution because of the magnitude of the issues that we face. In regions that face significant acceleration of their needs, the consequences of air, water, and soil pollution are too severe for any business-as-usual scenario to be maintained. Let's remember the figure the OECD provided on the evolution of air pollution costs in the coming decades. By 2060, these could be ten times larger than what they are today in new economies and represent up to 15–16 percent of GDP. In other words, new economies have no future if they do not address the problem of pollution (and climate change) firsthand.

Fortunately, new energy, digital, and atomic-scale technologies have the potential to reverse this trend. And because they are infinitely scalable and highly decentralized, and provide increasing rates of return over time, their adoption is possible. But will they be adopted?

Agriculture Revolution

Obviously, agriculture comes first. India's population is set to increase by 70 percent by 2050 while that of Africa will double (from a 2015 baseline). This corresponds to two billion additional people on the planet to feed, in regions that are already largely dependent on imported food. As I mentioned earlier, worldwide food demand will increase by 70 percent by 2050 and double in new economies alone. There are three possible options for them.

Food dependencies

The first one is to rely on increasing quantities of imported food. This may prove to be the only practical option and does not yield excessive pollution, particularly from the use of fertilizers and pesticides in unfavorable lands. However, this creates critical dependencies, which some countries may be reluctant to have. When considering the current leverage of energy exporters in world affairs and what this did to the general arms race worldwide, what would the geopolitics of food look like if they were to develop at a scale not envisioned today? After all, global food trade represents only 3–4 percent of the global goods trade, and a mere 5 percent of the sector's output. The problem with food is that it degrades fast. That is why the market is essentially local and also why short supply chains have always been favored. When long supply chains need to be used, special emphasis should be placed on products' conservation, using refrigerated systems and complex logistics. This adds to pollution from logistics but more importantly significantly increases costs.

Bridging the productivity gap

The second option is to upgrade agriculture techniques in those regions to reach modern levels. As I explained earlier, there is still a massive potential for better yields in traditional agriculture in new economies. Today, the sector employs only 3 percent of the workforce in mature economies, but over 60 percent in new economies. In these regions, people essentially survive from the product of their own labor, relying on antiquated techniques (World Bank, 2020).

Notwithstanding the potential increase in arable land, there is often a 50–60 percent gap of productivity potential in agriculture in new economies (Food and Land Use Coalition, 2019; Petit, 2021). The use of modern agricultural techniques could hence prove vital. Yet, as mentioned, this will come at the expense of significant air pollution and, more importantly, water and soil pollution if traditional fertilizers and pesticides are used. Traditional techniques of agriculture, combined with potential overexploitation in areas where there is limited suitable land available, will further contribute to soil erosion and degradation and thus aggravate the issue over time. The use of organic fertilizers and pesticides could be an alternative, but those remain to be further developed at an industrial scale. Traditional compost will take us only that far. Biotechnologies could help develop products that have not necessarily been invented yet (Hockfield, 2019). With modern computing techniques, nothing now prevents the redevelopment of chemicals at an atomic scale.

Irrigation also significantly increases agricultural yields, but it requires water. With many regions facing greater scarcity, the use of irrigation (which is mainly used in Asia today) is therefore likely to be a growing problem, particularly in India and many African countries, unless freshwater can be produced in mass volumes that is suitable for agriculture. I will come back to this.

Twenty-first-century agriculture

The third option would be to reinvent food production. This is what Tubb and Seba (2019) have looked at. I mentioned their research earlier on. Their view is that modern food production, based on modern technologies (and notably atomic-scale ones) could rebuild key nutrients and microorganisms instead of growing them traditionally through animal and crops farming. Their claim is that it would require 10 times less water, 5 times less energy, and 100 times less land use, with critical consequences for land use and obviously the cost of food. This transition would come at a fraction of food costs and is probably infinitely scalable over time. The claim I could make here is that it would significantly reduce pollution as well, and, provided the figures materialize, reshape the agricultural industry. The use of fertilizers and pesticides would cease, and the associated GHG emissions (methane from animal farming for instance) would also be significantly tamed. This industry would probably also be capable of becoming global, as the produced nutrients and microorganisms could possibly be better conserved.

We would just be at the dawn of a significant transformation in agriculture. After millennia of relying on subsistence agriculture, in the twentieth century we have turned toward industrialization, with machines, fertilizers, and pesticides used in vast quantities to boost yields. Not all regions have made that transition yet. However, the lesson has been that such "industrialization" led to significant pollution, and the long-term, sustained degradation of soil. Will the twenty-first century build on modern technology developments (like the twentieth century did) and reinvent agriculture and food production at the atomic level? The challenge is massive and up for grabs. It could be one that new economies, faced with the challenge of developing food at scale with limited capabilities, take on first.

Industrial Revolution

The second of the revolutions is obviously about modern industrialization. Again, the key issue of modern industry is that of waste: the waste of nondegradable materials and chemical substances in the production or manufacturing process, or the waste of used products abandoned in garbage dumps when they reach end of life. All these issues will probably form the heart of industry's future if pollution issues take center stage in the coming decades, and if the burden on billions continues to increase, as I discussed above.

Industrial waste, at end-use

A first way of reducing industrial waste is to reduce it at end-use. One of the major issues to handle is that more products made of complex artificial and nondegradable substances are ultimately dumped in garbage areas, over time leaking their way deep into the soil, rivers, and aquifers. Circularity measures could help mitigate this significantly, through any solution that makes it possible to first reduce the number of products circulating. Demand reduction measures (such as sharing), the optimization of products' utilization or an extension of their lifetime are all powerful contributors. They will mainly apply to large machines and assets at first (such as cars, motor systems, furnaces, etc.). I already discussed the central role of digital technologies in this area. Recycling is another option for mitigating waste at end-use. Mature economies are more advanced in this area, as we have seen, both in terms of recycling but also in terms of regulating landfilling activities. However, this all comes at a cost, and this is essentially why these measures have failed to pick up beyond a few environmentalist-driven countries. The cost is first that of sorting and collecting materials, and second of actually recycling them. To give an example, only 9 percent of plastics are recycled worldwide (Parker, 2018). The most cost-effective way of recycling plastics is mechanical recycling, but there are limits to its feasibility and this often comes with some quality degradation. Chemical recycling breaks the molecules down and reconstructs new molecules from original materials. This is much closer to virgin production, except it does not need to use raw products (Tullo, 2019). For mechanical recycling to thrive, product design and corresponding value chains need to be developed, and this is precisely what has fallen short thus far. Collection, sorting, and design-to-recycle solutions therefore need to be developed for the entire recycling value chain to reach scale. Digital technologies — once again — will be a major driver of progress in this field.

And even though the circularity concept has emerged in environmentally concerned mature economies, it could well be that it finally finds its way in new economies striving for economic growth and least-cost opportunities. These are all things that local and digitally enabled circular loops could well provide at scale if designed from the start. An opportunity for "reverse" innovation.

Industrial waste, in manufacturing

A second way of reducing industrial waste is to reduce it during production or manufacturing. We all have pictures in our mind of dirty factories releasing gallons of chemical products in nearby rivers or chemicals leaking from poorly managed landfills at the back of these same factories. The unfortunate truth is that this is still very much of a reality.

Again, the circularity measures described above lead to systemic effects on the entire industrial value chain, reducing the footprint of manufacturing and thus pollution. Moreover, resource conservation measures at the plant level are also a way to significantly reduce the amount of waste while improving productivity, and digital technologies help do just that thanks to greater granularity in controls.

Going further, additive manufacturing uses far fewer materials, up to 90 percent in certain cases, reducing waste by a significant amount and thus also its associated pollution. Additive manufacturing may ultimately come at a fraction of the cost and provide incredibly competitive solutions, at least for commoditized goods, and could also build on more decentralized economies. Therefore, it might become a significant option for sustainable industrialization in new economies. Another perfect opportunity for "reverse innovation."

Beyond wasting materials and resources, industrial production also generates significant GHG emissions. It accounts for 25 percent of total GHG emissions (Intergovernmental Panel on Climate Change, 2014; WRI, 2020). These emissions are related to process operations (beyond energy use) and generate various gases such as sulfur dioxide, nitrogen dioxide, fluorinated gases, and carbon dioxide. This is notably dependent on the lack of purity of raw materials used in processes. These impurities combine with oxygen in the atmosphere to form these gases. In steel production, they can be found in raw iron ore, in petrochemicals as part of crude oil or natural gas, and in cement as part of limestone, clay, shells, etc.

A new periodic table, with new materials

It seems extremely difficult or costly to remove these impurities prior to running the manufacturing process, hence why it will likely never happen. However, other options might exist, and they are all connected to our final way of reducing harmful industrial waste: working on materials themselves. Indeed, the main issue of modern industry is that it builds on nondegradable materials that therefore pollute air, water, and soil. Yet, if competitive degradable materials could be used instead, this would largely solve the problem.

Alternative feedstock could already be used in some modern processes. The two main routes explored today are biomass and hydrogen. Biomass is an alternative to oil or natural gas as a source of carbon. Let's remember that oil and natural gas deposits are in fact million-years-old, ultra-concentrated deposits of biomass. And carbon is at the heart of most chemicals we use. Obviously, these chemical processes tend to generate GHG emissions, notably carbon dioxide. If biomass can be grown artificially to substitute oil or natural gas as feedstock, then in theory the process can be thought of as carbon-neutral (since the same amount of carbon has been stored by the biomass at the time of growing). The only issue with biomass is scale. It is generally acknowledged that biomass is very unlikely to be able to disrupt a significant share of traditional fossil fuels (Energy Transitions Commission, 2018). Moreover, it will probably come at an increased cost due to the sheer amounts of biomass required.

Another route is hydrogen. Hydrogen has no carbon content, but it can contribute to certain processes. In the steel industry, the traditional process involves the use of coke to purify iron ore, thereby releasing carbon dioxide emissions (and other gases from impurities). An alternative technique, using hydrogen instead, would release only water (with impurities dissolved in it). Hydrogen is also thought of to be used as an alternative to traditional oil or natural gas, when combined with carbon dioxide that would have been captured preliminarily. This would require an entire carbon capture industry to scale up though, so it is unlikely to scale up very fast.

But let's take it to another level. These alternative feedstocks are considered as substitutes for traditional (and polluting) existing materials in order to mitigate emissions, but are meant to recreate the same types of products as the ones we currently use. It does not have to be this way, however, and research is not constrained to reconstructing the same old materials we have been using for centuries. Instead, new materials could be developed and fully replace the existing ones, such as steel, cement, or various chemicals. And they could be developed in such a way that they are degradable from the start. With current advancements of computing power, as well as the ability to control manufacturing at an atomic scale, new materials could be created. In short, a new periodic table (Hockfield, 2019).

New technologies therefore hold a number of keys to developing a sustainable twenty-first-century industry, one that is more circular, that leverages more efficient and precise process techniques, and that no longer relies on age-old processes that have developed on the backbone of cheap fossil fuels or nondegradable and polluting materials.

Energy Revolution

Global picture

The last of the revolutions needed to turn around the global issue of pollution is that of energy. In our modern economy, fossil fuels represent over 80 percent of primary energy resources (International Energy Agency, 2018), and they are the main reason of pollution. Other sources include nuclear resources for electricity generation and renewable resources (traditional biomass but also hydroelectricity, wind, and solar power). Fossil fuels are made of oil, coal, or natural gas. Oil is primarily used as a fuel for transport. The combustion of oil in car engines (or planes, ships, etc.) causes pollution. This includes carbon dioxide, created from the combination of crude oil with oxygen, as well as impurities and/or additives turning into gas when combined with oxygen and ozone as well. Coal is used for heating, cooking, and electricity generation. Its use for heating and cooking has largely been abandoned in mature economies as it is a primary cause of indoor air pollution. It remains widely used for electricity generation, however, and is one of the major causes of carbon dioxide emissions. Electricity generation alone accounts for 35 percent of energy-related GHG emissions. In addition, impurities also lead to emissions of other gases. Finally, natural gas is primarily used for electricity generation and heating. In both applications, natural gas has made great strides in recent decades as a cleaner option than coal. And indeed, burning natural gas creates 50 percent fewer carbon dioxide emissions than burning coal. The other resources of our energy system include traditional biomass, which is another energy source for heating and cooking, and renewable and nuclear resources for electricity generation (Intergovernmental Panel on Climate Change, 2014; WRI, 2020).

Figure 1 compiles only GHG emissions and does not include associated pollution from particles or aerosols, but it still gives a good idea of where to look when it comes to energy depollution. The breakdown of emissions shows a pretty clear route to depollution. This will take place in two ways: first, depolluting energy consumption, at the point of use, and second, depolluting energy supply.

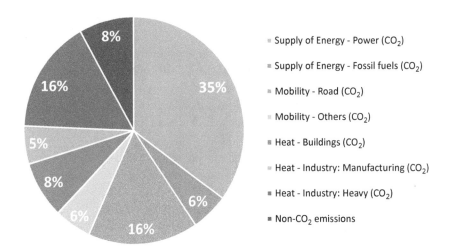

Figure 1   Greenhouse gas emissions from energy

Depollution at point of use

If we look at energy consumption first, the two main uses of energy are mobility and heat. Mobility for road transport represents around 75 percent of all emissions in the sector and includes light-duty vehicles (cars and small freight) and long-haul road transport, with light-duty transport accounting for two-thirds of the total (International Energy Agency, 2018). The remaining 25 percent is created by railways, ships, and planes, for both people and freight. Electrification at end-use is the obvious solution to the issue of pollution, as there is no fuel combustion, hence no gas exhaust, with the use of electric motors.

In addition, this transition comes basically at a fraction of the cost because of the inherent simplicity of design and expected long-term learning curves on battery technologies and electric motors, as I discussed already. Electrified mobility is already making its way through light-duty vehicle transport (including personal cars and small commercial vehicles), and recent progress made in batteries means that some believe that long-haul road transport will be accessible in the coming decade or earlier (Bloch *et al.*, 2019). Big companies such as Volvo, Daimler, Tesla, and BYD are already working on it (Downing, 2020).

Aviation and shipping represent the remaining share of demand in the mobility sector, around 25 percent of emissions. They are likely to be more difficult to electrify because of the sheer volume of energy that needs to be stored. Although electric motors will probably be more powerful, the issue lies with the energy storage solution and its ratio of conversion into electricity. However, again, since 75 percent of journeys through the air or by sea are short-haul ones, there is a belief that electricity could also take a share of those sectors (Energy Transitions Commission, 2018, 2020).

Then comes heating. Once again, burning coal or natural gas generates massive carbon dioxide and other pollutant emissions, even if natural gas is less harmful. And again, electrification emerges as an obvious solution that is economically competitive, with no emissions whatsoever at end-use. It will primarily apply to building and manufacturing heat, because these two sectors share some common needs.

First, temperature heating requirements are relatively low. Heating in buildings barely exceeds 25 degrees, while that in manufacturing usually remains below 250 degrees. It is in primary industry, where there is often a need to break down molecules, that heating requirements can exceed 1,000 degrees. At low temperatures, ultra-efficient and competitive heating solutions exist, notably the ones building on the ideal gas law of physics, such as heat pumps, which leverage pressure to build up heat (or to cool). When used, these solutions are so efficient that they will often be cheaper than conventional fossil fuel burning. Combined with hot water storage and radiant heating in households, as an example, they would prove to be extremely competitive (Griffith, 2020). And since they are very scalable, they are likely to further pervade markets in the years to come.

The second reason why electrification will happen in buildings and manufacturing is because both these sectors tend to have extremely specific needs. They require granularity and precision in controls, whether to heat a room (and not have to heat an entire building if it is unoccupied) or a specific part of a process (drying paint or paper, sterilizing food, etc.). Electrification solutions (and heat pumps are part of the score of solutions, among others infrared and microwave) are the only ones capable of achieving such granularity. In addition, and as described earlier, electrified heating is faster and shows great inertia, so it enables faster and more precise processing.

The ultra-competitive and infinitely scalable decentralized electricity solutions that I described earlier will be a powerful incentive to switch to increasingly competitive heating solutions, particularly in new economies and in buildings, as this is where people face the largest issues with indoor air pollution. Indeed, if the cost of electricity continues to drop alongside that of heating systems, it will soon become an obvious choice. Technology may partly limit its development today, but the reality is that science (and current developments) is going into the direction of a massive deployment of electrified heat pump systems, and that these generate no harmful emissions because there is no fuel combustion at end-use.

Of course, not all buildings or manufacturing processes may be fully suitable. There may still be pockets of demand where adopting electricity will prove complex. For instance, using decentralized heat pumps in heritage buildings in downtown Paris may prove to be complicated. Where to put them? It would hurt everyone's eyes to suddenly see cohorts of heat pumps on the beautiful nineteenth-century roofs around the "Jardin du Luxembourg." Nevertheless, the Energy Transitions Commission (2018, 2020) estimates that 80–90 percent of buildings and manufacturing will end up being electrified by 2050. This compared to fewer than 30 percent in manufacturing and 12 percent in buildings today (Author's evaluation, based on data from International Energy Agency, 2018; Shell, 2018).

These reductions in pollution at end-use will be complemented by digitally enabled energy savings with significant potential, as already discussed.

The situation will be more complicated in primary industry, because while electrified solutions exist, their costs are not yet competitive with those of current fossil-fuel-based solutions. Research on how to scale up electric furnaces, plasma heating solutions, or other forms of highly powerful infrared or microwave options is ongoing. Therefore, electrified solutions will prevail where it makes sense, and the Energy Transitions Commission (2018, 2020) believes they could account for around 25 percent of the mix.

The remaining applications are areas where research and technology developments will occur. Electric motors or electrified heat can provide the power required for such applications. Yet, what is missing is energy storage capability. A plane can fly perfectly well on electric engines. In fact, it will be much more efficient that way, and less energy is needed to do so. However, this requires such a large amount of batteries (at current density levels) that it will be impractical. The same will happen with ships, or with primary industry. I doubt the solution will come from a breakthrough in batteries, because their natural market for scale will not be these applications (at the edge of the energy system's needs). The solution might thus be a continued reliance on fossil fuels or other options. One that is seriously considered today is hydrogen, but biofuels could also play a role (Energy Transitions Commission, 2018, 2020). The role of digital technologies described above in generating energy and resource conservation at a factory level, or systemic benefits across the value chain (through reduction in demand), will hence be critical in curbing pollutant emissions as well. Thinking ahead, miniaturized nuclear reactors could ultimately present an alternative, but that is probably not a short-term option.

Depollution of energy supply, mainly an electricity problem

While the electrification of end-use clearly comes out on top of the solutions designed to mitigate pollution in every sector, electricity generation poses a critical issue, as it is one of the main contributors to pollution itself. Granted, electricity does not generate emissions at end-use because there is no fuel combustion, but there is a massive and inefficient combustion of such fuels for its production. Hence, a thorough plan for reducing pollution should activate the electrification of end-use alongside a switch away from fossil fuels for electricity generation.

Here, the options exist, and they have already proven to be competitive. Nuclear power, but more importantly renewable energies will play a critical role in depolluting the sector. The 2019 forecast from BloombergNEF (2019) estimates that the intensity of emissions will be cut by 2.5 by 2050 in a business as usual scenario. The intensity accounts for emissions per kWh of energy produced. The International Energy Agency Sustainable Development Scenario (2018) considers these could be cut fivefold. One thing is for sure: renewable technologies, and particularly solar, are infinitely scalable, meaning their costs will continue to drop over time while they provide increasing rates of return, and since they are highly decentralized, their penetration can accelerate as soon as the economic tipping point is reached and barriers to development are removed. And as the world electrifies, it will need much less fossil fuel and therefore, associated pollution will drop as a result.

Two-thirds emissions reduction

Although the intent of this book is not to provide detailed quantitative estimates but rather to suggest some possible routes for the upcoming energy transition that have not been explored to date, I can try to come up with a raw estimate.

Starting with end-consumption, mobility represents around 22 percent of total GHG emissions (discounting non-carbon dioxide). Assuming an 80 percent electrification of the road transport sector alone would result in a global reduction in GHG emissions of 13 percent. Assuming a 90 percent electrification of heating of buildings and manufacturing, and 25 percent of primary industries would result in another 15 percent of reduction in emissions.

If I follow these electrification rates — which are compatible with the latest Energy Transitions Commission (2020) report — for demand, electricity demand could grow three to four times. Yet, if power generation emissions are zeroed thanks to the complete switch to nonpolluting sources, then emissions would drop by 35 percent. However, if we follow the International Energy Agency projection of an intensity divided by five within 20 years, emissions would drop only by 10 percent. If we use the BloombergNEF (2019) forecast of an intensity divided by 2.5 with such levels of electrification, then net emissions would increase.

Since this exercise is purely theoretical, I will consider a power system that is entirely decarbonized, or 35 percent savings on GHG gas emissions. The electrification of the energy system leads in turn to a sharp reduction in fossil fuels demand of around 70 percent (Energy Transitions Commission, 2020), or, in greenhouse gas terms, of a further 5 percent reduction of total emissions.

This raw calculation adds up to a reduction potential of around two-thirds of emissions, with direct and clean electrification alone. The remaining share of emissions would be split between long-haul and non-road mobility, as well as — and more importantly — heat, particularly in primary industries. Circularity in industry would be a powerful mitigation of these emissions. The International Energy Agency (2019) says the same thing when elaborating on its Sustainable Development Scenario, and its analysis not only applies to GHG emissions but also includes pollutant emissions.

The striking conclusion of this is that pollution associated with energy can already be largely averted. Reaching a net-zero economy by 2050 becomes a less insurmountable prospect. Technologies for the biggest chunk of the issue are already here (while they also bring massive benefits to consumers as already explained). What to say then about their potential further adoption as they continue to improve and bring increasing rates of return?

The Central Role of Water

From the three main streams of pollution discussed above — agricultural, industrial waste, and energy — we have thus seen that technologies hold significant potential (if they are not available already) to significantly alter the dystopian scenario at play. There is a last resource and area of innovation that will significantly impact all of the above, and that we must hence spend some time on: water.

We tend to focus on materials, chemicals, or energy resources in every conversation about climate, industry, or even agriculture, and for good reasons. Yet, freshwater is at the epicenter of everything we transform and use. Freshwater is essential to agriculture. Land that is well fed by rain grows better crops and is more productive. Irrigation increases yields significantly, which is why it is widely used in Asia. Indeed, 70 percent of all freshwater demand is dedicated to agriculture.

Moreover, freshwater is also essential to energy, and the sector represents around 10 percent of total demand. It is widely used for the collection of raw energy resources (oil and gas exploration and production, coal mining, etc.) and for thermal power generation. The white smoke that escapes large chimneys of familiar power plants often consist (in part) of water vapor.

Freshwater is also widely used in industry, be it in mining (cracking rocks, cleaning materials), food and beverage (an essential component), or various industrial processes (to clean surfaces, as a dissolvent, or to mix with various chemicals). This represents another 10 percent of total water demand.

Finally, domestic demand represents a mere 10 percent of total freshwater demand, an interesting figure. When one is advised to conserve domestic water by not letting the tap run for too long or by shortening the time under the shower, one should not forget that such a contribution represents a fraction of the issue, and probably does not matter much if water is re-treated. Not that we should not do it, however!

There are two main issues with freshwater: one of geography, and one of quality. First, not everyone on Earth is blessed with the same amount of water resources. Asia represents 60 percent of the global population but benefits of only 33 percent of the world's water resources. Africa represents 16 percent of the global population (today — but will move toward 40 percent by the end of the century), with only 10 percent of water resources available. In comparison, the Americas have 45 percent of worldwide resources for only 14 percent of the population (Citi, 2017). Hence, water scarcity may be an issue in certain geographies, creating a huge burden on economic development (and survival). And, as we have seen, water is essential in virtually every sector.

The other key issue surrounding freshwater is that of quality. Indeed, in many of the processes described above, water is not lost per se. For instance, when water is used as a coolant in thermal generation, it escapes as vapor and remains within the water cycle (it is however withdrawn in the short run from available surface water). When water is used for fracking, it may eventually run off into aquifers again. Water is not lost. However, it is contaminated, and as a result it becomes unfit for consumption, harms biodiversity, and further pollutes soil and thus ecosystems.

Technologies could and certainly will come in to help solve these issues. Because these issues are most likely to materialize in Asia and Africa, one can expect that the corresponding innovations will emerge there. Only 1 percent of water is truly accessible to humanity, out of 2.5 percent of freshwater. The vast majority of water is seawater. As accessible freshwater resources become increasingly scarce, and unless new deposits can be accessed, seawater will become the new gold, and with it desalination. For long, this well-known process has remained too expensive to truly develop at scale, in part because it is a highly energy-intensive process. Yet, new digital technologies and atomic-scale material developments could provide significant benefits (AquaTT, 2020; Hockfield, 2019; Stover, 2018). The Life Dreamer project (in which Acciona Agua is involved), for instance, would help raise water conversion rates by 40 points and reduce pollution by 80 percent and energy use by 10 percent, while removing half of the chemicals used (I'mnovation, 2020). New distributed and cheap energy sources could also contribute to bringing costs down further. Another example would be Acquaporin, a water startup described by Susan Hockfield (2019) in her latest book, which developed revolutionary protein-based membranes to filter water more efficiently.

Beyond desalination, the optimization of demand will prove vital as well, notably in energy (more water-efficient processes) and agriculture (precision farming will help reduce and optimize water use). Finally, wastewater treatment will be the cornerstone of reducing contamination of water by all processes. It has already begun to develop for municipal water, domestic and industrial uses, and will continue to do so. The issue for agriculture and energy remains, as only systemic changes appear to be a solution: for agriculture, a transformation away from traditional, chemical-based fertilizers and pesticides; for energy, a move away from fossil fuels (and mining in general). Water scarcity will probably become a key driver of these changes going forward.

The Next Stage of Our Civilization Will Be About Reconnecting with Nature

Civilization progress, at the expense of the planet

Let's wrap up. The two industrial revolutions of the nineteenth and twentieth centuries have put the world on a fantastic course toward population explosion and economic development, much beyond anything that had been witnessed in centuries. For millennia, grandchildren used to live like their grandparents did, with little to no change. Quite often, they were born and raised on the same premises their own grandparents were born and raised. They used to marry neighbors and perpetuate the lifestyle. A lot of this was due to the relative isolation of these communities. When finally an end was put to this, everything changed. This historical transformation of the way people used to live and prosper has however come at the cost of pollution. Humanity's blooming is aggressive and detrimental to the rest of the planet. And humankind will have to take that problem and change its way of doing things before it actually backfires. One likely does not want to confront nature.

There are three sorts of pollution: of air, water, and soil. Today, 50 percent of the world's population lives in areas where air pollution is above safety limits (typically, a PM2.5 concentration above 35 micrograms per cubic meter). In other words, half of humanity breathes harmful particles 24/7, with obvious major health impacts and shortened life expectancy, but probably also more durable effects (such as a drop in fertility rates, children's diseases, etc.), most of which remain to be seen. Air pollution can also be more insidious, with the massive increase in greenhouse gas concentration in the atmosphere from human activities. These are not necessarily harmful (carbon dioxide is not dangerous for humans), but their concentration triggers (or is about to trigger) significant transformations of the climate, which are largely irreversible, and that humankind will have to adapt to in one way or another.

One of these changes is expected to be in water availability. By 2050, 50 percent of the world's population (notably in Africa and parts of Asia) could struggle to find water. Yet, climate change is only an accelerator of the trend. A key reason for water scarcity is pollution. Currently, 25–30 percent of the world's population already does not have access to healthy water. And the figure keeps going up.

With air and water pollution also comes the pollution of soil. In fact, the three are entangled in a "Dance of Death." Soil is mainly polluted by hazardous waste from human activities: plastics, chemicals, but also the vast amount of new materials (synthetic or composite) that we have invented and that nature cannot break down and turn back into essential building blocks of the planet. These will thus stay in the soil for centuries and pollute it. The consequences are severe. There are 10 million hectares lost to erosion every year, and another 20 million abandoned because they are unfit for agriculture. At this pace, the current issue could well turn in a global food crisis over time.

The significant pollution inherited from the first two industrial revolutions also comes with a cost. It is not fully known at the moment, because there is no standard to measure it everywhere, but some studies consider this cost to be around US$4,600 billion per year. This obviously hides all cost-reporting disparities that are not included in here. The figure could actually be much higher, and the share of new economies in it much larger. Projections are indeed pretty straightforward. While they expect that mature economies will see their costs double over time (which is largely acceptable considering GDP-projected evolution), costs for new economies could increase tenfold by 2060, and reach a level that could represent up to 15–16 percent of GDP.

And these costs represent pollution only. Climate change costs should be added to them. Despite what we may think, the sad reality is that these costs will add to the burden of these developing economies. On that, everyone agrees. Hence, and this is maybe the most important conclusion of this chapter, the global pollution issue will primarily affect new economies, and especially those that will face the largest increase in population and that need to catch up on living standards the most. Yet, it is truly a global issue that, if not properly handled, would ultimately concern all population groups. Migration and wars, on scales unimagined before, could follow.

Three revolutions to prevent a catastrophe and rebuild a contract with nature

To prevent this from happening, three revolutions must happen: in agriculture, industrial waste, and energy. Agriculture must have its revolution. The twentieth century witnessed the significant industrialization of agriculture, which pushed yields up while reducing the share of the population involved in it. The twenty-first century will first need to build on this progress by ensuring that productivity gaps in new economies (which may top 50–60 percent) can be bridged, as well as by developing new fertilizers and pesticides that are less harmful to the environment. Going further, however, this may not prove enough. A food revolution could also take place. With the momentous capabilities of modern computing power and the ability to now work at an atomic scale, a new approach to food production could emerge that would focus on directly producing the necessary nutrients and microorganisms rather than consuming them in the form of traditional crops or animals.

Industrial waste can largely be addressed with the accelerated development of circularity measures, including resource conservation at the production level, reduction in demand for goods hence resources (from sharing, lifetime extension, or asset utilization optimization), and the sharp acceleration of recycling. Additive manufacturing could also help to vastly reduce waste in those sectors where it would make most sense to develop it. Finally, the next frontier will be to develop new materials or new feedstocks that, by design, will be less harmful to environment.

Last, energy must also have its revolution. Pollution from energy use will largely be averted by the electrification of the system at end-use and then the "cleaning" of electricity generation through the deployment of nonpolluting power generation resources. Overall, direct electricity demand could increase three– to fourfold, and this at a competitive cost for consumers. Combined with a significant shift to renewable resources — notably decentralized solar, which will play the major role of accelerator — two-thirds of emissions from the energy system could hence be cut.

These three revolutions in agriculture, industrial waste, and energy will probably also contribute to solving the overarching issue: that of clean water and freshwater availability. They are also largely achievable, with technologies already available and new technologies in development. The accelerated deployment of infinitely scalable and highly decentralized digital, atomic-scale, and electrification technologies, which provide increasing rates of return over time, will prove key in accelerating the resolution of these issues. Innovation, building on these capabilities, will be essential.

Reverse innovation and a less Westernized philosophy of life

New economies will be hotspots of these innovations, as they are the ones who will face all the challenges at once. A crucial finding is that what has been referred to as reverse innovation may ultimately become the new norm; a historical shift that is probably not expected in today's forecasts.

Taking it a step further, such a transition could also have other consequences, such as a new relationship with and new respect for nature. Nothing forces us to live in filthy environments. Our human body tells us this every time we encounter a beautiful spot where nature is preserved. We are likely built to live in harmony with it. How long are we thus going to think that resources, water, and energy are free for us to spoil and use? A recent movement in mature economies has begun to advocate for greater "sobriety" (this is the term they use) to lower environmental impacts. In other words, focus on the essential, respect nature, and learn to limit humankind's footprint on the planet. This is a highly polemic and hotly debated theme, as some believe that behind this is the theory that we should accept and embrace economic decline, and probably civilizational collapse. Yet, without going to that extent, sobriety can also be understood as learning to preserve the planet's resources, and on this, everyone must agree. No matter what we may think about the concept of sobriety and the extent to which it materializes, pricing resources and focusing on their sustainable preservation could well be one of the significant shifts that will take place in the coming decades. Here again, digital technologies are likely to help foster change. The deployment of spectacular tools such as the World Air Quality Index, which I mentioned earlier, is just an example of the awareness and assertiveness that technologies can build across communities.

Additionally, these technologies are central to better understanding where the planet is heading. Climate change analysis and projections are advancing every year, despite their complexity, through increasingly sophisticated models that run on modern supercomputers. With the infinite scalability of such technologies, one can only imagine the level of awareness that we will collectively reach within the coming decades.

Major impact on the energy system

And obviously, all this will have significant impacts on energy. I already mentioned the accelerated deployment of decentralized energies in the mix and the accelerator role they are expected to play. But demand for goods and services will also evolve. New sectors could emerge, such as a twenty-first-century, electricity-based modern agriculture, adjacent to the current food and beverage sector, or a materials production industry that would ultimately substitute traditional materials, or greater use of water desalination. A revolution in the energy system, which will take place following significant shifts in demand and is driven by innovation; our argument all along in this book.

Drivers of and challenges to adoption

One of the main drivers of adoption will of course be pollution and its related health impacts. As I have discussed, pollution has reached critical levels in all regions of the world: six million people die from pollution-related effects every year, 25–30 percent of the global population has access to contaminated water only, and over 20 million hectares of land are abandoned every year due to irreversible soil degradation. And this is only the beginning. The problem could potentially turn into an all-out disaster in new economies, which struggle to balance population growth, economic development, urbanization, and industrialization, and their associated pollution. Beyond health issues, this could also trigger a significant food and water crisis, with massive consequences for sustainable living in those regions. Let's not be shortsighted. Such challenges in new economies would have ripple effects on all economies of the world, as they would probably trigger significant migrations from one region to another at a scale that has not yet been seen nor anticipated. Averting such a disaster will therefore become a critical driver of innovation in the coming decades. There is no better example than China, which is already tackling many of these issues. This is why President Xi Jinping has declared a war against pollution and set a long-term goal of becoming a fully ecological civilization by the mid-twenty-first century.

Besides pollution, climate change is the other big threat for humankind. While it is an undebatable reality, actions to mitigate it have so far fallen short. As the effects will gradually be felt everywhere, it is inevitable that rigorous actions will be taken to compensate for decades of denial and timorous action. The challenge is daunting, with the need to reach a net-zero economy by 2050 and halve our emissions by 2030. Beyond mitigation, adaptation will also pick up, notably in those regions most heavily impacted, if they can afford it. This transformation will indeed primarily affect new economies, and the question of international cooperation will be essential. If it is not already, climate change will be a powerful driver of change. Many governments and corporations have now embraced the topic. At the time of writing, Europe and China have for instance committed to reaching carbon neutrality by 2050 and 2060 respectively. Several large corporations have made similar commitments to invest in decarbonizing their operations; another powerful driver of change, as their commitment ultimately includes that of their supply chains, hence thousands of smaller companies.

Let's face it, however: there will be significant challenges. Apart from the challenges for technology and business models that I already reviewed earlier, and which will prove key to enabling a fast and competitive adoption of these new solutions, one fundamental enabler will be environmental and energy policies. They have so far fallen short, despite the evidence. I attended COP25 in November 2019, which turned out to be a disappointment for all. There were reasons for this, notably that the conference, initially planned to take place in Chile, was moved to Madrid, Spain, at the last minute because of social protests in Santiago. Government discussions fell short once again, and I vividly remember the general disappointment of all member parties at the conference. A sense of urgency was facing a stunning inability to collectively move the agenda forward. COP26, to be hosted in Glasgow, was supposed to pick up on this meeting's remains and build a powerful, multilateral frame for change five years after COP21 in Paris, which had marked the history of environmental politics as one of its critical milestones. Yet, COP26 was postponed due to the Covid-19 crisis, and not much has changed in the last year. Indeed, it is striking to see that while the global economy is facing the most dramatic economic downturn in recent history, carbon emissions are expected to fall by a mere 5–6 percent by the end of 2020. A drop in the ocean: 5–6 percent reduction is the annual trajectory that the world's carbon emissions should be following until 2050. Every year, a similar drop as the one experienced in 2020. This is a very unlikely scenario, unless major policies are put in place. And as already mentioned, these policies are unlikely to emerge if they fail to properly redistribute their benefits (or share the burden) across the society in a fair manner.

Another critical challenge will be that most issues described above actually concern new economies. Granted, mature economies need to depollute and decarbonize, and they have committed to doing so. But, as I discussed earlier, new economies will be a hotbed of all these issues combined. Pollution is staggering and bound to increase, while these regions will be the first areas to be impacted by climate transformations. This is also why there are many debates around the world on how to support them in making the right choices, so they can build a sustainable economy, with little action thus far. The opportunity is here; nothing prevents these regions from building their infrastructure right from the start, provided they effectively have access to the technology and to financing support. Yet, the challenge is certainly larger than that. The question of developing sustainable infrastructure in new economies is not limited to providing access to technologies and financing. It is obvious that the solutions that will be implemented will differ depending on the region, because of different needs and visions of what should be done. This is why, more importantly, creating the conditions for "reverse innovation" will prove critical. In the end, this kind of transition needs to also be an opportunity to create an environment favorable to economic development and to the integration of these economies into the global network of trade. This is probably to be one of the major challenges to adoption going forward, but it could also be one of the most rewarding ones to overcome in the end (Figure 2).

Figure 2   Demand-driven innovations

A civilization that reconciles itself with nature

There are thus three main revolutions that need to happen: in agriculture, industry, and energy. Available technologies can help alleviate the negative effects of pollution and climate change, and as they pervade these sectors further, they will continue to improve, following the law of increasing rates of return that governs them. In energy especially, they could potentially reduce GHG emissions by up to two-thirds, a major game changer, and arguably the only practical pathway available. Most of these challenges are however concentrated in new economies, and it is the ability of these countries to adopt and probably develop these innovations that will be tested.

If we take a step back, however, a greater ambition also takes shape: that of reconnecting humanity with a nature that is finally preserved and making peace with it. For millennia, people have confronted nature: first to survive, then to develop and thrive by controlling its resources. One could argue that humankind has finally prevailed. But at what cost? Could the developments I described above enable a new and harmonious relationship with nature, one that we seem to have forgotten, even if at times we reminisce about it when we leave our crowded urban centers?

References

Amadeo, K. (2019). "Climate Change Facts and Effect on the Economy." *Balance*, 27 January, updated November 3. https://www.thebalance.com/economic-impact-ofclimate-change-3305682.

AquaTT. (2020). "World Water Day 2020: Desalination Technologies Provide Safe and Sustainable Drinking Water." European Commission CORDIS EU research results. June 22. https://cordis.europa.eu/article/id/415568-world-water-day-2020-desalination-technologies-provide-safe-and-sustainable-drinking-water.

Berkey, The. (2020). "Water Pollution Facts: The Cost of Contamination." https://theberkey.com/blogs/water-filter/153003783-water-pollution-facts-the-cost-of-contamination.

Bloch, C., Newcomb, J., Shiledar, S., and Tyson, M. (2019). *Breakthrough Batteries: Powering the Era of Clean Electrification*. Report, Rocky Mountain Institute. https://rmi.org/insight/breakthrough-batteries/.

BloombergNEF. (2019). *New Energy Outlook*. Report, Bloomberg New Energy Finance. https://about.bnef.com/new-energy-outlook/.

Bosu, R. (2018). "China Redoubles Efforts Toward 'Beautiful China' by 2035." *China Plus*, May 22. http://chinaplus.cri.cn/opinion/opedblog/23/20180522/134276.html.

Bradford, A. (2018). Pollution Facts & Types of Pollution. Live Science, February 28. https://www.livescience.com/22728-pollution-facts.html.

Burke, M., Hsiang, S., and Miguel, E. (2015). "Global Non-Linear Effect of Temperature on Economic Production." *Nature* 527: 235–39. doi:10.1038/nature15725.

Citi. (2017). *Solutions for the Global Water Crisis. The End of 'Free and Cheap' Water.* Citi GPS: Global Perspectives and Solutions, April. https://www.citivelocity.com/citigps/solutions-global-water-crisis/.

Cohen, S. (2017). "The Human and Financial Cost of Pollution." State of the Planet (blog), Earth Institute, Columbia University, October 23. https://blogs.ei.columbia.edu/2017/10/23/the-human-and-financial-cost-of-pollution/.

Denchak, M. (2018). "Water Pollution: Everything You Need to Know." *NRDC*, May 14. https://www.nrdc.org/stories/water-pollution-everything-you-need-know.

Downing, S. (2020). "8 Electric Truck and Van Companies to Watch in 2020." *GreenBiz*, January 13. https://www.greenbiz.com/article/8-electric-truck-and-van-companies-watch-2020.

Ecavo. (2016). "Causes and Effects of Pollution." December 18. https://ecavo.com/pollution-causes-effects/.

Energy Transitions Commission. (2018). *Mission Possible: Reaching Net-Zero Carbon Emissions from Harder-to-Abate Sectors.* November. http://www.energy-transitions.org/mission-possible.

Energy Transitions Commission. (2020). *Making Mission Possible: Delivering a Net-Zero Economy.* September. https://www.energy-transitions.org/wp-content/uploads/2020/09/Making-Mission-Possible-Full-Report.pdf.

European Environment Agency. (2017). "Historic and Projected GDP in the EU, the Us, the BRICCS Countries and Other Countries." Last modified February 23. https://www.eea.europa.eu/data-and-maps/figures/past-and-projected-global-economic-output-1.

Everything Connects. (2013). "Soil Pollution." Last updated. November 20. https://www.everythingconnects.org/soil-pollution.html.

Food and Agriculture Organization. (2018). *Soil Pollution: A Hidden Reality.* Rome: FAO United Nations: http://www.fao.org/3/I9183EN/i9183en.pdf.

Food and Land Use Coalition. (2019). *Growing Better: Ten Critical Transitions to Transform Food and Land Use.* Global Consultation Report, September. https://www.foodandlandusecoalition.org/wp-content/uploads/2019/09/FOLU-GrowingBetter-GlobalReport.pdf.

Globe Water. (2020). "Water Pollution Statistics 2018–2019." https://www.globewater.org/facts/water-pollution-statistics/.

Griffith, S. (2020). *Rewiring America.* Rewiring America, November. https://www.rewiringamerica.org/handbook

Hariri, Y. N. (2014). *Sapiens: A Brief History of Humankind.* London: Harvill Secker.

Health Effects Institute. (2019). State of Global Air/2019. *A Special Report on Global Exposure to Air Pollution and Its Disease Burden.* Boston, MA: Health Effects Institute. https://www.stateofglobalair.org/sites/default/files/soga_2019_report.pdf.

Hirani, P., and Dimble, V. (2019). "Water Pollution Is Killing Millions of Indians. Here's How Technology and Reliable Data Can Change That." World Economic Forum, October 4. https://www.weforum.org/agenda/2019/10/water-pollution-in-india-data-tech-solution/.

Hockfield, S. (2019). *The Age of Living Machines: How Biology Will Build the Next Technology Revolution.* New York: W. W. Norton & Company.

I'mnovation (2020). "A New Approach in Desalination Could Make Use of Up to 90% of Treated Sea Water." I'mnovation #hub, https://www.imnovation-hub.com/water/a-new-approach-in-desalination-life-dreamer-project/.

Intergovernmental Panel on Climate Change. (2007). *Climate Change 2007: Synthesis Report. Contribution of Working Groups I, II and III to the Fourth Assessment Report of the Intergovernmental Panel on Climate Change.* Edited by the core writing team, R. K. Pachauri, and A. Reisinger. Geneva, Switzerland: IPCC. https://www.ipcc.ch/site/assets/uploads/2018/02/ar4_syr_full_report.pdf.

Intergovernmental Panel on Climate Change. (2014). *Climate Change 2014: Synthesis Report. Contribution of Working Groups I, II and III to the Fifth Assessment Report of the Intergovernmental Panel on Climate Change.* Edited by the core writing team, R. K. Pachauri, and A. Reisinger. Geneva, Switzerland: IPCC. https://www.ipcc.ch/site/assets/uploads/2018/02/SYR_AR5_FINAL_full.pdf.

International Energy Agency ©. (2018). *World Energy Outlook 2018.* November. Paris: IEA Publishing. https://www.iea.org/reports/world-energy-outlook-2018.

KPMG. (2014). "Future State 2030." https://home.kpmg.com/xx/en/home/insights/2015/03/future-state-2030.html.

Kuhn, R. (2013). "Xi Jinping's Chinese Dream." *New York Times,* June 4. https://www.nytimes.com/2013/06/05/opinion/global/xi-jinpings-chinese-dream.html.

Marshall, T. (2001). *Prisoners of Geography: Ten Maps That Tell You Everything You Need to Know about Global Politics.* London: Elliott & Thompson.

National Geographic. (2020). "Great Pacific Garbage Patch." https://www.nationalgeographic.org/encyclopedia/great-pacific-garbage-patch/.

Organisation for Economic Co-operation and Development. (2016). *The Economic Consequences of Outdoor Air Pollution.* June 9. Paris: OECD Publishing. https://doi.org/10.1787/9789264257474-en.

Organisation for Economic Co-operation and Development. (2020). *Environment at a Glance 2020.* June 9. Paris: OECD Publishing. https://doi.org/10.1787/4ea7d35f-en.

Pacific Institute. (2010). "World Water Quality Facts and Statistics." March 22. https://pacinst.org/wp-content/uploads/2013/02/water_quality_facts_and_stats3.pdf.

Parker, L. (2018). "Here's How Much Plastic Trash Is Littering the Earth." *National Geographic*, December 20. https://www.nationalgeographic.com/news/2017/07/plastic-produced-recycling-waste-ocean-trash-debris-environment/.

Petit, V. (2021). *The Future Global Order. The Six Paradigm Changes That Will Define 2050*. London: World Scientific Publishing.

Phys.org. (2019). "Water Pollution Can Reduce Economic Growth by a Third: World Bank." August 20. https://phys.org/news/2019-08-pollution-economic-growth-world-bank.html.

Pirlea, F., and Huang, W. V. (2019). "The Global Distribution of Air Pollution." World Bank, September 12. http://datatopics.worldbank.org/world-development-indicators/stories/the-global-distribution-of-air-pollution.html.

Ritchie, H., and Roser, M. (2019). Air pollution. https://ourworldindata.org/air-pollution.

Shell. (2018). "Sky Scenario." https://www.shell.com/energy-and-innovation/the-energy-future/scenarios/shell-scenario-sky.html.

State of Global Air. (2020). "Explore the Data." Health Effects Institute. https://www.stateofglobalair.org/data/#/air/plot.

Stern, N. (2006). *The Economics of Climate Change: The Stern Review*. Cambridge: Cambridge University Press. https://doi.org/10.1017/CBO9780511817434.

Stover, R. (2018). "Innovation Leads the Way to Solving Desalination Challenges." *Water Online*, July 12. https://www.wateronline.com/doc/innovation-leads-the-way-to-solving-desalination-challenges-0001.

System IQ & The Pew Charitable Trust (2020). Breaking the Plastic Wave. https://www.systemiq.earth/wp-content/uploads/2020/07/BreakingThePlasticWave_MainReport.pdf.

Tubb, C., and Seba, T. (2019). *Rethinking Food and Agriculture 2020–2030*. RethinkX, September. https://www.rethinkx.com/food-and-agriculture.

Tullo, A. (2019). "Plastic Has a Problem; Is Chemical Recycling the Solution?" *Chemical & Engineering News* 97, no. 39. https://cen.acs.org/environment/recycling/Plastic-problem-chemical-recycling-solution/97/i39.

Wade, K., and Jennings, M. (2016). The Impact of Climate Change on the Global Economy. Schroders, August 31. https://www.schroders.com/nl/sysglobalassets/digital/us/pdfs/the-impact-of-climate-change.pdf.

World Bank Group. (2020). "Employment in Agriculture (% of Total Employment) (Modeled ILO Estimate)." June 21. https://data.worldbank.org/indicator/SL.AGR.EMPL.ZS.

World Health Organization. (2019). "Drinking Water." June 14. https://www.who.int/news-room/fact-sheets/detail/drinking-water.

Woodford, C. (2020). "Land Pollution." *Explain that Stuff*, last updated April 22. https://www.explainthatstuff.com/land-pollution.html.

WRI. (2020). CAIT Climate Data Explorer. http://cait.wri.org/.

CHAPTER 7

The Future Will Be Very Different from the Way We Currently Conceive It

"There is nothing more difficult to take in hand, more perilous to conduct, or more uncertain in its success, than to take the lead in the introduction of a new order of things." (Machiavelli)

The World in 30 Years

Innovation-on-demand is truly at the heart of the upcoming energy transition

This chapter concludes the second part of this book. In Part 1, I set the debate straight and clarified that energy transitions, the topic of this book, were the byproduct of evolutions in "consumption," or demand, which were themselves driven by innovation and the quest for further abundance. This is important, because the harsh reality is that today's debates on the energy transition are totally off track regarding this evidence from energy history. Today's forecasts, scenarios, and conversations neither include innovation nor do they focus on demand.

Energy experts around the world try to answer this question:

"What new energy sources should we develop to meet existing demand needs and decarbonize the energy system?"

I commend the good faith of the intent, but the question is wrongly framed. It should rather be:

"What innovations will trigger demand changes that will, in turn, change and decarbonize the energy system, and how to foster their rapid adoption?"

The objective of Part 2 has been to explore the infinite potentialities of innovation (Figure 1). The approach I took was to build on three core issues of our current world: its inefficiency, the fragility of its construct, and its terrible impact on the environment. For millennia, humanity has tried to improve its fate and conditions of existence. Its quest has been that of abundance. This is why ancient foragers chose sedentarism and why nations and empires developed and prospered, and this is ultimately what modern industrial revolutions brought about. And abundance can only come if the current "operating system" is improved. Identifying its underlying issues and weaknesses and working solutions for these is the right proxy, I argue, to map out the upcoming innovations that will push civilization to its next stage of development and to a greater level of abundance.

Obviously, one could counter that building forecasts is a tricky exercise, and that innovations in demand are only one component of the equation. In other words, things could go wrong and innovations — as powerful as they can be — should be only one of the many parameters to take into account when predicting the future. I fully agree! And history has shown that sometimes, humankind had to grope in the dark, searching for a way forward. Yet, I would also argue that this should not be an excuse to not look for innovations that can (and ultimately will) change the world, hence the energy system; and I would also claim that the more we focus on the right things, i.e., life-changing innovations, the less time we need to spend crawling in the dark.

Finally, some could argue that despite being interesting, the map is incomplete. I would hope it is! Back to my earlier example. Do you remember what you did in 1990? As for myself, this is pretty much the period I started reading Jules Verne, and I was fascinated by "From the Earth to the Moon." I quickly learned that men had already landed on the moon, only 20 years earlier, and I had to picture myself in what must have been one of the greatest adventures of all times. Now, 30 years later, I have a computer in my pocket that is 100,000 times more powerful than the guiding system of Apollo 11. Granted, I do not necessarily use it to do extraordinary things, such as landing on the moon, but this says a lot about the surprises that might still come. Who would have envisioned we have such capacity at our fingertips in 2020, and what does it tell us about what to expect for 2050? What could we achieve that is truly useful with such already-existing capabilities in the coming 30 years? I truly hope that the next 30 years will be even more thrilling than the last 30 years have been, and I have reasons to believe that, with increasing awareness and a greater and more acute sense of issues, innovation will be blooming and blowing our minds. Hence, when forecasting what would happen to the energy system and what energy transition to drive, we would be better off taking those innovations into account.

Toward an ultra-efficient economy

Innovations	Drivers of adoption	Challenges to adoption
Buildings -blend -human-centric -autonomy	**Buildings** -convenience -productivity -cost -progressivity	**Buildings** -competency -business models -technology
Industry -BAT -process intensification -electrification -digital controls -circularity	**Industry** -productivity -cost -progressivity	**Industry** -policies -business models -technology
Mobility -multimodal -EV -TaaS -AV	**Mobility** -cost	**Mobility** -technology
Infrastructure -decentralized infrastructures	**Infrastructure** -productivity -cost	**Infrastructure** -competency

Human-centricity @ the core

Toward an ultra-resilient society

Innovations	Drivers of adoption	Challenges to adoption
Resources -circularity -new materials -sustainable food -energy	**Resources** -resiliency -progressivity	**Resources** -business models -technology
Trade -circularity -decentralized manufacturing -additive manufacturing	**Trade** -resiliency -inclusion	**Trade** -policies -business models -technology
Social -information -education -work -finance	**Social** -inclusion -progressivity	**Social** -policies

Decentralization @ the core

Toward an ultra-clean civilization

Innovations	Drivers of adoption	Challenges to adoption
Agriculture -precision agriculture -new fertilizers -atomic agriculture	**Agriculture** -pollution -climate change -health	**Agriculture** -new economies -policies
Industry waste -circularity -additive manufacturing -new materials	**Industry waste** -pollution -climate change -health	**Industry waste** -policies -business models
Energy -electrification -renewable energies	**Energy** -pollution -climate change -health	**Energy** -competency -business models -policies
Water -treatment -desalination	**Water** -pollution -health	**Water** -technology

Nature @ the core

Figure 1 Demand-driven innovations

In the three preceding chapters, I explored those issues in depth and have progressively developed a perspective on which innovations could emerge, alongside their key drivers of adoption and the associated challenges.

In every chapter, we have learned that a considerable potential for innovation exists to create systemic changes that will help drive further social progress, toward greater abundance. And as the world grapples with the threat of climate change (among others!), I argue that these positive transformations of demand can be the bedrock of rapid change.

Making the economy more efficient

The first one of the core issues reviewed was the efficiency of our economy. For as long as humankind has kept records of its development, it has traced and chased inefficiencies in order to do things better, at a lower cost, and with greater convenience. Despite the formidable strides of the last two centuries, with accelerated mechanization, a lot remains to be done. Consequently, many innovations will be spurred and bloom as the world becomes more conscious of these potential improvements. It is rather reassuring to imagine that further breakthroughs are possible, in every sector. There is no such thing as glass ceilings.

First, buildings are expected to evolve and transform. The historical paradigm that consisted of building a separate building for each use or commercial activity is being revisited. Blurring boundaries across time used and locations are the new norm. The quest for greater convenience and quality of service to the dweller will also lead to new use patterns that are digitally enabled, and to a main focus on putting the building "at the service" of its dweller. These new building types will enable a new level of granularity and speed in optimizing the utilization of space (and services) as well as the necessary utilities, such as energy, water, etc.

Next, industries are also in for a big change. The quest for productivity and greater competitiveness has always been the alpha and omega of industry all around. The deployment of best available technologies could already significantly raise overall efficiency, since many sectors in selected regions have had no access to them yet. The potential is significant already. Then, changes to processes can bring further benefits. Process intensification is a crucial area of research, especially in highly energy-intensive sectors such as the primary industry. Electrification has the potential to offer critical benefits, notably in manufacturing, as it provides more granular and faster control capabilities and thus higher precision and quality. Digital technologies have attracted considerable attention and enthusiasm in the last years. Coined as Industry 4.0, they indeed offer a greater level of granularity and control at higher speed, with significant support for operators and analytical capabilities. It is a foundational transformation, which goes hand in hand with electrification. Maybe more importantly, circularity could be the next wave of innovation, one that provides systemic benefits that we cannot begin to envision. Circularity is a broad concept that can basically be broken down into five key activities: energy and resource conservation, lifetime extension, utilization optimization, reducing demand, and recycling. These activities, particularly if they are taken together, can *systematically* reduce the footprint of modern industry, generating a major revolution that would have no equivalent except for the intense mechanization of the second half of the twentieth century.

Third, mobility will probably be the first area to transform. Mobility has been at the heart of the first two industrial revolutions: railways, then cars and planes. This is also because mobility has long been extremely inefficient. For millennia, people have been living in isolation. As poetic as sailing boats and ancient commercial routes of the Silk Road may appear in retrospect, the reality is that the global economy and life are way better since global trade has become safer, cheaper, and much quicker. Yet, progress can still be made, essentially around two main topics. First, private mobility assets (cars) are idle 95 percent of the time; a huge waste of capital, which translates into cost. Second, congestion has developed alongside urbanization, leading to a massive time waste for everyone, not to mention stress. Who remembers William Foster (impersonated by Michael Douglas) in *Falling Down*, the middle-aged engineer who loses it and starts shooting around because he gets stuck in traffic for too long? Greater multimodal mobility services, enabled by digital technologies and coupled with the electrification of mobility, transport as a service (TaaS), and ultimately autonomous vehicles will turn a sector that has made a living of building idle assets upside down. The potential benefits for the global economy are in US$ trillions.

Finally, infrastructure will also evolve, notably gas and electric utilities. Once again, and despite commendable efforts to manage them as well as possible, these infrastructures are by design unoptimized. Yet, unlike tunnels or railways, which depend on traffic, the flows of energy could end up being optimized in the next stage of innovation, considerably improving the systemic efficiency of these infrastructures and thus reducing their cost to the economy. This would however come with a significant change to the way these infrastructures are being accounted for in total costs of energy. A similar evolution as that in telecommunications could happen in the sector over time.

Building a more resilient society

The second of the core issues reviewed is the fragile construct of our current societies. Why is it that at times the world's history derails? When the inherent fragilities of our living together are exposed, then history takes side trails and progress can be halted for some time. Think of every war, epidemic, social eruption, and civilizational collapse. These have always been the consequence of inherent fragilities. The 2020 Covid-19 crisis has spilled a lot of ink on the topic of resiliency, and on how (Western) societies needed to develop a more resilient environment that would be immune to upcoming crises. I have little interest in shortsighted discussions that are often a manifestation of electoral ambitions, but one must recognize that resiliency (in everything) is a central driver of innovation. Taking some distance, I identified three areas where innovations could materialize.

First, resources. Materials, food and water, and energy. The world has grown so large that pressure on resources has intensified, and with it dependencies across regions. This could take a dramatic turn if scarcity were to emerge, particularly of food. Yet, many innovations are expected to prevent this from happening. As mentioned, circularity is a primary enabler of reduced dependencies: producing more economic output, with less resources. Materials depletion will however not be averted by efficiency alone. Research on new materials could significantly change the paradigm. Scarcity of food and water is also a reality in certain regions of the world and could turn into an even bigger issue in the coming decades. Yet, innovations in atomic-scale agriculture, developing essential building blocks such as nutrients and microorganisms, could contribute to alleviating the issue. Finally, renewable energies endowments have proven to be, in every region, much larger than today's energy demand. Innovations in harvesting this significant potential will redefine the sector in the coming decades: digital technologies, nanotechnologies and biotechnologies, and electrification will be its foundations.

Second, trade is also a key point of failure in the system. Circularity — once again — because it improves the use of resources and finished goods and helps tame trade volumes, thus reduce dependencies. Beyond, the rise of more distributed manufacturing is more than likely, powered by increased automation and digital capabilities. Additive manufacturing could also play a significant role in certain highly commoditized sectors. All these could significantly reduce dependencies across nations. It would not put an end to global trade, which is probably one of the best global achievements of the last decades, but create more buffers and fewer critical dependencies in the system.

Last, social inequalities are likely one of the greatest challenges our current construct has to face, particularly in a better-informed planet. Inequalities can exist within population classes in a given nation or among nations. Yet again, innovation has the potential to significantly improve the situation. Inequalities are less of an issue than their perpetuation. The "American dream" has been a source of inspiration for all those who have pictured the United States as a land of opportunity, where hard work could help climb the ladders of society. It is acceptable to start from a low position if one can elevate oneself during the course of one's life, and if one who sits on top because of where they were born can also fall down. Yet, inequalities tend to be perpetuated and passed along the generations, because someone who sits at the bottom of the ladder does not have the same access to opportunities as someone who sits on top. In this regard, digital technologies can and will be a powerful "equalizer," providing greater access to information, education, work opportunities, and financing to all. This could be one of the greatest legacies of digital technologies in the twenty-first century.

Reinventing a harmonious relationship with nature

The last of the core issues I explored is that of pollution. Interestingly enough, our modern civilization has developed based on the perceived abundance of God-given free resources, be it air, water, or soil (and its resources). The quest of the last two centuries has therefore been that of increased harvesting through mechanization and industrialization, with little regard for preservation. Yet, humanity has grown so large that the paradigm of the twenty-first century is probably more of a species sharing a "common spaceship," with the primary focus on preserving its resources so it will last longer. The new abundance may well be that of renewed natural endowments. And as there has been little focus on preservation so far, pollution is now taking center stage. The origins of this pollution are threefold: agriculture, industrial waste, and energy.

First, agriculture will likely undergo a new revolution. The twentieth-century revolution was already massive. Founded on mechanization and industrialization, modern agriculture has generated major productivity and yield improvements. Yet, this has been mostly in mature economies. As urbanization increases, the same now needs to happen in new economies. But this industrialization has also led to significant pollution. Significant efforts are being made to continue upgrading productivity levels while replacing polluting fertilizers and pesticides with less harmful ones. A twenty-first-century agriculture is within reach as well, one that explores the potentialities of working at an atomic scale to rebuild, rather than grow food. This would present a significant potential, particularly for economies most exposed to scarcity, such as new economies.

Second, industrial waste is a major source of pollution. Circularity, once again, is a major enabler of mitigating pollution by reducing the environmental footprint of industrial value chains. Additive manufacturing could help further reduce the need for materials and thus the associated pollution. Going further, the next frontier will be to develop new materials that are less harmful to the environment, leveraging atomic-scale nanotechnologies and biotechnologies.

Next, energy is both a source of direct pollution and the critical root cause of climate change through its release of vast quantities of greenhouse gases. These gases are not harmful to the environment per se, but their increased concentration in the atmosphere triggers climate evolutions that could turn into a global catastrophe. Electrification is the only energy vehicle that does not release emissions at the point of use, and so is the obvious solution to mitigate pollution. It is already a well-understood area of innovation for mobility or heating. As it substitutes fossil fuels, the associated pollution from extracting and refining these fossil fuels diminishes. Yet, the production of electricity is one of the most polluting activities, essentially since it heavily relies on combusting polluting fuels such as coal. The switch to competitive and clean energy sources to produce electricity is a critical area of innovation that has already made great strides in the past couple of decades with renewable energies and will continue to do so, as research continues to progress.

Finally, water is set to become a critical issue in the decades to come, due to the combined effect of increased water scarcity caused by climate change and significant water pollution. While wastewater treatment will become of the utmost importance and probably an area of further innovation in the decades to come, it is undeniable that humanity has had access to only a fraction of the water available on Earth, mainly because the overwhelming majority of it is salinized and thus unfit for consumption. Water desalination has existed for decades but has so far not managed to reach competitive levels, particularly in the sectors where freshwater is the most used: agriculture, industry, and energy. Further developments in this field, particularly through greater recourse to ultra-affordable energy sources, incremental improvements in process efficiency, or the use of new materials (based on atomic-scale technologies) could help further develop this industry.

A new world is taking shape

Innovation will thus build on making the economy more efficient, creating a society that is more resilient (or at least alleviating its key issues), and reinventing a (more) harmonious relationship with nature. These innovations will build on three main technology areas: energy sources, which will capitalize on renewable energies (especially solar) and storage solutions; digital technologies, which will build on increased computing power, ubiquity, and connectivity; and nanotechnologies and biotechnologies, which will make it possible to work at an atomic scale and redefine the building blocks humanity has traditionally been playing with.

What these three areas have in common is that they hold the potential for infinite scalability, highly decentralized setups, and increasing rates of return. They are infinitely scalable because they depend on production scale. The more production increases, the more costs go down, fueling a virtuous cycle of exponential adoption. They favor highly decentralized setups, since they can virtually be integrated everywhere. This is true for any of these three technologies, pushing the boundaries of decentralization to levels that have not yet been imagined. What if tomorrow's laptops or appliances could all integrate energy sources and become autonomous? What if connectivity could be associated with every appliance or device we use, such as glasses or wearables, or even be directly integrated into our bodies? What if nanotechnologies became the new frontier of medicine? Finally, they provide increasing rates of return. Every time the technologies progress — and they naturally do with accelerated adoption, which brings additional financing capabilities for innovation — the next upgrade creates additional benefits, at lowered costs. In other words, increasing productivity and rates of return.

It is because of these three fundamental characteristics that adoption is likely inevitable. And with adoption will come the opportunities for change I described above. They will be inexorable improvements.

My analysis in the previous chapters also demonstrates that these developments will achieve more than simple enhancements of our current condition. They will be foundational in reaching the stringent targets of a net-zero economy by 2050, i.e., very rapid decarbonization, because they hold the potential to pervade faster our daily uses than any other option available, as they provide increased benefits at the same time. Again, demand innovations are the true drivers of any energy transition. More importantly, they will also profoundly change our vision of how life, society, and the economy should be organized. Ultimately, they will transform our view of what matters and what does not, and how some of the big issues confronting us should be dealt with.

The world of tomorrow will be more human-centric and more decentralized, and nature is expected to make its comeback to the center of our civilization. The next stage of economic improvement will be that of human-centricity. The greatest part of the twentieth century has been about industrializing the production of goods through standardization in order to cut costs and make these products accessible to a greater share of people. The twenty-first century will change this. Why? Because we will reach a level where manufacturing will become more (and, why not, entirely) commoditized, so there will ultimately be a shift in economic value. The new value will be to develop and create goods that are personally relevant to everyone, and not to mass-produce them. Are we far from this reality still? Not at all. That is what Erik Sprunk (Nike COO) was talking about in 2018. It is only a matter of time. Buildings — and in fact every facility we live, work, or entertain ourselves in — will become an "electronic orchestra" entirely fit for individual experiences. Human-centricity, associated with manufacturing commoditization, will also change the way products are traded. Why put a price on a product whose manufacturing is worth close to nothing? What will now be of value will be the individual experience. Hence, economic trade will progressively become more service-oriented or experience-oriented. This will change the economy for the better, eliminating inefficiencies and creating new opportunities for more local and customized services, a picture at odds with the current situation.

Second, our societies will become more decentralized. For over 10,000 years, since ancient foraging groups gave way to agricultural societies, our organized systems have looked at further centralizing institutions to increase "control and power" over ever larger quantities of real estate and the population. Expansion and verticalized command have been core components of our modern societies. And with this have come conflicts, the rise and fall of empires, and sustained inequalities among people and societies; in other words, fragilities. I am not arguing that all this will change in one day, but the very practical transformations I described in the earlier chapters will reshape societies. They will likely become more egalitarian in the sense that they will offer greater opportunities to all. More importantly, they will also contribute to redefining boundaries of belonging and interaction. They will help local ecosystems become more independent, self-managed, and vibrant; more decentralized societies. The question is, to which extent? It will certainly be an order of magnitude more decentralized than current nations and states (even if it does not replace them per se). What is striking about this conclusion, how-ever, is that it provides a very different perspective on globalization than the one people are used to. From the 1990s until recently, globalization was per-ceived as a positive accelerator of development for all, but also one that tended to uniformize societies according to the same model, essentially the American one. From 2017 onward, however, the US administration has acknowledged its progressive retreat from global leadership, leaving the rest of the world rather unprepared. Some have therefore begun to advocate for regionalization, relocalization, or greater autonomy. Their claims have grown stronger during the Covid-19 crisis, which exposed some dependencies. These populist claims are dead-ends, because throughout history, civilizations have thrived when global trade was efficient. Global trade is the cornerstone of peace and devel-opment and will always be. What has happened between 2017 and 2020 could ultimately be a mere accident that no one will remember five years from now. But a third model of globalization seems to emerge: one of a peaceful, interconnected, decentralized world. Global trade and exchange remain because they are at the heart of peace and economic and social development. However, uniformization gives way to more decentralized societies, where local cultures and peculiarities are reinvigorated; once more, a picture of a world at odds with current visions.

Finally, our societies will probably reinvent their relationship with nature. Common wisdom once again is that people will continue to move to and live in urban centers, as they have been doing since the first industrial revolution. Why? Because they are in search of a better future and more opportunities. But the shift to more decentralized societies brings this continued movement into question. Could we be at the dawn of a radical turnaround in urbanization, one that nobody expects? Everyone in the entire world unanimously recognizes the feeling of fulfillment, blossoming, and appeasement that fills the heart when entering the countryside, particularly areas that we are emotionally attached to. What does this tell us? People are instinctively built to live close to (and as a part of) nature. If not, a part of them remains unfulfilled. The twentieth century brought wealth to billions, but also dramatic damage to the environment, which everyone laments. Early developments in the twenty-first century show much greater awareness of the issue, on the one hand thanks to new technologies that make it more transparent, and on the other hand because the effects of this damage are becoming increasingly visible. A large part of the twenty-first century will be about repairing that damage, and this will be unanimously demanded in every country and every community. One of the key outcomes of this will be that a value is assigned to natural resources. For ages, humanity has considered nature as the infinite realm in which it had to develop itself to prosper. In the nineteenth and the twentieth centuries, people thought they had finally learned how to control nature and make the best of its infinite endowments. Now that the population has expanded severalfold and humanity's needs have grown very large, people realize that nature is not infinite. This will be the great discovery of the twenty-first century. Some could argue that people already know that. Yes, but they have not yet changed their habits. How much time will it take: one generation, more or less? Time will tell, but it is almost certain that later in the twenty-first century, any sampling of nature's resources will come at a price, if not a cost. And that will probably change everything and shake up the economy in ways that are yet to be defined. Just picture this: every material, energy resource, or amount of water that we take from the ground costs zero today. The cost of the resource depends on the infrastructure needed to supply it. What if this were to change entirely?

The world of tomorrow will thus change alongside innovations. It will become more human-centric and more decentralized, and have a new relationship with nature. For ages, humanity has tried to improve its condition. The goal has always been, across all times and places, to have greater abundance, to prosper and thrive. These innovations will all contribute to greater abundance. A more efficient economy is also an economy in which the cost of accessing a good or service is lower, and thus it is more abundant. A more resilient society is one in which scarcity is reduced and opportunities are more evenly distributed; hence, a more abundant society. A civilization that reinvents its relationship with nature is one that offers to return to humanity its direct connection to nature's endowments and reconcile humanity with its inner instincts. In other words, greater abundance. And because these innovations will all contribute to greater abundance, they are all inevitable. They simply make sense.

Why is it important?

"Unfortunately, by dint of judging, one ends up almost fatally losing the desire to explain" (Marc Bloch). The biggest problem in history has always been anachronism and judgment. In other words, analyzing the past using the perspectives of the present. Well, the reverse is true for predicting the future: shaping the future with the perspectives of the present, as if nothing will change. In fact, everything will change, and it is inevitable. The entire purpose of this book is to demonstrate this evidence. One could argue that I did not need a whole book to reach such a conclusion, but fact is that nobody integrates this evidence into climate or energy transition forecasts, or, for what it is worth, any scenario or approach I have come across. The unfortunate outcome? Wrong expectations lead to wrong actions. This is why developing a sharp eye on what the future may look like is important. This will also save time by preventing us from groping in the dark, looking for an answer, or wondering why things did not happen the way we anticipated them to. And this is the key question, ultimately. At which pace will these innovations unfold? Will it be fast enough to mitigate some of the biggest issues at hand, including (but not limited to) climate change? I will come back to this.

The Age of Fire Is Over

Unexpected changes to the energy system

The detailed analysis I conducted in the last three chapters has laid out a score of transformations. I have demonstrated that they are largely inevitable. As I am closing this second part of the book, it is time to identify the potential impact they can have on the energy system.

We can make sense of the above by categorizing these innovations into three types of impact on the energy system. First, the extent to which they contribute to reducing demand for energy. Next, new demand patterns that emerge from these innovations and that come on top of existing services. Finally, the shifts in energy sources for each type of demand.

Final energy demand could be significantly decreased by the deployment of such technologies. In buildings, there is a large potential for more efficiency, as we have seen above, with benchmark energy intensities two-thirds below those of the existing building stock (and up to 50 percent for retrofits). The evolution of the building stock toward more blended uses is also likely to help reduce and optimize its footprint and thus have a positive effect on energy demand by reducing the volume of construction and repurposing some of the existing stock, essentially for commercial buildings (office, retail centers, etc.). In industry, circularity could play a systemic role in curbing the growing demand for final goods (manufacturing) and raw materials (primary industry). It would also have ripple effects on logistics and freight transport. The accelerated penetration of digital technologies is expected to mean less travel for all. In this regard, the Covid-19 crisis has demonstrated that "white collars" were as productive (if not more) with less travel. Moreover, the development of mobility services (TaaS; multimodal services; and ultimately autonomous vehicles) will probably lead to a drop in mobility-associated energy demand: among others, a greater recourse to services that help optimize the number of cars on the road and a reduction in congestion (less consumption).

New energy demand will also emerge that will in part compensate for these reductions. A potential halt or slowdown of urbanization could reboot private homeownership, particularly if homes become highly affordable thanks to new construction technologies (e.g., additive manufacturing). This would entail greater household surface per capita, hence energy demand. In the industry sector, the production of new materials as they emerge will represent a new source of energy demand that will (in part) replace traditional primary industry. Then, distributed manufacturing could come at the expense of highly efficient industrial setups, hence pushing energy demand upward. Both evolutions would also, and maybe more importantly, modify the geographical distribution of industrial energy demand, with a greater balance across regions. The agriculture sector is often forgotten in most energy balances, simply because the vast majority of the energy it uses is that of the sun, either directly (crops) or indirectly (livestock), through natural photosynthesis. The atomic agriculture revolution that I described would be a further step toward industrialization. While it would help decrease part of traditional energy demand (tractors, machines), it would also create new needs for modern forms of energy. The water industry comes next and is also likely to become progressively more energy-intensive, as the necessity to produce water becomes more patent across vital geographies. Finally, the deployment of digital technologies across all sectors will lead to an increase of associated energy demand. More computing in appliances will also raise the energy demand of those. More computing power and data storage needs will expand the footprint of data centers. Ubiquitous connectivity (notably mobile) will increase the energy demand of networks.

Last, there will also be changes in energy sources for selected demand types. Electrification will be paramount in most sectors as the most efficient, resilient, and clean source of energy, as we have seen. It is increasingly competitive across all sectors. This will concern heat in buildings and industry (up to a certain extent in primary industry — time will tell to what extent) as well as motion applications (motors and machines in industry, but also mobility, at least road transport). Electrification will also be the core energy source of most demand increases we have identified, be it to produce new materials for distributed manufacturing and additive manufacturing or to create twenty-first-century agriculture and water production systems. Energy production (in the form of electricity) will also be increasingly decentralized. This will contribute to the reshaping of energy infrastructure, which is traditionally centralized, but could also lead to an increasing number of appliances being partially or fully autonomous, with impacts on total "measured" energy demand (Figure 2).

This book is about the upcoming energy transition. So far, I have described transformations that were only indirectly related to the energy industry. I will now make sense of this description and connect these transformations to the impacts they will have on the future energy system.

We can thus ask the question: how sizable will these evolutions in the energy system turn out to be?

In one word: considerable. This is why any energy forecast that does not take these evolutions into account should be disregarded right from the start. This is also why all efforts to better comprehend the extent and pace of these changes should now converge.

Significant evolution of existing demand

One of the key aspects of my current work is to draw forecasts and scenarios that help inform my company's strategy going forward. As part of this exercise, I also spend considerable time reviewing forecasts by others, so that I can cross-check and compare my findings. Therefore, I know firsthand how complicated

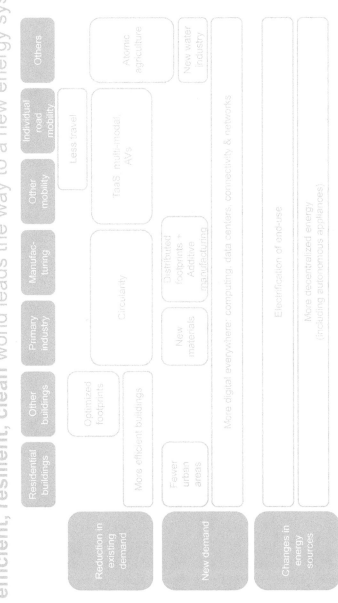

Figure 2 Changes in demand

it can be to do this kind of exercise, and how many forecasts can be challenged. Ultimately, they are only as good as their assumptions. This is also why I decided to write this book. I find that the assumptions made in current forecasts do not properly reflect what will happen: the set of innovations and transformations that I described before. Yet, this book is not about building a concurrent forecast. This would provoke too many rightful challenges to my argument, without serving a useful purpose. My intent, to recap, is to make a case for looking at the transition in the right way so that collective bodies and agencies set out to develop forecasts and scenarios with the right set of assumptions in hand.

But one could argue that this is too easy of an argument and that I cannot escape from outlining some of the large quantitative changes that we should expect, and one would be right. So, let's try to make sense of it all with some figures. Our current energy system fulfills around 120,000 TWh a year of final energy demand (International Energy Agency, 2019). Typically, data is reported using various metrics that depend on the energy type. I have decided to use terawatt hours as the baseline metric for all types of energy. Fossil fuels represent the vast majority of final energy demand. It is important to realize that electricity, which represents around 20 percent of final demand, is essentially produced from fossil fuels. In fact, total primary demand (i.e., raw resources) is even more dominated by fossil fuels. What is also interesting is that traditional biomass is still a large part of final demand. This form of

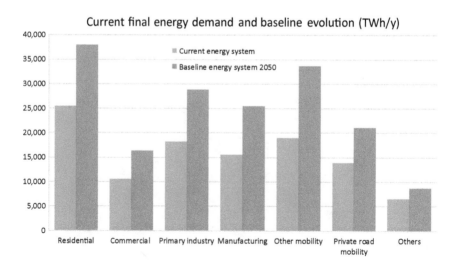

Figure 3   Current energy system and its evolution

energy meets cooking, lighting, and sometimes heating needs in low-income new economies.

In the following exercise, I will look at the final energy demand at a global level and use a 2050 baseline, which is extrapolated from data from the International Energy Agency (2019) that assumes a continuation of current trends (what the International Energy Agency refers to as the Current Policy Scenario). I have estimated the split across sectors for both today's and 2050 forecasts, assuming equal shares over time (Figure 3).

We can already acknowledge the theoretical aspect of the exercise, with baseline forecasts that could easily be challenged. In addition, nothing indicates that all transformations I described above will be fully realized by 2050. I will look at what challenges their unfolding in the last part of this book. Yet, I use this timeline as a basis on which to evaluate the transformations' full potential impact. As said, my intent here is to briefly assess the impacts of the transformations mentioned above, not run a precise modeling exercise.

The existing demand footprint will first evolve from the combined effects of reduced demand and electrification. We can take the list I provided above and make some assumptions (Figure 4):

- Buildings: I assume that optimized building footprints will deliver a 10 percent optimization in the stock, while new technologies will make it possible to reach 70 percent efficiency in new buildings and 50 percent in existing ones. At the same time, the building stock will be up to 80 percent electrified in residential buildings and 90 percent in other building types, and most low-density applications will become autonomous (I assume that represents around 10 percent of demand: lighting, IT, security, etc.).
- Industry: I assume circularity will deliver a reduction of 20 percent of the footprint through better sharing, lifetime extension, and asset optimization of the stock, while energy and resource conservation measures will bring 20 percent efficiency to plants' performance, and recycling will apply to 50 percent of primary materials production. Next, 90 percent of the manufacturing industry stock will become electric for heating, with only 25 percent of that in primary industry.
- Mobility: Overall travel volume will be reduced by 10 percent because of fewer commutes and trips abroad thanks to digital technologies. TaaS and autonomous vehicles will enable a reduction of 75 percent of cars in cities. Freight transport will also be impacted by the reduction in final goods demand. Finally, 100 percent of the road transport stock will be electrified (individual cars as well as trucks).

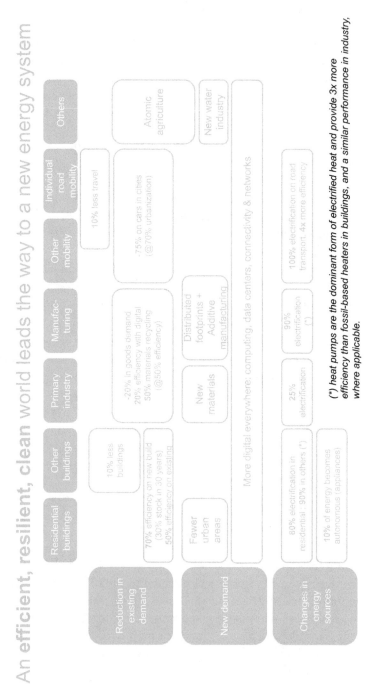

Figure 4   Existing demand evolution

Rise of digital technologies in the energy mix

We must add the actual new demand that will emerge from these innovations to the analysis. The first of these is the energy demand from digital technologies. According to Andrae and Edler (2015), who have conducted what is probably the most comprehensive study to date, energy demand associated with digital technologies could grow between 3 and 13 percent on a yearly basis, with an expected annual growth of around 7–8 percent. This matches other studies (Mills, 2013; Shift Project, 2019). Andrae (2020) later revised his forecast to an annual growth of 4 percent to 2030. The difference between forecasts is related to assumptions about the efficiencies that can be realized on these technologies in terms of computing and storage power demand and use, but also network performance (for instance, 5G is 10–20 times more energy-efficient than 4G, International Energy Agency, 2020). The International Energy Agency (2017) has estimated that overall growth will be rather flat in the coming few years due to efficiency gains. It declined to provide a long-term perspective because of the inherent uncertainties associated with technology developments, a position I can fully understand. Nevertheless, and for the sake of the exercise, I can take a 5 percent annual growth rate and use 2050 as our baseline to estimate what demand could look like and obtain a perspective on the rising share of digital technologies in total energy demand.

The energy demand associated with digital is divided into that of data centers and networks, connected devices, and manufacturing. Andrae and Edler (2015) have estimated that in 2015, data centers and networks accounted for around 500–1,100 TWh, devices for 600–1,200 TWh, and manufacturing for around 200–800 TWh. In absolute terms, this is a total energy demand of 1,300–3,100 TWh, accounting for perimeter changes and uncertainties. In his 2020 forecast, Andrae (2020) estimated demand to range around 1,700 TWh. He also recognized that devices' demand is likely to drop over time due to their convergence and increased efficiency. This drop could be even larger if we consider that part of these devices could become autonomous.

Overall, with such assumptions, and taking 2,000 TWh as a baseline, digital technologies would account for around 9,000 TWh by 2050. This increase would mainly be driven by increased computing and connectivity, in data centers and networks.

New demand for twenty-first-century agriculture

The second new source of demand will be that of twenty-first-century agriculture. Here, we must rely on the work of Tubb and Seba (2019), which has laid the groundwork for this transformation. Total energy demand for agriculture includes the energy required to produce fertilizers and pesticides and that to carry out on-farm activities (using diesel engines) and off-farm activities (refrigeration, etc.). The estimate of on-farm energy requirements is negligible, at around 200–300 TWh a year. However, fertilizers and pesticides represent around 30 percent of petrochemicals output, around 2,000 TWh a year. This includes feedstock, which is essentially of fossil-fuel origin (Levi and Cullen, 2018). Finally, food refrigeration would represent around 6 percent of total energy demand (Tubb and Seba, 2019), or around 6,000 TWh annually. Tubb and Seba estimate that these needs (in total around 8,000 TWh) would collapse with the rise of atomic-based modern food production systems.

Yet, additional electricity demand would be required to power the new facilities. Food intake per year can be estimated at around 8,500 TWh globally today. I compute this value by considering the average calory intake per person per year. Food demand will also evolve with the increase in population and increased food intake, growing by an estimated 70 percent by 2050 (Petit, 2021). Proteins correspond to around 8 percent of that, according to my estimate (based on data from the New Zealand Nutrition Foundation, 2020). The efficiency of traditional protein production (animal-based) is around 4 percent, but that of modern production could reach 60 percent (Tubb and Seba, 2019); in other words, an additional energy demand of 1,900 TWh for protein production facilities (essentially electric). The ability to scale up beyond proteins has not really been demonstrated, so I will assume only a switch to modern protein production here. This could have a significant effect on refrigeration needs (reducing their footprint): I estimate that 10 percent of that energy would be displaced, or around 600 TWh. This translates into an additional electricity demand of 1,300 TWh.

New demand in a water-scarce world

The third source of new demand will be water production. Annual fresh water demand adds up to nearly 4,000 cubic kilometers, and it could increase by 50 percent by 2050 (Citi, 2017; International Renewable Energy Agency, 2015; UNESCO, 2017). The overwhelming majority of supply comes from direct extraction from freshwater sources (surface or groundwater). Desalination represents less than 1 percent of water supply (International Renewable Energy Agency, 2015). All this needs energy to be extracted and distributed. Groundwater pumping is ten times more energy-intensive than surface water sampling. Desalination is 100 times more energy-intensive (International Energy Agency, 2016). Water distribution is as energy-intensive as groundwater pumping. Wastewater represents around 50 percent of total water withdrawals, essentially in agriculture drainage (UNESCO, 2017). Also, 80 percent of that wastewater is not treated, as we have seen above. The rest is processed through water treatment plants, which demand energy to run and operate with an intensity similar to groundwater pumping (International Energy Agency, 2016).

I can make sense of all of this and come up with a total energy demand of around 2,500 TWh per year today. A large majority is devoted to distribution. The majority of demand is electricity, but some diesel engines can be used for groundwater pumping in remote agriculture, and natural gas for some desalination applications (a minor share of the total).

Based on this knowledge, it is possible to estimate the evolution of water demand in a (more) water-scarce world. I assume first that displacement of protein production would have a 30 percent impact on water demand devoted to agriculture since this is the share of crops farming devoted to feeding livestock (Plumer, 2014). I then assume that the increase in water demand will be almost entirely supplied by desalination (since the increase happens for the most part in water-scarce regions), and I assume that water treatment is maximized for municipal and industrial wastewater. Corresponding energy demand is around 7,500 TWh, or three times today's and over two times the 2050 baseline, and is mainly driven by a significant rise in desalination needs. We can also consider that by then, cheaper, renewable-based (electric for the most part) solutions will have substituted the remaining fossil fuels in use.

Other rebounds in new demand

The last section includes other transformations, such as the slowdown of urbanization, the advent of distributed manufacturing and additive manufacturing, and the development of new materials. I assume (arbitrarily) a rebound of 10 percent of demand in residential due to the slowdown of concentrated urban landscapes.

I also assume that 10 percent of manufacturing demand will turn into decentralized applications with additive manufacturing (effectively consolidated in the building demand and no longer in the industrial sector) and that these will generate a relative increase in demand of 10 percent.

New materials will also come in and substitute some existing ones. Since the potential is still unclear, I assume 20 percent substitution, and no efficiency between the two processes (which remains to be proven!). New materials are however primarily built on electric energy, unlike historic ones, which rely more on fossil fuels and other sources such as biomass (Figure 5).

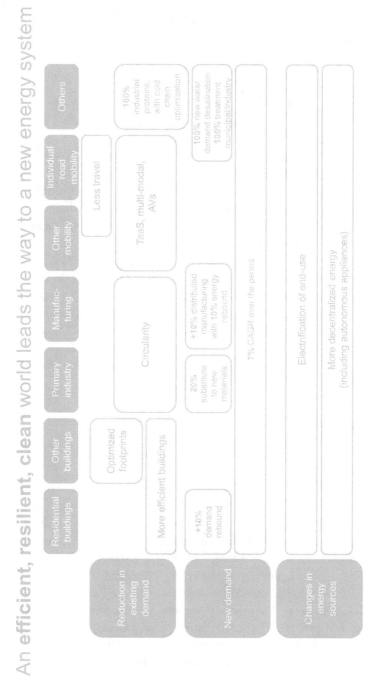

Figure 5   New demand

The Age of Fire Is Over

If we consolidate all the work above, on both existing demand evolutions and new demand evolutions, we come up with a new final energy demand of around 96,000 TWh, slightly below that of today and representing a 45 percent reduction compared to the baseline.

Existing demand will actually drop by around 50 percent, thanks to massive efficiency improvements and electrification, while new demand sources (digital, water, and agriculture) will come in and partially compensate this optimization.

The other remarkable outcome is the share of electricity, which will climb to constitute from around 20 percent to around 70 percent of the energy mix, at around 67,000 TWh per year. In the meantime, the need for fossil fuels and biomass will drop by 70–80 percent, depending on the source.

This transition marks the end of an era in which humanity relied on combusting fuels to procure energy. This is a transition that moves away from the paradigm that has prevailed for millennia. In effect, the Age of Fire, or that of combusting fuels to harvest energy, is over.

Hence the title of this book

Innovations in demand will transform the energy system into a more electric one, effectively removing fossil fuels from the energy system. This is because they will provide solutions to existing issues in our economy and society, and because they are infinitely scalable, highly decentralized, and characterized by increasing rates of return.

Scenarios and forecasts for the future are as good as their assumptions. I have made this argument all along in this book. The above thought experiment does not escape this rule! Notably, there could be other rebounds in demand that have not been anticipated. In a world of greater abundance, demand could in fact rise faster and outstrip part of the efficiency generated. Yet, I did not want to turn this book into a detailed and precise forecast, but rather use it to propose some interesting insights into how we can build one. The above quantitative estimate should thus be taken for what it is: a first attempt at describing what innovations could provide in terms of benefits. My only intent is that it triggers debates and further refinements in collective works around these topics (Figures 6 and 7).

A few others have already begun to explore some of these potentialities. The Energy Transitions Commission (2020) has developed a scenario in which final energy demand would drop by 15 percent and direct electrification reach 70 percent of the final energy mix by 2050. These results are not far removed from the ones presented above. However, although assumptions about electrification are

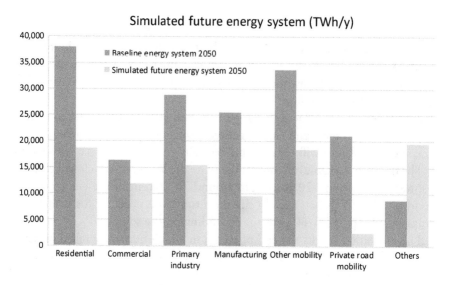

Figure 6   Future energy system

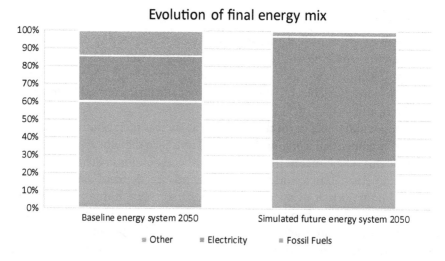

Figure 7   Future energy mix

very similar, those about existing demand are quite different. My forecast is much more aggressive, but also considers additional and new demand patterns that the Energy Transitions Commission has not taken into account.

Another interesting forecast is that of Grubler *et al.* (2018), which was published in the well-known *Nature* magazine in 2018. It introduces the

"Low Energy Demand" scenario, which builds on some technological advancements described above (not all). Their scenario refers to them as "granular" technologies (I call them infinitely scalable, highly decentralized). Final energy demand is nearly 40 percent lower than baseline demand (close to my own findings). Direct electrification reaches around 55 percent of final energy demand. A critical outcome of their study is also that these technologies are likely to penetrate the economy more quickly and provide higher learning rates (and increasing rates of return). This is a critical point as it shows a feasible pathway to decarbonize the economy at a pace consistent with current commitments (halve emissions by 2030, zero by 2050). Hence demand transformations are more suitable to rapid turnaround while they also provide increased benefits to consumers (greater abundance). My argument all along in this book.

All these efforts are obviously highly commendable and bring interesting and fresh perspectives to the upcoming energy transition, which differ greatly from traditional approaches used by other organizations, despite the latter's intrinsic qualities. Results differ because models and assumptions differ. I can only hope that more research on demand patterns will emerge in the coming years, and that this movement of looking at what truly matters in energy transitions will progressively take center stage.

Critical impact on power infrastructure

As part of the transition described above, another change will occur as well: that of the increased decentralization of energy production, especially with the increasing number of rooftop solar systems. The building stock today is around 200 billion square meters and is expected to reach 350–400 billion by 2050 (International Energy Agency, 2013; SDSN and FEMM, 2019). The bulk of new constructions is expected to happen in Africa, China, and India, in that order.

Yet, not all that surface translates into solar panel surface. Roofs typically correspond to a share of the size of the ground surface, and it varies across building types. Hence, global rooftop surface must be evaluated. We can try to create a rough estimate. Individual household roofs typically measure around half of the total habitable surface, while small buildings' roofs measure around 25–30 percent and large buildings' roofs around 10 percent of the surface. Individual households represent around 50 percent of total surface, small buildings around 30 percent, and large buildings the remaining share (I use data from France's stock as a proxy, which I extrapolate, Institut Montaigne, 2019). This data is obviously highly challengeable. Yet, it enables us to convert total building surface into rooftop surface. The calculation shows that around 70 billion square meters is available for solar panels.

A current solar panel's power output is around 150 W per square meter. Assuming an average of ten hours' daytime across the year (not at full power), this equates to 250–300 kWh per square meter per year. Combining this with the above yields around 20,000 TWh of rooftop solar energy. Some of that energy is likely to be in excess during parts of the day and missing during others, hence the importance of storage to fully harvest it. It will also be significantly more widely available in distributed building areas (suburbs, rural areas) than in dense urban ones.

This rule of thumb exercise can obviously be challenged. It matches however quite well similar and more detailed analyses. Deng *et al.* (2015) found a rooftop solar potential of 18,000 TWh by 2030, increasing to 34,000 TWh by 2070 thanks to technology improvements. The International Energy Agency (2019b) also estimates the total potential of rooftop solar at around 9,000 GW, or 60 billion square meters addressable (if we assume 150 W per square meter).

This raw evaluation provides an indication of the size of rooftop solar's potential in the whole energy system. It will not be the silver bullet that will replace all energy sources (this share could however dramatically increase with third-generation PV, particularly if building envelopes and surfaces can all become photovoltaic: Deng *et al.* find an additional potential of 25,000TWh of energy if the potential of photovoltaic facades is harvested). It could however significantly transform the way power infrastructures are designed. Requirements for power networks' availability in low-density areas are expected to drop significantly, while they will remain significant in concentrated urban areas. We could hence see a significant evolution of network architectures, which will be more concentrated on centers of demand, with less service to (expensive) low-density areas. We are already seeing signs of this in the vast land areas of Australia or some regions of the United States, and this will continue to grow. In the end, it would have a positive impact on the costs of infrastructures overall, because it optimizes assets utilization. This resembles railway systems focusing on the most utilized and profitable routes and dropping the distant rural connections. Except this time, the transition will not come at the expense of the service provided. This is important, because most estimates assume that the addition of more variable renewable energies into the mix will entail a sharp rise in investments in infrastructure. This could actually be questioned.

Moreover, the share of energy that is effectively distributed through these networks will diminish through the combined effect of reduced demand and more decentralized production, increasing the fixed cost of these infrastructures in the overall price mix of electricity supply, as I discussed above. In the end, centralized power infrastructures are likely to become more of an "insurance" of availability, with a greater share of fixed cost and certainly a concurrent evolution of pricing systems (more fixed access tariffs, and greater locational pricing schemes). Energy as such might not be traded anymore; rather, its availability will be sold. This would be a major change of paradigm.

What if energy was to become a "near-free" commodity, similar to what happened to the telecommunication sector a bit over a decade ago?

This would no doubt have major implications for economic development and energy demand. It would be a new source of abundance, an advancement of our civilization that is hard to believe in. Yet, it seems to be no longer impossible in the coming decades.

The world in 30 years will look very different from what we think

Energy transitions are driven by the evolution of demand. They are a byproduct of innovations that aim to bring greater abundance, hence social progress. Therefore, if one wishes to understand energy transitions, one must first explore the wider ocean of innovations and structural transformations. The upcoming energy transition will inevitably follow the same rule.

The coming decades will be driven by innovations that will build on key technological advancements. Renewable (solar) energies, digital technologies, and atomic-scale capabilities will be the underlying foundations of upcoming progress. Innovations will naturally focus on solving some of the main issues at hand: building a more efficient economy, a more resilient society, and a cleaner civilization. Several opportunities exist to do existing things better and to do new things that were unthinkable or inaccessible before; in one word: embrace progress.

More importantly, these technologies show that there are unique patterns to these upcoming innovations. Because they are infinitely scalable, highly decentralized, and characterized by increasing returns over time, they drive a transformation toward more human-centricity and more decentralization. They will also make it possible to rebuild or rediscover our relationship with nature. The economy, society, and civilization that will take shape as a result will differ from the stage of advancement that humankind has reached today, which for centuries was founded on greater centralization, standardization, and control.

Even more important, these innovations and the transformation that they will engender will provide, if not always greater abundance, a greater sentiment of abundance. In one word, people will live wealthier, safer, and happier lives, and has that not always been the ultimate goal after all?

Obviously, all this will have major impacts on the energy system. Often neglected by forecasts, these evolutions have the potential to turn the entire energy system upside down, and I hope that — at this stage of the book — I have convinced you about their potential. This raw analysis tells me that total energy demand could slightly decrease, despite significant economic progress. In fact, existing services have the potential to run at half their baseline energy demand, while new services are likely to pick up at an accelerated pace, notably around digital, agriculture, and water; the new "gold resources" of the twenty-first century. Alongside these changes, a transition to new energy sources will take place, moving us away from fossil fuels and traditional biomass to embrace electricity (and notably decentralized solar electricity), which could reach 70 percent of the energy mix. The Age of Fire would thus finally be over. There would be no more fuel combustion to generate energy. This transition would definitely be remembered as the landmark of our century, after thousands of years of humans being dependent on fire. Another critical aspect is the cost of energy, which is probably to approach near zero. The amount of energy consumed would no longer matter; rather, the reliability of the access to it would be paramount. This is an entirely new paradigm, and a great source of renewed abundance.

Of course, one must be careful with scenarios and forecasts. The trends are here, and the developments I described will all occur, but to a certain extent and at a certain pace. The impacts on the energy system that I explained above are stretched-out visions of what these transformations could ultimately look like. But the unfolding of each one of them will depend on how fast and to which extent adoption materializes. All along, I have made the point that these innovations will be at the heart of the energy transition to come. Yet, the extent and pace of the development of each could lead to several scenarios. I would love to see these possible developments become the center of current debates, scenarios, and projections, particularly as the world focuses on reaching a net-zero economy by 2050. There is a pathway to advance jointly progress and climate mitigation, which, if designed right, could resolve both issues at the same time. Let us thus move to the last part of this book, in which I will outline some elements to help us think through this unfolding.

References

Andrae, A. (2020). Hypotheses for primary energy use, electricity use and CO_2 emissions of global computing and its shares of the total between 2020 and 2030. September. https://www.researchgate.net/publication/339900068_Hypotheses_for_primary_ energy_use_electricity_use_and_CO2_emissions_of_global_computing_and_its_ shares_of_the_total_between_2020_and_2030.

Andrae, A., and Edler, T. (2015). "On Global Electricity Usage of Communication Technology: Trends to 2030." *Challenges* 6: 117–57. https://doi.org/10.3390/challe6010117.

Citi. (2017). *Solutions for the Global Water Crisis. The End of 'Free and Cheap' Water.* Citi GPS: Global Perspectives and Solutions, April. https://www.citivelocity.com/citigps/solutions-global-water-crisis/.

Deng Y., Haigh, M., Pouwels, W., Ramaekers, L., Brandsma, R., Schimschar, S., Grozinger, J., de Jager D. (2015). Quantifying a realistic, worldwide wind and solar electricity supply. *Global Environment Change* 31, 239–52, Elsevier. https://www.sciencedirect.com/science/article/pii/S0959378015000072.

Energy Transitions Commission. (2020). *Making Mission Possible: Delivering a Net-Zero Economy.* September. https://www.energy-transitions.org/wp-content/uploads/2020/09/Making-Mission-Possible-Full-Report.pdf.

Grubler, A., Wilson, C., Bento, N., Boza-Kiss, B., Krey, V., McCollum, D., Rao, N., *et al.* (2018). "A Low Energy Demand Scenario for Meeting the 1.5°C Target and Sustainable Development Goals without Negative Emission Technologies." *Nature Energy* 3: 515–27. https://doi.org/10.1038/s41560-018-0172-6.

Institut Montaigne (2019). *Rénovation énergétique: chantier accessible à tous.* July. https://www.institutmontaigne.org/ressources/pdfs/publications/renovation-energetique-chantier-accessible-a-tous-rapport.pdf.

International Renewable Energy Agency. (2015). *Renewable Energy in the Water, Energy and Food Nexus.* January. https://www.irena.org/publications/2015/Jan/Renewable-Energy-in-the-Water-Energy--Food-Nexus.

International Energy Agency ©. (2013). *Technology Roadmap. Energy Efficient Building Envelopes.* December. Paris: IEA Publishing. https://www.iea.org/reports/technology-roadmap-energy-efficient-building-envelopes.

International Energy Agency ©. (2016). *Water Energy Nexus. Excerpt from the World Energy Outlook 2016.* Paris: IEA. https://www.bt-projects.com/wp-content/uploads/documents-public/Environment/IEA-2017-Water-Energy-Nexus.pdf.

International Energy Agency ©. (2017). *Digitalisation and Energy.* November. https://www.iea.org/reports/digitalisation-and-energy.

International Energy Agency ©. (2019/2019c). *World Energy Outlook.* November. Paris: IEA. https://www.iea.org/reports/world-energy-outlook-2019.

International Energy Agency ©. (2019b). *Renewables 2019. Analysis and Forecast to 2024.* October. https://www.iea.org/reports/renewables-2019.

International Energy Agency ©. (2020). *Data Centres and Data Transmission Networks.* July. https://www.iea.org/reports/data-centres-and-data-transmission-networks.

Levi, P., and Cullen, M. (2018). "Mapping Global Flows of Chemicals: From Fossil Fuel Feedstocks to Chemical Products." *Environmental Science and Technology* 52: 1725–34. https://pubs.acs.org/doi/pdf/10.1021/acs.est.7b04573.

Mills, M. (2013). *The Cloud Begins with Coal. Big Data, Big Networks, Big Infrastructure, and Big Power.* National Mining Association and American Coalition for Clean Coal Electricity, August. https://www.tech-pundit.com/wp-content/uploads/2013/07/Cloud_Begins_With_Coal.pdf.

New Zealand Nutrition Foundation. (2020). "Energy." Last modified May 14. https://nutritionfoundation.org.nz/nutrition-facts/nutrients/energy.

Petit, V. (2021). *The Future Global Order. The Six Paradigm Changes That Will Define 2050.* London: World Scientific Publishing.

Plumer B. (2014). "How much of the world's cropland is actually used to grow food?". *Vox.* https://www.vox.com/2014/8/21/6053187/cropland-map-food-fuel-animal-feed.

SDSN and FEMM. (2019). *Roadmap to 2050. A Manual for Nations to Decarbonize by Mid-Century.* Sustainable Development Solutions Network and Fondazione Eni Enrico Mattei, September. https://roadmap2050.report/static/files/roadmap-to-2050.pdf.

Shift Project, The. (2019). "Lean ICT — Towards Digital Sobriety. March. Paris: The Shift Project. https://theshiftproject.org/wp-content/uploads/2019/03/Lean-ICT-Report_The-Shift-Project_2019.pdf.

Tubb, C., and Seba T. (2019). *Rethinking Food and Agriculture 2020–2030.* RethinkX, September. https://www.rethinkx.com/food-and-agriculture.

UNESCO. (2017). Wastewater: The Untapped Resource. UN World Water Development Report 2017. Paris: UNESCO. https://unesdoc.unesco.org/ark:/48223/pf0000247153.

Part 3

Riding the Inevitable

CHAPTER 8

Let's Not Be Disappointed: It Will Mostly Look Like an Imperfect Patchwork of Changes

"Life can only be understood backward; but it must be lived forwards." (Kierkegaard)

Different Innovations, Different Adoptions

Energy transitions are driven by demand, demand is driven by innovations, and innovations are enabled by new technologies. The key technologies in our current toolbox are renewable energy, notably solar photovoltaics, digital technologies, and atomic-scale bio- and nanotechnologies. They share common patterns: they are infinitely scalable, highly decentralized, and characterized by increasing rates of return. Together, they will reshape buildings, industries, and mobility, but also our reliance on an extractive economy and global trade, while mitigating inequalities, pollution, and climate change. They will be the fundamental building blocks of an evolution toward a more human-centric economy, more resilient societies, and a civilization in greater harmony with nature. Ultimately, they will provide greater abundance or greater perceived abundance, which has been the quest of humankind in all times.

However, these transformations will not happen all at once. If the drivers of adoption are clear, and the potential of disruption significant, challenges could also slow some of these evolutions, or even halt them, at least for a while (Figure 1). We must therefore comprehend these inner dynamics of adoption to better lay the groundwork for their unfolding. It is time to explore at which pace they will materialize.

The S-curve is the traditional reference for adoption dynamics. At first, innovations emerge in early adopters or innovator circles: those who are keen to adopt new technologies and test their benefits. When a certain tipping point arrives, an early majority forms and adopts these innovations, which begin to

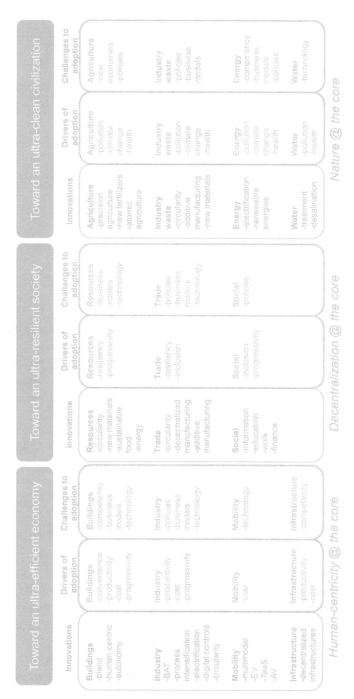

Figure 1   Demand-driven innovations

scale up. They quickly reach maturity and convince a larger set of people, the late adopters. When the innovation becomes fully mature, it continues to expand and capture the remaining customers.

Dynamics of adoption and tipping points will vary depending on the type of innovation. Tony Seba, for instance, classified innovations into four categories. First, innovations that bring increased benefits but at a higher cost. A good example are smartphones. Progressively, the technology becomes simpler to use and costs go down. As costs fall, adoption increases. Second, innovations that do not bring increased benefits, but that come at a fraction of their past cost. Personal computers are emblematic of such a transformation. This innovation did not bring increased computing capacity but made it available to everyone at a fraction of its cost. Adoption accelerates immediately, and progresses as increased benefits from technological advancements kick in. Then, some innovations may change the way products or services are delivered or sold. Solar panels are a good example; online retail platforms another. They modify the "architecture" of an industry. Such innovations reshape the rules of the market and kick off when increased convenience or reduced costs become a given. This is what made online platforms such as Amazon so successful, and what will ensure the success of solar panels in the short term. Finally, some innovations break all boundaries. They provide increased benefits, at a cheaper cost, and potentially transform the delivery models at the same time. Seba highlights Google maps, which completely disrupted traditional GPS systems (Arbib and Seba, 2020). In such cases, adoption is all the more rapid, because they combine all benefits at once.

The score of innovations I identified above falls into these categories. Several bring increased benefits but come at extra expense. Better buildings, with blended uses and more consumer-centricity, provide additional benefits that will help differentiate these buildings and increase convenience, hence the value of assets. In industry, process intensification, electrification, and circularity provide increased performance, but come at extra cost (most of the time), at least for now. Autonomous vehicles are a fundamental disruption, but they have only begun to pervade the market for luxury cars. Precision agriculture or new fertilizers all bring increased benefits (better yields, greater environmental performance), but come at a cost, at least initially. Finally, water treatment and desalination serve many purposes, from depollution to maintaining sustainable access to water, but also come at great expense.

One could argue that the best available technologies are no longer innovations, although their deployment lags behind. Their further deployment makes increasing sense, however, as it optimizes productivity. The same applies to digital controls, which become increasingly pervasive with costs going down.

Additive manufacturing has also been around for some time. Cost reduction will propel these technologies' use in new sectors of activity. These innovations are about the mass deployment of proven technologies.

Some of the identified innovations will also change the way services are delivered. This will be the case for decentralized energy infrastructures based on renewable (solar) energy and batteries, decentralized manufacturing, multimodal transportation, and TaaS. New work structures enabled by digital will also radically transform the landscape of business.

Finally, some innovations are truly disruptive. New materials could come at a fraction of the cost with improved properties, radically changing the landscape for some crucial resources. Electric vehicles will soon be cheaper than cars with traditional combustion engines, and they provide greater convenience of use and reduced wear and tear. Atomic agriculture could also be a disruption of traditional agriculture. Developments in information, education, or finance are all significant disruptions as well (Figure 2).

Different innovations will follow different drivers of adoption. Tony Seba makes the point that true innovation comes at the point of convergence between decreases in technology cost, a good business model, and product innovations (Arbib and Seba, 2020). A first key driver of change is obviously cost. I identified it and expanded the concept to productivity, which is also a cost driver, based on return on investment. Beyond this, other drivers — such as resilience, inclusion, the fight against pollution, climate change, or health issues — are all critical. They are non-cost drivers that meet significant objectives or hurdles. Convenience of use is also a major enabler of accelerated adoption, as is progressivity: the ability of a technology to scale up progressively through compatible applications, with the adopter being able to try, test, adopt, and expand the applications over time. These drivers fit well into existing reference frameworks of innovations (Dearing, 2009; Grubler and Wilson, 2014; Ham, 2018).

Enabling Adoption: A Deeper Look

Yet, despite clear drivers of adoption, these different innovations need to find the right playground for them to scale up and remove some of the concerns or some of the existing roadblocks associated with their development. Let's look at them one by one.

Buildings

The building sector will undergo significant changes, from a greater blend of building uses to more consumer-centricity, with greater energy autonomy and

Innovations		Better product, more expensive at first	Cheaper product, getting better over time	New model of delivery and service	Better, cheaper, different
Buildings	Blend	X			
	Human-centric	X			
	Autonomy (energy)			X	
Industry	BAT		X		
	Process intensification	X			
	Electrification	X			
	Digital controls		X		
	Circularity	X			
	Decentralized manufacturing			X	
	Additive manufacturing		X		
	New materials				X
Mobility	Multimodal			X	
	EV				X
	TaaS			X	
	AV	X			
Agriculture	Precision agriculture	X			
	New fertilizers	X			
	Atomic agriculture				X
Water	Water treatment	X			
	Water desalination	X			
Social	Information				X
	Education				X
	Work			X	
	Finance				X
Infrastructure	Decentralized infrastructures			X	

Figure 2 Different types of innovations

space optimization. The initial playground in which all these innovations can pick up will naturally be new buildings. The existing building stock will likely switch later and more slowly.

Deep retrofits are a key enabler of change and can be encouraged through proactive policies. The main reason why retrofitting the existing stock is more difficult is simply that it costs more. Providing provisions for digital and energy infrastructures within a new building is inexpensive because all overhead costs (origination, project management, etc.) are already taken care of, and remaining hardware and labor costs represent only a fraction of total costs. Since they are negligible ahead of global construction costs, they are extremely easy to integrate, provided proper provisions have been made upfront and the required competencies are available. The right business model for retrofit will however be a significant roadblock. The ability for a specialized channel to deliver an upgrade at cost will be vital in deploying the technology throughout the stock (which represents the overwhelming majority of buildings). Technology could come in handy to support the emergence of such a new channel. Digital technologies could indeed lower origination and administrative costs, which can represent a significant share of total costs. As I demonstrated in the above example on deploying solar panels in households, they can constitute up to 70 percent of total costs. Not negligible!

Yet, technology could also support adoption in the existing stock in a variety of innovative ways. Native connectivity of appliances, or their energy autonomy (third-generation PV, integrated batteries) could help diffuse innovations throughout the existing stock simply through upgrades of appliances, with no additional cost of deployment. Finally, the ability of these technologies to scale up progressively will be decisive in enabling a progressive adoption of these technologies. There should be no need to redefine the complete IT infrastructure of a building to be able to benefit from some of the advantages I described above. It should be possible access some of these applications progressively and build on this. In this regard, mobile connectivity will — again — prove a prime enabler of "infinite scalability." In short, competency, business models, and technology will be the significant roadblocks or enablers of the transition.

Industry

Industry will also transform, at a pace that will depend on how main roadblocks are being addressed. Many improvements will be driven by the modernization of factories: the deployment of best available technologies, process intensification, electrification, or the digitization of the industrial process and the enterprise (to better manage decentralized manufacturing for instance). The primary playground for such a development will therefore be new factories or deep modernization programs. In this regard, increased productivity will probably be the main driver, but the return on investment must be attractive.

The main roadblock that could prevent accelerated adoption is likely to be technology. Will integrated offerings be available that cover the full suite of needs of a given facility: from design to operation and maintenance, from shop floor to facility level? Though it seems obvious, my own professional experience suggests that the industrial sector is so complex that there is virtually no company that can offer a full suite of applications for all needs of a given sector. Take as an example the concept of Industry 4.0. This has been the landmark concept of the annual "Hannover Messe," which is one of the largest trade fairs for industries in the world, and certainly one that aims (successfully) at showcasing the industrial power of Germany. Industry 4.0 (or, as they call it in Germany, Industrie 4.0) is the critical concept that all industries rally around in that fair, which I had the chance to attend several times. There are fantastic stories of what digital technologies can do. Some commendable consultants, such as Roland Berger, have made insightful calculations of the potential benefits of Industry 4.0 deployment in certain sectors, and they are impressive, as I discussed earlier.

Yet, all this takes time to deploy. Why? The reason is that, despite the concept being clear, software is an ocean of complexity, and nobody has yet fully cracked the nut of how to provide a suite that can be fully customized for every end-user while being built on standard blocks. Adoption takes time because needs differ, and because the platform is not fully there yet. Don't get me wrong, however. It will come, but it may take years. A first roadblock to adoption is thus the ability to provide an integrated suite of offerings. A second one will be the ability to scale up the innovation progressively. As for the case of buildings, modernization programs may not enable a full-scale implementation. Also, the ability to try, test, and expand progressively is critical, as it makes decision-making a whole lot easier. Again, these technologies have a significant potential, but their materialization depends on how solutions are shaped.

Like the deployment of innovation in facilities, the deployment of circularity will also face critical roadblocks. Many of the pillars of circularity (energy and resource conservation, lifetime extension, asset utilization optimization, demand reduction) are tied to the ones above. Here, I look in more detail at the creation of a circular supply chain, one that enables the recycling of materials. One of the main nonstarters may be the inherent degradation of the material when it is recycled. Some processes involving high-quality materials may not accept degradation. Until this is resolved, if it ever is, the use of recycled materials in such sectors is unlikely. As a consequence, the best playground for scaling up recycling value chains is likely to be those sectors that do not face such requirements.

Yet, even in those sectors, the challenges to overcome may be significant. Let's take an example to illustrate this. Plastics recycling has gained a lot of traction in recent years due to the sheer amount of pollution associated with it. An estimated 8–10 million tons of plastics are dumped in the ocean every year (as I discussed above). Plastic is widely used in a variety of applications. Packaging is one of them, which does not require high quality. This includes the plastic wraps in cardboard packages, or bottling, and other uses; a good target for recycling. However, several issues appear. Basic mechanical recycling is much cheaper than other options, and 80 percent energy-efficient (there is no need to break molecules again), hence considerably more interesting. Yet, for mechanical recycling to be eligible, primary plastics must be designed to be mechanically recyclable. Many plastics are combined with other materials, which make them more difficult to recycle and reuse afterward. Therefore, a critical question to start with is the design of the final product and how plastics are used, even for packaging.

A second issue will be the actual collection and sorting of plastics. This must be done at minimum cost, and needs significant supply chains to be deployed, to first recover the used products and then sort out those eligible for recycling. Today, there are limited automated operations for that, so costs are prohibitive. Once again, technology can make the case for efficient design, collection, and sorting, but the entire industry of producing (and recycling) plastics must be thought out as circular from the start. That would include the design of products, tracing them through every stage of their lifetime, collecting them, and sorting them automatically (thanks to their digital ID for instance) to channel them to the right recycling and second-life use.

Scaling up such a new industry will not come without an initial stimulus, however. This is what policies may (or may not) provide. Strong environmental policies will be needed to ensure the initial takeoff of circular value chains, which will probably be more expensive at first but will optimize over time.

Next, such supply chains also require a completely new approach to the materials industry, a critical shift in how to "think" traditional business models. That reminds me of one exciting conversation I had with the head of strategy of a large mining company whom I asked about her priorities. One of them, she replied, was to develop further remote operations to help optimize costs and increase the safety of mining operations. The second one was circularity, the ability to champion a circular value chain throughout the life cycle of a raw material. This is a pretty big change of business model, which entirely redefines the boundaries of such companies. The value may not be in the extraction of the raw material itself, but in the optimization of its use over the longest possible lifetime. Technology, policies, and business models will prove key in enabling (or not) circular value chains to emerge.

The fate of additive manufacturing is also not a given. On paper, the potential of disruption is significant. In practice, we are still at a very early stage of adoption, despite the technology having existed for over three decades. However, there is reason to believe that this time, adoption could accelerate, because the digitization of information now makes it possible to share design files at a scale that was unimaginable only a decade ago, and design files are the true value of additive manufacturing. This innovation resembles that of personal computers and could be as disruptive. It is all about deploying a well-known technology throughout the masses and enable new uses and business models to emerge. The initial playground is likely to be basic consumer goods, such as plastic or metal tools or even sports shoes (to echo Eric Sprunk from Nike). The challenge will essentially be technology. Additive manufacturing solutions need to become affordable enough, and simple enough to use, so that they enable fast, mass-scale adoption. When the first Apple of additive manufacturing finally emerges, the technology is likely to see increasing adoption. Business models will then evolve, such as the delivery of raw materials suited for this application, and ultimately, an entire ecosystem of digital design applications will exist.

Finally, new materials are the latest innovation in the industry sector that I considered in this book. New materials will build on emerging bio- and nano-technologies, or what I have referred to as atomic-scale design. The success of this innovation will mainly depend on the amount of effort devoted to it. There are great hopes that designing new materials could alleviate some of the most pressing issues involved in traditional extractive mining: distant dependencies on scarce resources, decreasing rates of return, price volatility, and associated pollution. Moreover, new materials could also come with improved properties and help advance the traditional paradigm in which certain industries operate. Let's take one example: solar panels. Traditionally made of silicon, first-generation panels are generally thick and can only be deployed on rooftops or fixed supports. Under this constraint, forecasts of solar PV deployment cannot go much beyond the existing surface of roofs!

Today, however, a lot of effort is devoted to exploring new material properties that could help change this paradigm. And consequences could be significant. Graphene is one of the new nanomaterials that has received a lot of attention lately. Atomic-scale capabilities could now enable the industrialization of its production and its use in a variety of new applications. In particular, flexible photovoltaic surfaces could be made, which would make it possible to deploy PV on a much larger scale in virtually every surface available. Performance is not there yet, and we are still in the trial stages. However, this provides an idea of the potential disruption that new materials could bring to this industry. And this is only one example. The bottom line is that bio- and nanotechnologies could help reinvent a new periodic table of elements that would significantly transform most paradigms and constraints that we are currently used to. So much for precise forecasts after that! Technology development will however be the main enabler.

Mobility

Mobility is the next area of interest and, as I detailed earlier, probably one that will experience the quickest transformation. The electrification of mobility, notably private cars (as a starting point), the development of multimodal systems and TaaS thanks to digital technologies, and ultimately the rise of autonomous vehicles are all major evolutions that are already on their way. The initial playgrounds for such innovations were luxury cars and cities, which so far have been enough to start the industry. Nothing however prevents us from believing that with technological progress, these frontiers can be extended.

Technology development will define the pace of change. Advances in vehicle electrification will depend on innovations in battery technologies. As we have seen, there is significant hope that battery densities will radically improve in the coming decade (as they have in the previous one). They have already reached a point where they compete on range with traditional combustion engines for light-duty vehicles, but they could outcompete them in the coming years. With increases in battery density, more compact batteries could also be used, enabling new applications, notably heavy-duty freight. Interestingly enough, many proponents of alternative options, such as the use of hydrogen, point to the inability of current batteries to serve the heavy-duty market. Many scenarios are therefore built to 2040 and beyond, creating a space for such alternative options. They basically all assume that there will be no progress in battery technologies in the coming 20 years, despite the immense resources that are currently devoted to it. This is just another example of the general inability to include innovation dynamics in long-term projections.

Autonomous vehicles will also depend on technology development, and again, the continuous improvements in computing capabilities and connectivity will be critical in enabling this. This is also a massive point of focus for a number of automotive companies, which have devoted significant budgets to it. The pace of change will depend on technology progress in those areas. But, as for electrification, changes seem well underway.

Beyond electrification and autonomous vehicles, the rise of multimodal transport systems and TaaS is essentially dependent on the deployment of digital technologies. Significant steps have been taken in certain areas and regions. The technology's ability to scale up and ensure the progressive extension of services as adoption grows will be a prime enabler of a faster transition. Yet, all these transitions are already largely underway, which is why I argue that mobility is probably a sector that will transition more quickly than others. To a large extent, roadblocks have already been removed or are on the verge of being removed.

Agriculture

The development of sustainable agriculture will follow a very different course and remain a key question for some time. Among the different innovations identified were precision agriculture techniques (and their deployment across all regions), new fertilizers, and what I called atomic agriculture, which builds on the work from Tubb and Seba (2019). One of the issues is that many of the innovations are likely to emerge in mature economies first, while their broad use is more critical in new economies. Adoption here will be a mostly regional conversation.

The development of new fertilizers or even atomic agriculture will probably be enabled by proper environmental policies that will force change. Agriculture is indeed a very fragmented market, with massive inefficiencies in the system (let's remember that the US$10,000 billion market has US$12,000 billion dollars in hidden costs, hence a net negative contribution to world's wealth creation).

Culture could also be a prime enabler, if the young generation will pay greater attention to environmental damage or have an appetite for modern atomic agricultural production. Both could also happen at the same time and even oppose one another. On the one hand, there could be a greater willingness to adopt sustainable food habits through veganism and short supply chains. On the other hand, there could be an appetite for proven healthy diets, developed in labs. Both outcomes are possible and might ultimately overlap.

Beyond policies however, the critical topic will be new economies. The traditional perspective is that new economies will need to follow the example of modern agriculture techniques that are in place in most mature economies, the challenge being the inherent fragmentation of the market in those regions and the ongoing reliance on subsistence agriculture. The story so far has been increased dependency on foreign imports in the face of increased demand. Therefore, agriculture in new economies will need a complete reboot to confront the upcoming challenges of demography and urbanization. I would thus argue that the question is not so much about how to provide the multitude with support for the adoption of modern agriculture techniques and tools, but rather about how to create the conditions for local innovation, based on these new technologies — what I referred to as reverse innovation earlier. This is probably one of the biggest challenges to adoption that the world is currently facing, and nothing indicates to date that it will be resolved in time.

Water

Water will face similar challenges, since the combined issues of water pollution and scarcity primarily concern new economies. About 1 percent of the water on Earth is currently available for use. The rest is either unreachable to date or salinized, hence unfit for consumption. At the same time, water pollution has become a plague that endangers biodiversity and sustainable access to freshwater in many regions of the world. As stated before, this is a critical challenge of our time. In fact, food and water form the base of Maslow's pyramid. Without these, nothing else truly matters. Yet, they are both sectors that struggle to reinvent themselves. We are used to thinking about the spectacular nineteenth- and twentieth-century developments as an industrial revolution, but it was primarily an agricultural revolution. The mechanization of agriculture and the recourse to fertilizers and pesticides enabled huge productivity gains, which moved societies away from a subsistence economy while freeing up cohorts of labor to move to cities and participate in other productive activities. Agricultural modernization has been the bedrock of economic development. Today, the agriculture sector represents 3 percent of the workforce in high-income economies, but nearly 60 percent in low-income ones (World Bank Group, 2020).

The ability to depollute available water and supply increasing quantities of it will thus become a paramount challenge in the decades to come. Solutions such as water treatment or water desalination exist. Yet, they are also expensive and require significant infrastructure in order to be put in place. Technology development will thus be a key enabler in accelerating access to suitable and affordable freshwater. It will certainly become a critical area of innovation in the coming decades, beyond what is already happening in the field. Going further, since the effects of water pollution and scarcity will be prime concerns of new economies, this is another field of activity that calls for reverse innovation. These are promising, yet highly uncertain prospects.

Society

Social innovations also hold the potential for significant improvements. Potential developments of emerging technologies, notably digital ones, include improved access to information, knowledge, and education, greater opportunities for remote work in areas not blessed with a well-structured local job market, and innovative financing solutions to enable entrepreneurship and development. Combined, these could fuel economic growth and reduce social inequalities, particularly in terms of access to opportunities, within and across regions.

These innovations are also highly disruptive and true game changers, whether they create new job market structures and conditions or provide access to online education for most people and innovative financing schemes for low incomes, for instance. The revolution of information that happened in the early 2000s and has expanded since — and without which a book like this one would not have been possible — exemplifies this potential.

There will be major challenges to adoption, however. Technology will play a role. The ability of technological developments to build on scalability to enable platform effects, optimize opportunities and choice, and significantly reduce costs of acquisition will be essential. Poorly designed systems will go only that far.

Business models will also be important, particularly for financing. Financing is always a balance between volume and the security of returns. Weighing risks over returns is at the heart of finance. This is why interest rates are higher and more volatile in new economies than they are in mature economies, impeding long-term economic growth by preventing the leveraging of the economy with debt. The result is a lack of access to financing, which translates into slower growth profiles, despite significant pressure from demography and urbanization (Petit, 2021). New financing schemes, made possible by digital technologies such as blockchain for instance, could help mitigate risk and enable lower interest rates, favoring debt contracting and economic growth.

Finally, and more importantly, the future of such developments will rely heavily on how policies are shaped in various regions. Let me take the example of the well-known and recent controversies around TaaS. At the time of writing, such controversy had emerged in the California birthplace of two major service providers: Uber and Lyft. A judge ruled to force these two companies to requalify their drivers, who were independent contractors, as employees, so that they would be able to receive minimum wages and basic social benefits, which they were not entitled to in the original construct (Lee, 2020). This is an emblematic example of how an innovation in work structure could be short-lived because of regulation. Is the right solution to shut down these operations? They do provide jobs, many jobs, but the social systems to support these contractors with adequate protection are not in place. Whether we think this decision is right or wrong, this example shows that innovation struggles to develop because of an inadequate policy environment. It remains to be seen how policies will develop to enable the creation of new jobs while ensuring rightly deserved social welfare. And what is true for work applies to information, education, and financing as well. Access to free and reliable information is not a given in many economies around the world. The same holds true for education and access to finance. Policies will thus play a critical role in maximizing (or not) the opportunity that these new technologies present.

Infrastructure

Finally, all these potential transformations will also significantly impact infrastructure. Decentralized infrastructures are the last of the innovations I discussed, fueled by mobile connectivity and decentralized energies. Their natural playground will be where techniques for deploying these technologies are most developed. In this regard, Australia is a living laboratory of decentralized energies, while China could soon become a leading area of mass mobile connectivity through the deployment of 5G networks.

There will be some challenges to the accelerated adoption of these critical advancements, however. One of them will be policies. These technologies require significant markets to enable fast upscaling and cost reduction. This is true for energy technologies such as solar panels or batteries and for digital technologies such as 5G or artificial intelligence. Today, China has outcompeted all world regions in picking up on those. It is without doubt the first provider of new energy technologies, arguably the running champion of 5G connectivity, and a leading front of artificial intelligence development. This technological dominance leads to new international dependencies and raises fundamental questions, as these dependencies essentially concern critical information and energy infrastructures. As a result, they are at the heart of the current trade conflict between the United States and China (Petit, 2021). Therefore, how policies evolve in this regard will play a critical role in enabling these technologies to ramp up. If these countries are reluctant to allow the free trade of such technologies, the transitions I described are likely to be slowed down significantly, and possibly halted, at least for some time. If they are more open to trade, however, the transition could accelerate.

Beyond policies, the other critical challenge will be competency and culture. These technologies are new, by design, and they will have to be deployed by contingents of people that, in certain sectors, are not familiar with them. This is very much true for energy utilities, for instance, and it is likely to be a key challenge in their ability to rapidly adjust to the new paradigm. In addition, there is a cultural aspect that could also work against the deployment of new technologies. The bedrock of most energy companies' cultures is always safety, while their mission purpose is often tied to providing the service they deliver in a reliable manner. No shutdowns! This is because these companies handle the bloodline system of the economy. If they fail to deliver, the rest of the system collapses. With such a commendable mission purpose and supporting culture, the appetite for switching to new technologies and paradigms is obviously limited. While it may still generate excitement for a few, the ability of such companies to drive change at the right pace while not compromising their core foundations will be a major test for most of them. In regions where these companies hold dominant market positions and have the ability to influence policies, it could prove vital in enabling or slowing down the adoption of certain innovations. This is already apparent in several European countries and a number of states in the United States, with some lagging behind others despite there not being significant differences in opportunity potential (Petit, 2018).

Five Key, Entangled Challenges, and What to Take Away from Them

Each of the innovations above ultimately faces similar challenges to adoption, even though these materialize differently from one sector to another.

Technology

The first challenge is the progress of technology itself. In certain areas, cost curves still need to go down enough to trigger adoption. In others, the inherent capabilities of technology remain to be improved. This is for instance the case for battery densities, or fully pervasive and native mobile connectivity, or third-generation solar PV. It is, however, only a matter of time before these improvements in both capabilities and cost are realized.

A second potential issue has to do with how the technology will effectively be developed. A key pattern of the technologies I discussed in this book (decentralized renewable (solar) energy, digital technologies, atomic-scale technologies) is their infinite scalability. This does not necessarily mean that the innovations developed to address some of the main challenges and trends above will build on this, and that they will ultimately be scalable. Yet, progressivity in adoption will be a major driver. If one can scale up one's installation progressively, without fully committing to it from the start, then the adoption of one's innovation is expected to be much more widespread and quicker. What is striking in my exploration above is that it concerns most areas. In other words, if solutions are not scalable, then there is little chance that the adoption of such innovations will be as fast as we may anticipate.

Once more, my own professional experience suggests that building scalable solutions — some would say "open" solutions — is far from being a given. It may even prove to be counterintuitive in new markets that have not yet been structured. Indeed, most established markets are structured around value chains, in which every actor has their place and receives the revenue assigned to them in the chain. This "structure" is the result of decades of friction and convergence in the business. Established markets are stable and would actually never be disrupted if it was not from outside innovations. Yet, many of the innovations I described above tend to disrupt the competitive balance across the value chain. They also often represent new market opportunities, which have not yet been well structured. The outcome of this is that incumbents are likely to try to preserve their place in the value chain by preventing outsiders from bursting in, especially small and nimble startups led by inspiring leaders.

Taking the example of electric vehicles, it took years for incumbents to finally adopt the technology, and they were forced to do so by regulations, particularly in Europe. The innovation came from the outside and reshuffled the value chains. The incumbents certainly tried to resist it and will continue to fight for their place in the value chain, even though their operating model may have to evolve. The same applies to digital controls deployment in industries. I was making the point earlier that integrated offerings are still rare in most segments because of their inherent complexity. Open platforms could help accelerate adoption but would also open the door to small and nimble players, who could in turn be more agile and less expensive than large incumbents and ultimately commoditize the industry. This is probably why such a transition is likely to take time and may never fully materialize.

Business models

A second significant challenge is that of business models. We have seen that these will play a critical role in enabling innovations in the existing build (buildings, factories), in industry for circularity, and in a number of possible social organization changes. In buildings, they will be crucial in addressing the retrofit market at cost and scale, with this market representing the bulk of opportunities. In industry, circularity breaks traditional supply chains and will need entirely new models, which remain to be invented. Some of the social innovations I described, for instance in financing, are also likely to cause changes in value chains, with the traditional role of banks or trusted parties being progressively challenged by technology.

Yet, these new models are not consequences of the inherent properties of the technology, as people often tend to believe. I would argue that we should regard them as key enablers of adoption. If these models do not materialize, then the innovations will not spread beyond the early adopters' category. This is why they are innovations, by themselves. And I would even argue that they are the prime innovations to focus on.

Let me take an example to illustrate this. New buildings may be fully equipped from the ground up with digital and energy technologies and be a new haven for augmented experience by its dwellers, but this will still concern a tiny minority of the population. The stock turnover is indeed around 1–2 percent per year (slightly higher in new economies because of population growth and urbanization). At this pace, it would take 100 years to fully convert the stock of buildings to new technologies. Technologies are there, but they simply do not "pervade" the market. Whoever finds the way to cheap and accessible retrofits for all will access a market that is many times larger and truly foster adoption. And the same will apply to industry, whether it is modernization of the industry stock (same issue as buildings) or the transition to circular value chains. For the latter, the heart of the transition is a change of business model, as we have seen in the examples of plastics recycling (the need to handle the full life cycle of plastics) or mining (life cycle of raw material).

Actually, what matters across all these use cases is enabling adoption without friction. Frictionless experience will be central in speeding up adoption. If you can upgrade your household with a new energy system in a couple of clicks or a request sent to your home interface without having to pay anything upfront (the initial cost comes as installments on your energy bill, and the energy savings you realize nullify it), then you might be interested in switching. On the contrary, if it takes you months to get there and if you have to coordinate different contractors to get the thing done, then you may as well drop the case right from the start. Similarly, if you can transition from virgin plastics to recycled plastics without having to worry about supply and waste-handling afterward for a minor premium (initially), and claim that you are cutting your supply chain emissions (the hardest ones to abate) by a significant factor, then you might be very interested in switching. Frictionless adoption is key to accelerated adoption, and it will depend on the development of smart business models.

Competency and culture

This leads us to a third critical challenge to adoption: competency. Adopting new technologies or new business models is not a given! I explained the digital competency gap issue above, as well as the major disparity between utilities' internal way of thinking energy systems and the capabilities of new technologies.

Without competency and even cultural change, adoption is extremely unlikely. As we have seen, this affects many transitions, particularly those in buildings, industry, agriculture, and infrastructure. In the end, generational changes may well remove the roadblocks, in one way or another. If we take the example of retrofitting buildings, one of the issues today is that one has to rely on a channel of small and fragmented contractors often not capable of deploying these new technologies. This channel will naturally renew itself for the better when the new generation enters, as they are more digital-savvy and probably had the opportunity to learn some of these concepts in class.

The only issue is that it may take a couple of decades to get there! As mentioned, rapidity of adoption will depend on how to accelerate a well-understood process. Training will be key. There have been many claims about the importance of lifelong learning, but this has never been as relevant as right now for some parts of the industry, notably small and medium enterprises. And despite everyone recognizing the need for it, very limited efforts are put into it by major technology companies looking at deploying their solutions. It is another way to shoot oneself in the foot. Hence, deploying an innovation requires the technology (given), the right business model (I discussed it), and the channel to deliver it! If one piece is missing, then it simply does not work. This is why considerable emphasis must be placed on training the channel, at an order of magnitude higher than what is being realized today.

Culture may also have to be changed, and this is where thought leaders must play their role. Storytelling is a principal way of engraving new changes in people's minds. Our species truly made itself over stories that our ancestors repeated to their descendants, until it became possible to get them into print. We still have a genuine appetite for stories that make a case. Culture will thus change when stories change. Marketing innovations are therefore a major challenge to adoption, one that is seldom addressed in most technology companies working on such innovations. An emblematic example of good marketing for me would be Apple or Tesla, at least in their early days. Their story was beautiful. As a matter of comparison, does anyone remember any good story on the energy transition? Impossible — because they are all dull. They lack a storyline that grabs our attention. The result is lack of traction. Would the "Age of Fire is over" be a good one to follow? I will let you judge or propose something else.

These competency and cultural evolutions also entail critical responsibilities for technology companies to bridge gaps and increase inclusion. Otherwise, it becomes highly likely that entire population categories get downgraded or are left out of the opportunities, a further inequality chasm that would lead to social disorder and in turn hamper evolution.

Policies

This naturally leads us to policies as the next challenge to adoption. If an innovation requires a suitable technology, the right business model and channel to thrive, it also requires a favorable landscape. This is ultimately what policies are here for. And defining policies is a complex exercise. To quote the notorious Max Weber, "the final result of political action often (…) stands in completely inadequate and often even paradoxical relation to its original meaning." But policies are not here to direct what people should and should not do; this would be too easy. What they are here for is to create conditions for the sustainable progress of large groups of human beings. In this regard, policies are at the heart of innovation. They either favor innovation or prevent it from happening.

Policies cover a large array of issues. Environmental and energy policies will be key to triggering the adoption of new energy innovations but also to the move to circularity or more sustainable agriculture and water practices. The scope of their application will extend across all critical sectors of the economy, including construction, industry, mobility, agriculture and water, and infrastructure. If these policies do not take stock of and do not favor the many transformations I described, they can ultimately constitute a roadblock to deployment. An interesting example of that is the electrification of transport. The rise of electrified mobility in Europe has been accelerated thanks to aggressive policies in the region regarding private car emissions, which left automotive manufacturers no choice but to switch to electric powertrains. This triggered a risky disruption of the sector, which employs millions in the region. And we can expect more policies to kick in as time goes by. The UN Principles for Responsible Investment initiative (2019) expects environmental policies to expand rapidly after 2023, following the global climate stocktake scheduled to happen that year.

More general policies will also have a main role to play in enabling some of the innovations I reported on. Trade policies for instance have a potentially high impact on their deployment, because innovations highly depend on scale to reach competitive cost tipping points. To take an example, China dominates the global solar PV and battery markets. Nearly 50 percent of solar panels installed in the United States in 2017 came from China (Energy Sage, 2019). The Trump administration then imposed a 30 percent tax rate on solar panel imports, forcing some Chinese companies to localize their production in the United States (Meehan, 2020). This obviously came at an extra cost for the consumer. The same type of battle also happens in the digital field, and particularly for some of its vital core components, namely semiconductors (Petit, 2021). The extent to which trade conflicts are resolved will thus have a critical impact on the transitions I described above.

Social policies will also play a vital role in enabling education (hence competency development) as well as new work practices or financing opportunities. These can be key enablers or slow or even halt innovation. The current conversations on the future of TaaS in California that I mentioned above are an interesting example of this.

The bottom line is that policies should not be taken for granted. They will play a critical role in enabling (or not enabling) most innovations I outlined above. More importantly, success will also (and maybe primarily) depend on the ability of these policies to be truly inclusive, i.e., to ensure no one is left behind, particularly low-income classes, which cannot shoulder the burden of a rapid transformation and its possible short-term consequences on jobs displacement and living standards. This may ultimately prevent some innovations from truly emerging, at least rapidly.

New economies

Finally, new economies will be the hotbed of all these transformations. The transformations may emerge in mature economies first, at least a certain number of them, because the overall policy, competency, and financing landscape is more favorable. Yet, it is in new economies that most challenges will ultimately have to be faced, particularly those concerning sustainable agriculture and water, as well as new opportunities for economic development.

There are two main differences between these two categories of countries. First, mature economies have stable low-growth economic environments. This is because their population has already stabilized and service-driven productivity levels are low. On the contrary, new economies face significant increases in their population and face accelerated urbanization and industrialization. The early adoption of innovations that provide greater and more sustainable economic prospects is thus a critical opportunity for such countries, which could help bolster development.

Moreover, mature economies have already well-rounded infrastructure, for the most part, while new economies are in the process of building it. They have an opportunity to leapfrog on innovations and develop, right from the start, more efficient, resilient, and sustainable infrastructure. To go against common wisdom: there is no reason why new economies should follow the pathway of mature economies — urbanize and industrialize first, with technologies from the nineteenth and twentieth century, then switch to modern ones. It would actually be nonsense, even though it is a fundamental principle of most existing forecasts.

The way new economies will embrace change is thus a critical question going forward, and one that will have ripple effects on mature economies.

The threats of pollution and climate change are indeed so significant that failure to mitigate those could lead to accelerated migration, with some forecasts anticipating ten times current levels in the decades to come (Petit, 2021). Moreover, failure to develop the right ecosystem for accelerated economic development would further extend the gap between mature economies' and other economies' wealth, with similar consequences. New economies' rapid and sustainable development will thus be crucial, and innovations are a fantastic opportunity for them to seize.

Yet, the way these innovations will ultimately develop may significantly differ from how they may have been conceptualized in mature economies, or in this book, for that matter! Needs, constraints, and cultural approaches are different, so new economies will need to develop their own ecosystem of innovation. To take it one step further, I would also argue that innovation is driven by the new generation. As Kettering puts it, "if you have always done it that way, it is probably wrong." And a striking fact that tends to be overlooked is that the young generations live in new economies. The share of population under 19 in mature economies barely reaches 10 percent of that of global youth, and this ratio falls year after year (United Nations, 2019). Hence, many innovations I talked about above may ultimately have their breakthrough in new economies first, before they potentially come back to mature economies. And they may also take different forms, which we may still struggle to anticipate fully. This is what I referred to as reverse innovation. Creating the conditions for sustainable reverse innovation will be essential in alleviating the challenges I have just described.

Entangled challenges

These five key challenges are at the heart of accelerated adoption. Technology, business models, competency and culture, policies, and new economies will be the main enablers or roadblocks of the upcoming energy transition. As we have seen, these innovations are likely to unfold no matter what, simply because they make sense. The question will be at which pace, however, and this greatly depends on how these challenges are being addressed.

Additionally, these challenges are entangled in a complex network of dependencies. Technology and policies are prime enablers. They will both influence how competency and culture are addressed. Policies will obviously play a role in creating conditions for learning and a rapid scaling up of capabilities, while they enable more profound cultural changes. Technology will prove indispensable as a critical tool for realizing the increase in competency.

Policies will also influence business models. As stated, they can provide the legislative framework and necessary incentives to bolster the emergence of new models. Good examples are retrofit policies in both building and industry, as well as circularity policies. But technology will also play a prime role. If we take the example of building stock retrofit I mentioned earlier, a sustainable model will necessarily involve a five- or tenfold reduction in current ownership costs. Digital technologies are a powerful enabler of systemic effects of this kind, erasing all inefficiencies within the process. Combined with forceful policies, they could be essential to a fast scaling up.

Last, policies will also influence new economies' challenges. The way in which these countries construct the right frame of policies and support incentives will obviously prove key and has been a roadblock to accelerated development in some of them. Similarly, in some cases, technologies may have to reach a certain level before they can be adopted by these economies. An example is the global digital gap between mature and new economies. While Internet access tops 80 percent in most mature economies, it is below 30 percent in India and Africa (Petit, 2021). Part of the reason is the lack of communication infrastructure. It takes time and money to develop networks of communication (cables!) across large land areas, and this is often not a priority. However, things could change if satellite communication becomes more broadly available and affordable. I refer to the Star Link project, for instance, which aims at offering broadband access to the Internet to everyone in underserved areas by 2025 (Starlink, 2020). This is one example where technology advancements could kick in and shift the paradigm (Figure 3).

What to take away?

These innovations have the potential to significantly shift our economy, societies, and civilization toward greater (possibly perceived) abundance. And I am likely to have omitted some that are yet to come and surprise us! As they unfold, they will massively transform the energy system, to a level that has been barely explored by most existing energy forecasts, and likely for the better when considering current commitments to decarbonize it by 2050. This book has been written to fill this gap. These innovations will pervade all sectors of human activity: buildings, industries, mobility, agriculture and water, social systems, and infrastructure.

The innovations are not all of the same nature. Some are incremental improvements. They either provide increased benefits at a premium, or, to the contrary, deliver an existing service at a fraction of its cost, enabling it to further penetrate the economy. Some can entail more radical changes in delivery models or architecture, or even fundamental disruptions that provide new services or existing ones in an innovative way, and at a fraction of their original cost.

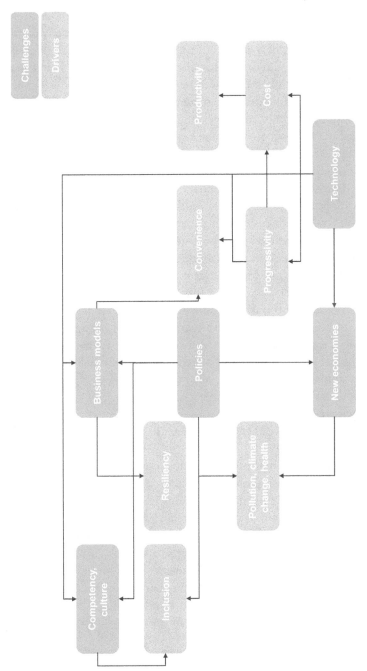

Figure 3   Challenges to and drivers of adoption

All these innovations make perfect sense and support a progressive transformation of our world for the better. As a result, they are all likely to materialize at some stage. However, a fundamental question will be the extent of their unfolding and, more importantly, the pace at which they develop. There is no certainty, and ultimately it may not matter. When they will eventually have transpired, this is likely all we will remember. But for those of us who live in this era, confronted with many issues including that of climate change, it is important to understand these transformations and influence them so that the transition accelerates. We thus need to know what will be the key challenges to their adoption.

I have identified five critical challenges to adoption, which equally apply (though in different forms) to the score of potential transformations. Technology comes first. Further technological enhancements are likely needed to see step changes in adoption in certain areas, both in terms of costs and capabilities. Most difficult could be to ensure that the application of underlying technologies makes the best use of their inherent potential, notably that of infinite scalability. Most of these technologies provide a unique platform for rapid adoption because they can scale up over time. However, it is not a given that this is how they will be used.

A second challenge is business models. To enable fast adoption, some areas will need innovative business models that will bolster change at a more rapid pace than what traditional upgrades are likely to yield. In fact, business models are a vital area of innovation in and of themselves, possibly as important as the actual innovations they help bring to the market. The key issue will be to design business models that enable frictionless adoption. Several of the innovations I have laid out are already available with current technologies, at least to a certain extent. What has prevented their development has been the lack of suitable business models. If this problem is not resolved, adoption will likely be much slower.

A third challenge is that of competencies and culture. This is often overlooked by those who are involved in debates on innovation, and is a major roadblock to adoption. Most innovations described above require a competent and enthusiastic value chain to channel them through. Training of the channel, and of the value chain if we look at it in a broader sense, will hence be of the utmost importance and is a crucial missing part in most of today's innovations. Moreover, culture will also play a role. Humanity develops based on storytelling, and culture is a critical element of accelerated adoption and the willingness to embrace change. Without the right culture, innovations are doomed to fail. Competency and culture will therefore be of the utmost importance for accelerating adoption.

Policies are a fourth challenge and probably one of the most difficult ones to address. If innovations require good technology, an effective business model, and a competent channel to thrive, they also need a favorable landscape. This is where policies come into play, and they have to strike a difficult balance between protecting what exists (notably for those most exposed to rapid changes) and embracing innovations that, by design, disrupt the existing order. Yet, and more importantly, policies are not meant to direct what needs to be done. It is a fundamental flaw to believe that legislation is the answer to everything and that everything can and must be the object of a rule. Rather, policies create conditions for progress, and thus innovations. Well-designed policies will be key to creating sustainable and positive conditions for innovations to find their way in existing markets and deliver on their promise, without destroying existing benefits.

Finally, new economies will be at the epicenter of change. This is undisputable because of the sheer size of the opportunity that change represents for them, the absence of a legacy to deal with, and the fact that many will combine all issues at once and will be forced to innovate. This evidence goes against common wisdom, however, which tends to believe that these economies will follow in the footsteps of mature economies. Nothing could be further from the truth. This is why these economies will need to create the right conditions for innovation through the right policies and access to the right technologies. When they do, they are likely to trigger reverse innovation; a major shift in leadership that will have massive consequences for the entire world.

What should come as a surprise following this exploration of adoption challenges is that almost none of them are related to technology per se. While technology initiates the process of evolution, the adoption of related innovations will depend on how these are designed, marketed, and channeled, and on the surrounding policy landscape. Energy transitions are not driven by energy, but by innovations in demand. And the unfolding of these innovations in demand is not driven (only) by technology, but more likely by changes to the environment. Our current journey has thus taken us even further away from our starting point of energy technologies. This is probably why there is so much to be done to further improve the quality of existing scenarios.

To conclude this part, I will come back to one of the findings from the first chapter of this book. I recognized that a key pattern to past energy transitions was that they overlapped with one another. I described how oil or electricity infiltrated the energy system toward the end of the nineteenth century and how they modified some, but not all, of the demand. I also took stock of the current energy system, which still relies on biomass for 10 percent and coal for 27 percent of its needs. These are energy sources from distant centuries. The reason for this complex evolution is that innovations in demand affect the demand or service they seek to improve, and nothing else. They transform this part of demand, but not the rest. Moreover, not all innovations necessarily spread through the market at the same pace. This is why, as an example, 30 percent of the world population still lacks access to a convenient form of energy. The extent and pace of changes brought about by these innovations will depend on how the challenges I described out in this chapter are resolved. Some may rapidly yield opportunities for change, and some may not. In the end, the upcoming energy transition will be a complex and imperfect patchwork of separate transformations.

Why is this important to understand?

Because, as stated, forecasts are built on models, and models on assumptions. And the volume of assumptions that needs to be made in order to be accurate has just gone up by an order of magnitude from what was traditionally the case. Let's therefore be careful with radical statements and shortsighted conclusions that are based on highly imperfect data. What will truly matter in the coming decades is not so much predicting accurately what could happen but working effectively at making these changes happen, as rapidly as possible, particularly now that we understand their positive effect on mitigating climate change. For that, however, we need to know where to start.

References

Arbib, J., and Seba, T. (2020). *Rethinking Humanity: Five Foundational Sector Disruptions, the Lifecycle of Civilizations, and the Coming Age of Freedom.* RethinkX, June. https://www.rethinkx.com/humanity.

Dearing, J. W. (2009). "Applying Diffusion of Innovation Theory to Intervention Development." *Research on Social Work Practice* 19, no. 5 (September): 503–18. https://doi.org/10.1177/1049731509335569.

Energy Sage. (2019). "Where Are Solar Panels Made and Should You Care?" January 2. https://news.energysage.com/where-solar-panels-are-manufactured/.

Grubler, A., and Wilson C. (2014). *Energy Technology Innovation.* Cambridge: Cambridge University Press.

Ham, M. (2018). "Theories of Innovation Adoption and Real-World Case Analyses." In *Driving Educational Change: Innovations in Action,* edited by A.-P. Correia, 15–37. eBook, available at https://ohiostate.pressbooks.pub/drivechange/chapter/chapter-1/.

Lee, D. (2020). "Uber and Lyft's California Operations Hang in Balance." *Financial Times,* August 17. https://www.ft.com/content/6e351f6b-4c15-4110-bb3b-19e2e58988ce.

Meehan, C. (2020). "Top 5 American Solar Panel Manufacturers in 2020." *Solar Reviews,* last modified December 8. https://www.solarreviews.com/blog/best-american-solar-panel-manufacturers.

Petit, V. (2018). *The New World of Utilities: A Historical Transition toward a New Energy System*. Cham, Switzerland: Springer.

Petit, V. (2021). *The Future Global Order. The Six Paradigm Changes That Will Define 2050*. London: World Scientific Publishing.

Principles for Responsible Investment. (2019). *The Inevitable Policy Response: Policy Forecasts*. UNPRI, December. https://www.unpri.org/inevitable-policy-response/what-is-the-inevitable-policy-response/4787.

Starlink. (2020). "High Speed Internet Access across the Globe." https://www.starlink.com/.

Tubb, C., and Seba T. (2019). *Rethinking Food and Agriculture 2020–2030*. RethinkX, September. https://www.rethinkx.com/food-and-agriculture.

United Nations. (2019). "World Population Prospects 2019." UN Department of Economic and Social Affairs, Population Dynamics. https://population.un.org/wpp/DataQuery/.

World Bank Group. (2020). "Employment in Agriculture (% of Total Employment) (Modeled ILO Estimate)." June 21. https://data.worldbank.org/indicator/SL.AGR.EMPL.ZS.

Chapter 9

What Will Matter Now Is to Roll Up Our Sleeves

"I'm looking for a lot of men who have an infinite capacity to not know what can't be done." (Henry Ford)

Accelerating Adoption: What It Will Take to Change

Unpacking the issue

In the previous chapter, we have better understood the main challenges to adoption of these new innovations. We have understood that there are five key challenges. The first is technology advancements, but also the ability to build on the inherent capabilities of these technologies. This is particularly their scalability, which makes it possible to make incremental and progressive changes. New business models, which enable frictionless adoption, are a second challenge. The availability of competency and the willingness to do things differently (the culture) are a major enabler of or roadblock to adoption. Policies are a next challenge, as they are a powerful conditioner of change without which innovations are likely to be slowed down. Finally, a large part of the change will in fact happen in new economies, and they will be a major potential reservoir of reverse innovation if the proper conditions are created. These challenges are also entangled. Technology developments and policies are at the heart of solving some of the other critical challenges, such as enabling innovative business models, accelerating on the competency front, or developing the right environment in new economies.

What will truly matter in the coming decades is to work effectively at making these changes happen. For that, we need to know where to start. And to know where to start, we need to unpack the issue, starting with these challenges. The challenges become enablers once resolved, and we can see how their resolution drives the unfolding of these innovations. We can then focus on the timing of their resolution and ultimately provide a tentative timeline for the innovations to materialize.

This is what I aim to do in this chapter. However, a word of caution: I have been challenging forecasts from the beginning of this book and argued that I did not mean for it to provide an accurate forecast of the upcoming transition. Despite temptations, I stick to this. The purpose of putting this transformation on a roadmap is not to provide a precise timing but rather to illustrate the dependencies between different developments. In this way, we can better inform subsequent roadmaps that will be worked out by collective efforts. Let us thus not take timelines for granted! That said, my personal outcome from the following analysis is that these transformations could occur more quickly than we expect. Indeed, the resolution of some of these challenges does not seem insurmountable, nor does it seem feasible in a distant future only. As the world confronts with the challenge (among many others) of reaching a net-zero economy by 2050, this inevitable evolution toward greater progress and a low-carbon world could in fact be accelerated. There is reason for hope!

Different timings per sector: Buildings and infrastructure

I explained above that the initial playground for innovations in the building sector is likely to be new buildings. However, what will truly create rapid scale transformation is the retrofitting of the existing built environment. For that to happen, certain challenges need to be addressed. First, environmental policies will force the transformation when implemented; something that is otherwise unlikely to happen, at least from an energy standpoint. The articulation of these policies will play an important role in doing things in the right way from the start.

Next, the right business models need to be developed: those that enable frictionless (and cost-effective) adoption. Without these, and despite policies, retrofit rates are likely to remain low because of the cost and hassle it entails. The development of business models will build on new digital technologies as well as a sharp increase in competency within the channel.

Over time, progress in new materials designs will further enhance current technologies (notably in energy, with both solar PV and battery enhancements moving toward more native energy provisions), which will accelerate adoption. Both the scaling of retrofits and ultimately native energy will decentralize infrastructure over time as penetration expands.

Different timings per sector: Mobility

New mobility solutions will emerge in cities, and innovations will first appear in luxury segments before they further penetrate entry-range vehicles and freight transport as technology develops. Electrification, multimodal transport systems, and TaaS will develop concurrently over the decade to come. There are incentives for this (congestion in large cities) and these alternative options are increasingly competitive with traditional, combustion-engine-based private transportation. The transition has already started.

A true game changer over time will be the rise of level 5 autonomous vehicles. This will bring a step change in terms of mobility competitiveness (among other things) and thus significantly accelerate the adoption of TaaS and multimodal systems, as well as the electrification of the fleets. With autonomous vehicles, intra-city transportation — which represents the bulk of mobility — will be entirely reshaped.

However, the advent of autonomous vehicles is dependent on technological development and, ultimately, favorable policies. Yet, policies will be a byproduct of technology if it can prove that it operates at levels that are safer than current. The technology for autonomous vehicles will rely on the advancement of digital technologies, both in terms of native and ultra-resilient connectivity and mass and affordable computing capabilities. As digital technologies continue to progress, they will make this transition possible.

Different timings per sector: Industry

The transition has already started in the industry sector as well. The digitization of controls, the progressive adoption of best available technologies, and new processes (including for instance process intensification or electrification) are already on track. They already provide significant benefits in terms of circularity, especially in terms of better energy and resource conservation or assets lifetime extension and utilization optimization. The acceleration of these transformations will depend on policies that enforce a faster rate of retrofits, as for the building stock.

Similarly, a larger decentralized manufacturing setup will largely depend on the progress in competitive digitization of manufacturing, the ability to remotely (digitally) control a larger set of facilities, and possible trade policy evolutions in the coming years that will foster greater reshoring.

But other innovations are also coming. The development of circular value chains (which will create a new economy of materials) will depend on advancing digital technologies, particularly ubiquitous connectivity, which will enable lifetime tracing and new forms of "closed-loop" supply chains management.

New materials will also be a crucial innovation route. They are already on the agenda, but their development will possibly accelerate as further progress is made in atomic-scale technologies, fueled by increased and more affordable computing power.

When these new materials kick in, they will also help accelerate the rise of alternative circular supply chains, which could develop from scratch for more widely available, localized, and designed-to-recycle products.

Finally, additive manufacturing could disrupt some of the current industrial value chains, allowing for a more distributed, decentralized, and commoditized industry to emerge. Additive manufacturing already exists, but it has not yet made its way to mass consumer adoption. This situation is similar to the emergence of personal laptops in the 1970s and 1980s. For mass adoption, technology needs to scale up and keep improving. Cheaper computing and broader connectivity capabilities will certainly help make it happen. Another powerful driver will be the emergence of new materials in circular supply chains. This is because one of the roadblocks to additive manufacturing's scale development is likely the frictionless and cost-effective procurement of cheap raw materials for a fragmented ecosystem, something current supply chains of materials have not been designed for. Instead, they are set up to provide large quantities of cheap materials to large consumers. The business model is thus entirely different and would require a new logistic approach, which could emerge alongside the rise of new circular supply chains based on new materials. Additive manufacturing could possibly build on a circular industry of new materials.

Different timings per sector: Agriculture and water

Precision agriculture is currently a reality, but it struggles to develop across all world economies. Its development will largely depend on policies in new economies, but will also rely on the ability of private farmers to both master these new techniques and invest in the associated productive means. This will be highly dependent on the level of development in these economies, and some innovations in education and finance are likely to play a critical role in making this possible.

Going one step further, the emergence of new fertilizers is likely to significantly pick up with the developments in atomic-scale research, which are dependent on further enhancements in computing. As for new materials, new fertilizers are likely to depend on a reinvented periodic table of elements.

Atomic agriculture will develop on the same foundational technology developments. But culture will play a role as well, because further adoption of this novel approach to food is also highly dependent on people's acceptance. Finally, a large part of the challenge is once again centered around new economies. Adoption will be more rapid when it is truly needed, which is primarily the case in these countries. Their ability to scale up a reverse innovation ecosystem will thus prove key. And this will build on social policies on and technology developments in information, education, work structures, and finance.

Last, this reverse innovation ecosystem is likely the key to the further improvement of innovations in other fields, such as new water treatment or desalination techniques, that would alleviate major scarcity and pollution issues. This is again a topic that will essentially concern new economies.

Different timings per sector: Social innovations

Finally, powerful innovations in information, education, access to work opportunities, or finance are within reach. Yet, their development will require favorable social policies that are able to strike the right balance between forceful transformation and social protection.

These social innovations, provided they emerge, will play a critical role in a number of adjacent innovation areas, notably in new economies.

Putting a Timeline to Change

I can summarize the exploration above in a simplified conceptual framework for transformation (Figure 1) and begin to make sense of these findings.

Only at the beginning of the change process

A first key finding is that we are only at the beginning of the process of change. In fact, many of the current developments are only precursors of what is to come. New advanced building techniques only prefigure a more radical transformation of the entire building stock. The electrification of private cars and the rise of TaaS platforms only show us the huge potentialities of completely new mobility design within cities. The digitization and modernization of industrial setups is only a first step toward a more radical transformation of the industry value chain through the combined effects of new materials developments, circularity, and additive manufacturing. Precision agriculture in mature economies is reminiscent of the twentieth-century agricultural revolution and is slowly ramping up in new economies. It provides a glimpse of what new innovations can theoretically provide in terms of productivity. Existing water supply infrastructures are not yet up to the coming challenge, which will likely be met only through massive innovations in the field. Finally, our current social system is bound to significantly transform for the better if the right policies are put in place to leverage the potential of upcoming technologies.

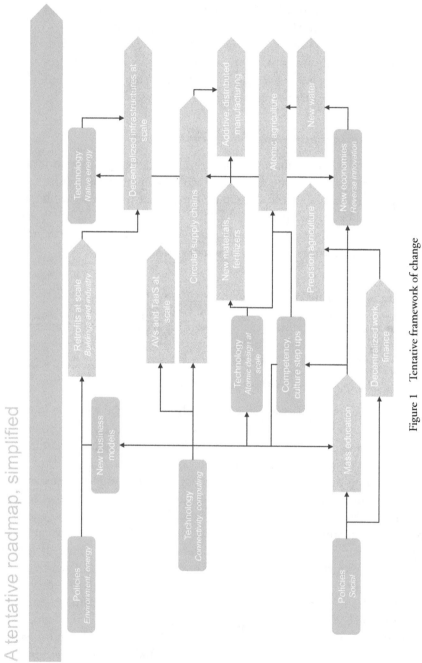

Figure 1   Tentative framework of change

Interdependent innovations

Another striking finding of this analysis is that all these innovations are dependent on one another. Social innovations in education are fundamental to ramping up competencies, which will in turn enable new business models to emerge and a reinvention of buildings and industries to take place. This requires upscaled retrofit activities and not just innovations for the happy few. Innovations, including in work and finance, will also prove central in creating a favorable ecosystem for new economies to develop their own set of innovations ahead of the pressing challenges they face.

Further advancement of digital technologies will entail a cascade of adjacent progress as well. It will be crucial in the emergence of new frictionless business models and in the further development of digitally enabled capabilities, such as in mobility. Yet, it will also be at the heart of further developments in atomic-scale technologies' scaling up.

Finally, and maybe more importantly, atomic-scale technologies will fuel a revolution of materials that will spread across all sectors of activity, as Susan Hockfield (2019) described in her book. These developments, enabled by computing power, and growing more competitive over time, will trigger a revolution in industry by changing the actual materials and their supply chains, likely also propelling a further reinvention of those to fit more circular approaches. They will probably also drive significant innovation in energy-harvesting technologies, potentially leading the way toward a native energy supply and autonomous devices. They furthermore hold the keys to reinventing agriculture and ultimately developing better water processes. Hence, all technologies and innovations are entangled. The power of computing allows for a new scale of atomic-precision design and manufacturing, which in turn reshapes the periodic table of elements and gives way to a multitude of transformations across all sectors of activity, particularly energy.

Who said borders could not be crossed and step changes could not happen? When this revolution materializes, the main concepts that have defined our way of seeing what is and is not possible are likely to become outdated, and an infinite set of possibilities will emerge.

Policies key enabler

Yet, all these transformations will depend on how prepared we are to embrace them. If nothing is to change in the current landscape, these innovations will certainly take time to develop and benefits are expected to be less disruptive. Let's remember Vaclav Smil's (2017) estimate of 50–60 years for an energy transition to complete. This is without forceful policies. Indeed, policies hold the key to accelerating these changes. Either they are favorable — in which case they create the right conditions for accelerated adoption — or they are not, in which case innovations follow slower S-curves of adoption.

Environmental and energy policies will be at the heart of accelerating the transition of the existing building and industry stock to modern technologies. If these policies do not force change, it may take several decades for the stock to naturally transition, as its lifetime may exceed four to five decades. Let's remember for instance that the annual rate of new construction barely tops 1–2 percent of the existing stock.

Yet, social policies will also play a critical role. Innovations are not all about technology, they are also about people and their interactions. Strides in education and reforms in work and finance are key to unlocking the potential of people to embrace innovations, create the groundwork and means for adoption, and ultimately foster change.

Policies are not about dictating what needs or does not need to be done. They rather create the conditions for success or failure. They are essential for holding societies and economies together, helping them move forward. At the same time, they are not all about change. They must take stock of what exists and of the way things work, and strike the right balance to ensure a positive change, not one that comes at the expense of certain populations. There is no such thing as "creative destruction." Destruction always carries a cost for society. It may well be inevitable, but policies are designed to alleviate its impact.

The way current policies will be shaped in the foreseeable future is thus of the utmost importance. In this regard, the debate around the Green New Deal in Europe is a good example to learn from. Here, we have the epitome of a difficult balance between environmental (and energy) objectives — to become carbon-neutral by 2050—, and to make that transition a positive one for the European people, what is often referred to as a "Just Transition" (European Commission, 2020). Time will tell to which extent this policy approach will be successful.

Can we sketch a timeline?

We can now try to make sense of Figure 1 and explain when the critical challenges I described above could be resolved. This is where we leave the comforting shores of theory and dive into predicting the unpredictable. I therefore repeat my word of caution on what to do with such timelines. These are intended to provide a frame for debate and to identify the driving forces of change.

Let's start with policies. In the first chapter of this book, I referred to another observation that Vaclav Smil (2017) made in his momentous history of energy.

Smil identified what he called innovation "pulsations," which would occur repeatedly in the course of history, generally after major economic depressions. He notably identified the diffusion of mobile steam engines between 1898 and 1924, the development of modern commercial transport post–World War II, etc. When will thus be the next economic depression? Some well-known economists, such as Ray Dalio or Nouriel Roubini, tend to believe that it will happen in the coming decade (Huddleston, 2020; Roubini, 2020). These economists build on the Covid-19 crisis that has been raging for over six months at the time of writing and is far from over, but they had made the argument before. I remember attending a conference in Geneva in 2018, at which a panel of economists addressed a crowd of around 200 large Fortune 500 companies' strategy executives. The panel began by asking the crowd whether they believed that a major economic crisis was looming on the horizon. Of the 200 people in the room, around 180 raised their hands. The panel then went on to explain why there was consensus on this. Whatever we may think of it, whether major economic depression is in sight or not, Smil has a point when he says that economic downturns prompt innovations. Time will tell whether we are about to enter this stage.

Yet, policy responses can also be driven by other elements. The United Nations Policy Response Initiative (Principles for Responsible Investment, 2019), which I mentioned earlier, believes that stringent policies will be made between 2023 and 2025. Their rationale is that a global climate scandal is about to erupt. The year 2023 will be a key tipping point, because this is the year when the global carbon stocktake will take place, eight years after the Paris Agreement of 2015. They expect that, since results will probably be completely off track, the reaction will be an inevitable flurry of policies on environment, energy, and associated social issues.

I think that, based on this evidence, we can all be cautiously confident that policies will be implemented within the coming five years, in one form or another, and progressively expand. Exogenous factors could derail this for some time. Scenarios for the coming world order that I developed in another book (Petit, 2021) showed quite clearly that the pace of these policy evolutions would depend on whether the world is confronted with a massive crisis, and on whether the international community would come together to coordinate the response to these issues or on the contrary collapse in a downward spiral of self-reliance and competition. In other words, how inclusive and coordinated regional policies will be. Of the four scenarios that I sketched, three anticipated a significant transformation on this front by 2025–30 latest.

A second key question revolves around the pace at which digital technologies and atomic-scale technologies will mature. Granted, digital technologies are already largely mature, but further progress in computing and connectivity is expected. Computing will advance to increase the potentialities of some other emerging technologies, such as atomic-scale technologies. Connectivity will make progress to provide ubiquitous and mass-scale connectivity capabilities to all sectors (e.g., mobility with autonomous vehicles for instance) and all regions (e.g., new economies). Building on the evidence of improvements in these different fields, we can reasonably expect step changes in the coming decade. I only need to mention once more the current progress in new forms of computing — such as quantum computing, the development of broadband satellite-based connectivity, or the ongoing deployment of 5G infrastructure — and the massive ongoing innovations in the field of atomic-scale materials, which I described in the previous chapters of this book. Could we position 2030 as a key year for the world to see massive changes in the capabilities of these different technologies, in other words a new frame of what is possible?

The pace at which new business models are expected to emerge will depend on progress in digital technologies (but the potential is already largely here) and, more importantly, on the emergence of competencies and new channels. These competencies will be founded on training and education, which digital technologies could probably accelerate. The scaling up will be progressive and probably differ from one region to another. In some mature economies, these new models have already started to emerge. This is the case for building retrofits in the United States, Western Europe, or Australia for instance, but it is not yet a full-scale development. In new economies, adoption is still very limited. Yet, if policies are well structured and if large efforts are dedicated to learning and development, we could expect early changes within the coming ten to fifteen years. It will not take longer to partly renew the workforce. The period 2030–35 would then be a suitable moment to see a new workforce on the field and the ramping up of scale retrofits and transformations.

Finally, the development of a proper ecosystem of innovation in new economies could take more time. On the one hand, it will depend on how social innovations (in part based on policies) penetrate these regions. The pace at which they do will probably differ significantly from one country to another. Let me take one example: online education. Online higher education has grown rapidly over the past decade, as we have seen earlier. It will continue to grow and become increasingly accessible (at increasingly affordable tuition) to students in remote locations. But for them to be able to enroll, they need to be eligible; in other words, the education system (up to high school) needs to be good enough for students to receive such advanced education. We are already there in many countries of Asia (not to mention India or China), which have very strong education systems, and who have benefited from international education for a long time. The master's program at the University of Texas that I attended 20 years ago was already full of Indians and Chinese — and just one French student. However, the same accessibility is much less of a given in several African countries, for instance, which have to further develop their primary and secondary education systems. Adoption rates are thus likely to differ between one region and another, and the same will be true for work habits or access to finance, not to mention potential regional confrontations and social or political disorder that could derail these efforts for some time.

Next to the unfolding of social innovations, the emergence of opportunities for reverse innovation will also depend on the pace at which the technologies I described above become widely available. When they are, conditions will be here for the process of change to begin. Arguably, we could set the year 2040 as the moment when all these conditions are in place. It could be closer to 2030 in countries like India or some parts of developing Southeast Asia, and further away in other regions.

If we combine all these assumptions, what we see is that the next decade is probably the turning point of the transition to come. By 2030, policies and technologies will be in place, and changes will have begun to ramp up. Conditions will be here for an acceleration in adoption to occur during the 2030s. To overcome some critical challenges — such as agriculture and water — further innovations are required. These innovations will probably take more time to realize, especially if they unroll in new economies.

Priming the Pump of Change

To recap, the purpose of this chapter is not to provide a roadmap for transition. In fact, if I were to develop a roadmap, I would most certainly come up with a set of scenarios, depending on how this score of assumptions is most likely to evolve. The purpose of this book is rather to lay the foundations of what could ultimately become a collective effort toward a roadmap. The aim of this chapter was to provide a framework to help us better understand how these changes will take shape over time, and ultimately what they depend on. In other words, it clarifies the assumptions.

A key outcome of this exploration is that the coming decade will prove critical and will probably be the turning point of the transition. We can rightfully expect that by 2030, most conditions for the transition to accelerate and begin to scale up will be in place. Policies will be there, at least in part. Technologies will also have reached new capability levels that should further bolster innovation.

Yet, this transition will not happen everywhere nor at the same pace. Some of the transformations described above may well have ramped up earlier in certain geographies and sectors. New buildings may exemplify some of these transformations, as they have started to do. Retrofit programs, such as the one currently under discussion in the European Union as part of the Covid-19 recovery, may help kick off the renovation of the existing stock. New business models may scale up as well and help retrofit infrastructure and large asset classes. Energy-as-a-service programs are a good example, where financing helps overcome initial investment hurdles. The digitization and the modernization of industrial footprints, potentially combined with some level of reshoring, will also have made significant progress, and this has already started. Circularity policies may be in place, and new models may have begun to emerge, such as a greater use of recycled materials in key productive activities. Mobility-as-a-service will almost certainly have gained further ground, as well as the electrification of the fleet. Even atomic-scale agriculture may have made significant progress by 2030, as suggested by Tubb and Seba (2019).

Yet, I would argue that those changes will not be systemic within that timeline. What I mean by this is that they will remain limited to a number of sectors in a few key geographies. To take just one example, Tubb and Seba (2019) predict an atomic agriculture revolution by 2030, but their study is limited to protein production in the United States. Similarly, Arbib and Seba (2017) predict a complete mobility disruption by 2030, but again limit themselves to cities in the United States. We could build such examples at will. The reality is that the underlying foundations of change will take time to materialize, in particular ubiquitous access to technology and competencies to drive change at scale. These are not minor transformations; they are spectacular evolutions. And as long as they do not materialize, the transformations will not occur at scale. Let me take another example. Energy-as-a-service models are already scaling up in several mature economies as a new way to further accelerate the retrofit of existing infrastructures' and buildings' energy systems. They will certainly continue to develop until 2030. Yet, over 75 percent of the existing stock consists of residential and small commercial buildings. This fragmented segment will require a more significant change of the actual value chain that serves it. This cannot happen overnight; it requires new solutions and new competencies to create the conditions for affordable scale adoption. It is under these conditions that systemic transformations occur. Hence, the extent and pace of changes up to 2030 will probably look hectic to some, as if we were collectively groping our way into a new industrial revolution. However, and hopefully I have made that case by now, there is a frame to this change, and what appears to be unstructured is only a manifestation of a typical transition to new innovations.

I would also argue that we cannot know for sure when all this will eventually scale up. The future is not written. Ultimately, some of these transformations and their key enablers (policies, technological enhancements, competencies and new business model innovations, and the overall development in new economies) will depend on a multitude of external factors. In the end, I believe policies will be the key, as they will determine the landscape and the pace for change. And the most impactful policies may not be those that focus solely on environment and energy, but on the contrary those that focus on our social structures (access to information, education, work opportunities, and finance) and those that look after global trade and international cooperation. There are many things that could derail these changes and postpone them by a decade or so. Political and social disorder could turn the agenda of governments upside down. Geopolitical confrontations could halt international trade and close certain markets to innovations that are emerging in others. Moreover, unanticipated black swans could pop up and reshape all priorities at once. We have seen this in 2020 with the Covid-19 crisis. We could see it again, in the form of another health crisis, a major climate event (or a series thereof), a regional conflict, a global financial crisis, or something else.

The future is thus not written, and it actually does not matter. What matters is rolling up our sleeves, focusing on what is important, and accelerating the changes that make sense, while working to resolve the different challenges to adoption. If we take a step back, I see three priorities that we should follow in the coming decade. The first one is to invest in the future and focus on innovation. The more we concentrate on research and technology development, the faster the innovations and positive outcomes emerge. There is no such thing as a dystopian future. The world is what we ultimately decide it to be, and, at all times, innovation has been a powerful driver of progress. Digital technologies, atomic-scale technologies, and new energy technologies will be the foundations of a new world of greater abundance. The focus must be placed on this. It may seem like an obvious thing to say, but I am alarmed by some of the debates that occur here and there on digital technologies being bad for the planet, atomic-scale developments being God mimicking activities that should be banned, and many others. Let me take the example of digital sobriety, the new mantra of some in Europe, which is gaining ground in an attempt to return to the good old days when nobody had access to the Internet and when one needed to go to a dusty library to find some information. Those who turn their backs on innovation turn their backs on the future. There is no other way. Policies are meant to ensure that these developments are done, with the right set of concerns in place. Again, embracing the future while supporting those who are most affected by its changes.

A second priority will be education, and by this I refer not only to lower or higher education but also to lifelong learning practices. Education, which is competency acquisition, will be key to embracing change and preparing for new technologies and new innovations. Earlier in this book, I mentioned the famous French historian Francois Furet, who pointed to the small difference in lifestyles between the seventeenth and the middle of the nineteenth centuries, and showed how everything suddenly changed in the twentieth century. The twenty-first century could be another systemic transformation, and by the end of it people will perhaps wonder how we could ever have lived the way we did. For this to occur, however, and to prevent a generation from being sacrificed or the transition from slowing down, lifelong education will have to become the new norm. And it will need to be available not only to the wealthiest (by design those who need it the least) but to everyone. If done well, this could also change culture, with a vision of the future that is deliberately looking forward and optimistic, while removing the last dinosaurs who advocate for no change from the equation. Digital technologies will play a key role in making this possible, by removing barriers to adoption while enabling personalized course developments.

The last priority will be to create the opportunity for scale. I mentioned it already: the key of buildings' transformation will be the existing stock. This applies to all industries as well. Well-rounded policies that focus on accelerating change should look at accelerating rates of retrofits. By doing so, they will artificially increase the size of the opportunity and thus drive massive innovation efforts. A long-tail legacy is not necessarily a problem but rather a golden opportunity to accelerate change.

These three priorities will be critical in setting up the right frame for change in the coming decade: a focus on technology and innovation, lifelong education, and increasing the market opportunity. This is not only going to be a challenge for government and policy, but also for corporates, who will need to adapt and prepare for change. As a start, these innovations must be at the core of all research and development efforts of these companies, whatever their sector of activity. Public research only goes that far. The amount of private capital injected in research is several orders of magnitude larger. Moreover, they must take stock of the significant challenge of transforming their value chain and invest much more radically in lifelong education — for their employees, but also for their entire ecosystem. It is only through this type of activities that they will ultimately be successful. Finally, they will probably have to develop alternative approaches to testing and trying new innovations in new markets. Aside from traditional matrix setups, specific vehicles are probably the right way to thrive in a fast-changing world.

To conclude this chapter, I call on energy and climate agencies to take stock of this evidence and rebuild their approach to long-term scenarios. These agencies have a critical responsibility: that of informing the debate on what can and must be done in the long-term future. Despite their very commendable research outcomes, they need to further embrace innovations as a key element of change in long-term perspectives. If they fail to do so, the conversation will probably remain centered around recipes from the past to solve the challenges of the future. By now, we already understand that the transformations I have described earlier are largely inevitable, because they make sense. As we grapple today with the threat of global climate change, I argue that the only way to reach a net-zero economy by 2050 (not to say halve our emissions by 2030) is to embrace these transformations and accelerate their unfolding, a perspective often overlooked in current plans. This is a heavy burden, but knowing most of their practitioners personally, I can only testify to their ability to embrace this change and finally trigger a much needed debate on solid ground, something this book has been able to only briefly and inaccurately sketch.

References

Arbib, J., and Seba, T. (2017). *Rethinking Transportation 2020–2030. The Disruption of Transportation and the Collapse of the Internal-Combustion Vehicle and Oil Industries.* RethinkX, May. https://www.rethinkx.com/transportation.

European Commission. (2020). "A European Green Deal. Striving to Be the First Climate-Neutral Continent." https://ec.europa.eu/info/strategy/priorities-2019-2024/european-green-deal_en.

Hockfield, S. (2019). *The Age of Living Machines: How Biology Will Build the Next Technology Revolution.* New York: W. W. Norton & Company.

Huddleston, Jr., T. (2020). "Ray Dalio Predicts a Coronavirus Depression: 'This Is Bigger Than What Happened in 2008,'" *CNBC*, April 9. https://www.cnbc.com/2020/04/09/ray-dalio-predicts-coronavirus-depression-this-is-bigger-than-2008.html.

Petit, V. (2021). *The Future Global Order. The Six Paradigm Changes That Will Define 2050.* London: World Scientific Publishing.

Principles for Responsible Investment. (2019). *The Inevitable Policy Response: Policy Forecasts.* UNPRI, December. https://www.unpri.org/inevitable-policy-response/what-is-the-inevitable-policy-response/4787.

Roubini, N. (2020). "Here Are the Biggest Economic Challenges We Face over the Next 10 Years," *World Economic Forum*, May 1. https://www.weforum.org/agenda/2020/05/depression-2020s-economy-pandemic/.

Smil, V. (2017). *Energy and Civilization. A History.* Cambridge, MA: MIT Press.

Tubb, C., and Seba, T. (2019). *Rethinking Food and Agriculture 2020–2030.* RethinkX, September. https://www.rethinkx.com/food-and-agriculture.

CONCLUSION

It's Only the Beginning ... Good News!

"Now this is not the end. It is not even the beginning of the end. But it is, perhaps, the end of the beginning." (Winston Churchill)

Change the lens through which we look at energy transitions

History is the mother of all sciences. I began this book by looking at the history of energy transitions, a lesson full of surprises. Having spent a large amount of time in meetings with world-renowned energy experts from some of the most prestigious agencies, it always strikes me that the way current debates around the energy transition are framed do not build on the evidence that it provides.

The biggest lesson of this brief history is that energy transitions do not proceed from energy. They are merely part of a much bigger picture, what people have referred to as industrial revolutions. Energy transitions are a byproduct, a consequence; in no way a starting point. There may be energy innovations, but these do not evolve in isolation from bigger transformations in the economic and social orders. They contribute to these transformations.

The reason why we tend to forget this evidence in our expert debates is probably a kind of endogamy. Since only energy experts are in the room, the only topic we talk about is energy, our common passion. In addition, climate studies have now demonstrated that energy lies at the heart of the current issue of human-induced climate change. So, my colleagues and I finally found a critical reason to assemble. Together, we are tasked with saving the world from a disaster! We thus explore what we know of the world, which mainly relates to energy, and we look at how to tweak our big drilling holes, big pipes, big cable networks, and large infrastructures to create different large and clean infrastructures. The dream of engineers! And we are at ease with the mounting pressure to mitigate climate change, because that means more funding to research, develop, and invest, all this hopefully within our career time frame!

Let me be clear. All this is obviously done in good faith. This is not the point. The point is that a hundred years from now, nobody will remember these passionate debates. History is cruel to those who do not write it. It forgets them. What people will remember from this time is more likely to revolve around some of the critical economic, political, and societal transformations of our time. Climate change will certainly be part of it. I am much more doubtful about energy. I call this a form of "reverse anachronism." Anachronism is when people tend to judge the past with the eyes of the present, a common mistake in history. "Reverse anachronism" is when people tend to anticipate the future with the eyes of the same present, a common mistake in forecasting and scenario planning. This is something that a professor at Oxford taught me years ago, and that was a revelation (Ramirez and Wilkinson, 2016). Therefore, let us not be victims of reverse anachronism and look frankly and genuinely at what the future will be like.

Energy transitions are driven by social progress. Humanity has always aimed at one thing and one thing only: to improve its condition. This has been a long quest for greater abundance in everything. And social progress, abundance, has been fueled by innovations. Energy innovations are part of these developments, among many other forms of innovation.

Today's upcoming transition, or revolution, will build on three key underlying technologies: digital technologies, atomic-scale technologies, and new energy technologies. These technologies fuel one another. Without progress in mass computing and connectivity, the ramping up of atomic-scale technologies would be impossible. And with a new periodic table of elements within reach, infinite prospects for new energy harvesting capabilities are opening up, notably for solar energy, a near infinite and free source of energy.

At the same time, these technologies share common patterns. First, they are infinitely scalable. They can progressively grow from small systems into very large systems. At the same time, they are produced in mass, scalable quantities, which provides them with large learning curves and thus significant cost reduction potential. Moreover, they are highly decentralized in nature. They can be integrated into virtually anything. To illustrate this, we already see innovations in nanoscale robots that could tomorrow be inserted into our bodies to fight infections, or in solar technologies that could turn screens, building envelopes, or windows into photovoltaic systems. Finally, they provide increasing rates of return. Because they are infinitely scalable and highly decentralized, they build on adoption and provide network effects, which increase rates of return. This is true for digital platforms, where services get cheaper as the number of platform participants increases. This is also true for solar technologies, where the cost of energy decreases over time as technology improves.

Why is this important?

The transformations to come will build on these critical patterns. They will redefine the boundaries of what is achievable at an unprecedented scale. It is thus a critical challenge for us to integrate this reality into our common frame of thinking. When we set limits of what is doable and what is not, we need to keep in mind that these inherent boundaries we impose on our imagination may well be broken within a decade or two. Who would have imagined in 1990 that 30 years down the road (today), half the world's population would walk the streets with 100,000 times the computing power of the system that guided Apollo to the moon in 1969 in its pocket? What does this tell us about what to expect in 2050, or later?

Moreover, this invites us to reflect on how we conceive changes. It is a normal course of things that new technologies are first used to replicate existing system structures. However, this does not prefigure the changes to the system itself as new technologies further spread and are better understood. A good example is the current approach to building large solar farms across the country. A new technology is deployed to mimic existing centralized power plants. Instead of building coal-fired power plants, we build solar farms and try to reach similar technical capabilities. But solar panels are designed to be decentralized. Their core value is that they can be integrated anywhere. As they pervade the energy system, they will become more distributed, because this is their true nature and advantage. Yet, very little consideration is given to this evidence in most forecasts. And what is true for solar farms also applies to a score of other self-proclaimed innovations. Our ability to sort out short-lived experiments (mimicking the existing) from long-lasting innovations based on the inherent patterns of the technologies we deploy will prove key in accelerating the transition.

Last, this also tells us that we are far from having seen it all. To paraphrase Churchill, we might just be "at the end of the beginning" — and this is not even certain!

How will this work then?

The Age of Fire Is Over

Innovations will pop up in any area where a key opportunity or challenge to abundance presents itself. A good way to unpack the upcoming energy transition is therefore to identify where those "industrial revolutions" will take place. This is what I have set out to do.

We found first that there is a stunning potential for increased efficiency in our economy. Looking at our building stock, industrial facilities and supply chains, mobility system, and infrastructure, it comes as a shocking surprise that most are largely underutilized and that significant resources are wasted in the process of building or running them. This is a first area of innovation!

It also became clear that the large growth of our current societies has exposed inherent fragilities that our future could stumble on if they are not properly addressed. The sheer size of our global population and economy have led to new points of failure. Our reliance on an extractive economy is now exposing our dependencies on long, distant, and growingly scarce resources. Our interconnected economy is also revealing the potential fragilities of our trade system, vulnerable to numerous disputes and power games. We cannot achieve everything we seek to achieve without working together on these common goals, but we have to get over millennia of competition. Finally, the way our system works tends to aggravate inequalities over time. Inequalities have been here forever, although to a large extent the last century has been a parenthesis. But we are now back on track, and these become unbearable in a world of free and real-time information flows. And what is true within societies also applies across them.

Finally, we have begun to realize the massive impact that our civilization has on the planet. On the one hand, immense cohorts of people suffer from increased pollution effects. On the other, we now see that if the world were to continue on this course the way it always has, we would quickly see disruptions in some of our most basic needs: food and water. And a more pernicious challenge is also upon us: that of irremediable climate transformations, the consequences of which could be so dramatic that they could threaten our very subsistence. To avert this, major revolutions in how we handle our food production, the production of all modern goods we depend on, and the sourcing of energy must happen quickly.

A hundred years from now, these opportunities and challenges, and the way they were or were not resolved, will be taught in history classes. And the technological advancements we have described above will significantly contribute to addressing these. We have identified a number of them. Is it exhaustive? Probably not. It is merely a beginning to trigger debate and thinking.

Buildings will probably evolve toward a greater blend in uses, increased consumer-centricity, and a new approach to space and energy optimization. Industries will progressively modernize, adopting better proven technologies, transforming processes, and digitizing rapidly. Circular supply chains will transform the dependencies across industrial sectors as well as their footprints. Finally, research on new materials and additive manufacturing could entirely reshape the current industry system. Mobility will become electric and move toward service models, until autonomous vehicles redefine the entire mobility system, within cities at least. Agriculture will continue to modernize based on proven precision agriculture techniques from the twentieth century, but the twenty-first century will see the arrival of new fertilizing techniques and atomic-scale food production, with ripple effects on many other activities. Water supply will be a key issue that will probably be addressed by further innovations in water treatment and more importantly desalination. Our social structures will probably transform as well, with greater access to information, education, and work and finance opportunities. This transformation will be particularly important in new economies, where it could become a critical enabler of accelerated development. Finally, our infrastructures will become more decentralized as a result of all these changes, a considerable disruption from the way they were designed in the twentieth century.

If we take a bit of distance though, these transformations will also reshape the way we live and interact. Building on these innovations, our economy will become more human-centric. This is the next "frontier," a fundamental change from the twentieth century, in which standardization was the alpha and omega of rapid development. Our societies will additionally become more decentralized. This is a critical shift away from the centralized structures that have developed since the end of foraging societies 10,000 years ago. Our living standards and interactions, entertainment, education, work: everything will probably become more decentralized or localized. There will be no global village, nor will we be back in the dark ages of self-reliance. What these innovations will bring is a more interconnected network of small villages, hopefully at peace with one another. Finally, our civilization will find its way back to nature. Ancient religions from around the world have always developed a particular relationship with nature: one of harmony. We can probably acknowledge that this faded away with the spectacular development of the three monotheist religions, which reinforced the primary role of humans and their particular relationship with the beyond at the expense of nature. These original beliefs are still here; they have not been entirely removed from our subconscious, and they are expected to take on a rejuvenated form in the civilization that is taking shape before our eyes.

These transformations will thus greatly transform our economy, our societies, and our civilization, moving us toward greater (possibly perceived) abundance. Greater abundance from more human-centricity (I get what I want for myself). Greater abundance from more decentralization (what I need to fulfill myself is right around the corner, and I interact, depend upon, and develop relations with people I know). Greater abundance from a more harmonious relationship with nature, a missing part of our core constitution as a species finally put back in place.

This book, however, is about the upcoming energy transition. But, and this is the point, all this will have dramatic impacts on the energy system. These innovations, the inevitable advancement of our societies, will obviously change what we need from our energy system. I have tried to sketch it, even though I must acknowledge that much greater work is obviously needed. The opportunity here is to optimize our current energy demand by a factor of two. With new services appearing along the way, mainly for agriculture, water supply, and digital infrastructures, and all other things being equal, our energy system could run at levels slightly below current levels of final demand, despite economic growth.

The energy system would also change in nature. Up to 70–80 percent of traditional biomass and fossil fuels could be eradicated, leading the world toward a truly net-zero economy, at likely a greater pace than current conventional approaches, effectively solving the dilemma we are currently confronted with. These traditional fuels would also be replaced by modern and ultimately near-free electricity.

It is this fundamental and disruptive shift that led to the title of this book. The Age of Fire, a millennia-long history of how we harvested energy, will be over, and will give way to a new energy system whose backbone would no longer rely on burning materials. Science and modern technology finally prevail!

Not all this will happen overnight though

Innovations are only as good as the extent to which they get adopted. And there are many challenges to adoption. First, technological progress. Significant advancements are still ahead of us, and their materialization will need to be supported. Moreover, the inherent capabilities of the technologies I described — infinite scalability, high decentralization, and increasing rates of return — must be preserved while these technologies develop into practical innovations. This is not a given!

Next, building up competency will be at the heart of adoption. Innovations can only develop at scale if the right set of competencies is available, at scale, to make it possible. As mentioned, this is not a given. The challenge is enormous, since an entire generation could be caught in the line of fire, with the destruction of traditional jobs and a lack of opportunities for those unable to adapt. Beyond competency, culture may also have to evolve, alongside the appetite for change. This is probably one of the biggest issues in growingly conservative and aged societies.

Business models will also have to transform, alongside traditional value chains. Such transitions may be beneficial to some and highly detrimental to others. Yet, these evolutions are inevitable if adoption is to accelerate. Some already argue that innovations from the past decade, such as online retail platforms, have created more damage than benefits. To a certain extent this might be true, as benefits have not necessarily been evenly distributed. Yet, this is nothing in comparison to the transformations that can emerge as a result of the score of innovations I identified above.

Policies will be at the heart of enabling these transformations. The challenge for them will be to strike the right balance between creating favorable conditions for innovation while preserving and protecting those who might be most impacted by it. The European Commission calls this a "Just Transition." There is no certainty that upcoming policies on environment, energy, social structures, and global trade relations will move the needle in the right direction. On the contrary.

Finally, new economies will be at the heart of the change, going against common wisdom. This is because they represent the largest share of the global population, the largest opportunity for development, and the last area of population and economic growth in the world. And, more importantly, this is because all challenges I described above are concentrated there at the same time, at a level that has no comparable equivalent in the past. This also means that most of these innovations will unfold and blossom in these new economies first, a phenomenon I refer to as reverse innovation. This is at odds with current thinking. The ability for new economies to develop the right landscape and ecosystem to bolster reverse innovation will thus be a key challenge to large-scale adoption.

These challenges are significant and, as in the past, this is maybe why transitions take time. What we find as well is that some of these challenges are entangled and apply differently across the different innovations they help materialize. But the bottom line is that the decade to come will prove critical in resolving them and put the world on the right course of change.

The reality however is that it might take more time, and that we could find ourselves groping in the dark for a while, looking for the light at the end of the tunnel without being able to frame and fully comprehend the changes at play. This book had no other intent than to try and illuminate this course, hence provide materials for debate. There would be no better outcome for this book than to become an object of heated debates and conversations. At least we would be talking about the right topic!

And as we are getting ready for the COP26 in Glasgow in 2021, we might just have the ideal opportunity to steer our efforts toward a transition which not only will help the world mitigate further impacts on climate, but also accelerate a collective transformation toward greater abundance for all.

Lead by hope

In this exercise, I have tried to develop a new frame of thinking that builds on evidence from energy transitions in the past. My key finding is that energy transitions are a byproduct of larger transformations, which are driven by innovations (in energy and elsewhere), serving the purpose of an eternal quest for greater abundance. I hope this will bring interesting insights into ongoing conversations and ultimately enable the development of a new approach to the issues at hand.

What I take away from this exercise too is that good sense does not come from expertise alone. What actually gives meaning to changes, a reason and a pathway for them, is located at the convergence point of different disciplines. The truth lies in the middle of different practices, and history is a powerful revealer of how things work. This makes the exercise tricky and strongly challenges how current advisory bodies and policies are framed.

Another outcome of this work is that we should break with current dystopian scenarios. Innovation is what has made humanity thrive, and it will continue to do so in the future. Those who refuse to recognize this will fail and ultimately be forgotten. Our future is bright because we have the means to change it at will, if we really and collectively put our minds to it. The key question is whether we will do this smoothly, or whether it will take us decades of hesitation to finally get there. This is what will make this generation be remembered in the future, or not.

Finally, the upcoming transition I have described in this book is only a beginning. In no way should we walk away thinking that we have laid out what 2050 will look like! As we found out in the initial chapter of this book, transitions tend to overlap with one another. They are progressive transformations that unfold one step at a time, like the waves of the sea that reach our shores. You can bet that more are coming, which will provide new opportunities or even reframe what has been discussed in this book. Let me take one example that I discussed in the second chapter: nuclear technologies. Nuclear power, which essentially mimics the way the stars of our solar system produce energy, in theory offers a considerable step change in the volumes of energy we could harvest. So far, it has mostly been a story of a missed opportunity, not to say an industrial disaster. Yet, research continues, and nothing should prevent us from believing that a breakthrough is possible in the coming decades. When this happens, and it ultimately will, it will change everything once again.

These technological developments, or waves of innovation, are not to be opposed to one another. To the contrary, they complement and nurture each other in a permanent course toward greater abundance. And this is what makes it all so exciting!

Vincent PETIT
Hong Kong, September 2020

Reference

Ramirez, R., and Wilkinson, A. (2016). *Strategic Reframing. The Oxford Scenario Planning Approach*. Oxford: Oxford University Press.

Index

CPSIA information can be obtained
at www.ICGtesting.com
Printed in the USA
JSHW010502250222
23235JS00001B/29